THE NEW NATION
1800–1845

Books by Charles M. Wiltse include

The Jeffersonian Tradition in American Democracy
John C. Calhoun, Nationalist, 1782–1828
John C. Calhoun, Nullifier, 1829–1839
John C. Calhoun, Sectionalist, 1840–1850

The Making of America

The Formative Years: 1607–1763 by Clarence L. Ver Steeg
Fabric of Freedom: 1763–1800 by Esmond Wright
The New Nation: 1800–1845 by Charles M. Wiltse
The Stakes of Power: 1845–1877 by Roy F. Nichols
The Search for Order: 1877–1920 by Robert H. Wiebe
The Urban Nation: 1920–1960 by George E. Mowry

THE
NEW NATION
1800–1845

By

CHARLES M. WILTSE

The Making of America

GENERAL EDITOR DAVID DONALD

American Century Series

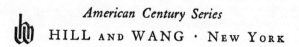

HILL AND WANG · NEW YORK

Standard Book Number (paperback edition): 8090–0102–0
Standard Book Number (clothbound edition): 8090–7290–4
Library of Congress catalog card number: 61–7561

Manufactured in the United States of America

FIRST EDITION FEBRUARY 1961
SECOND PRINTING SEPTEMBER 1962
THIRD PRINTING (FIRST AMERICAN CENTURY SERIES EDITION)
JANUARY 1964

12 13 14 15 16 17

For Kelly
in token of her constant interest
and unfailing aid

Foreword

THE AGE OF Jefferson and Jackson is one of the most controversial periods in American history. In our older histories the years between 1800 and 1845 have generally been viewed as a kind of prelude to the Civil War, a period marked by the emergence of sectional feeling, centering on the hotly disputed issue of slavery expansion. In the last few decades, however, other interpretations of the era have become fashionable. Some writers have found the central dynamic of these years in the growth of the democratic spirit, as expressed in the extension of political suffrage and the rise of the common man. Others have argued that the most important development of the age was the economic revolution which separated the American people into classes with opposing social and political interests. Still other revisionists maintain that the triumph of laissez-faire capitalism was the unifying theme of the era.

Charles Wiltse, the author of *The New Nation*, is, of course, familiar with all these interpretations. As historian of *The Jeffersonian Tradition in American Democracy*, he could hardly be unaware of the implications of equalitarian thought for his period. As the biographer of John C. Calhoun he has done much exploration of the economic developments of the age and has written a brilliant analysis of their consequences in the growth of American sectionalism.

But, admitting that all these earlier views of the age of Jefferson and Jackson have considerable justification, Mr. Wiltse argues that they slight a more basic theme of the era, the rise of American nationalism. No one can be more fully aware than he of the obstacles in the way of American national unity during these trying years. The Essex Junto, the Hartford Convention, the Missouri Compromise, the South Carolina nullification episode, and the bitter sectional rivalry over the annexation of Texas receive full and fair treatment in his pages. Yet his signal contribution is to emphasize the neglected countercurrent of the period, the slow and at times imperceptible evolution of the bonds of national unity.

Mr. Wiltse's pages are frankly revisionist. He stresses the nationalistic consequences of the territorial acquisitions of the Jefferson administration, the unifying results of the War of 1812, and the economic nationalism that emerged from the "American System." In his view the Jackson period, whatever other significance it may have, is important because it marks the "practical destruction of the whole state rights doctrine." "United States," he observes toward the end of his volume, "became a singular rather than a plural noun, and the entity for which it stood was well on the road to becoming a nation."

Mr. Wiltse's lively and informed study precisely fulfills the objectives of The Making of America series, six volumes designed to make the best of historical scholarship available to the general reader who is not a specialist in American history. *The New Nation* is based upon an extraordinary mastery of the public documents and private manuscripts of the period; in addition, as Mr. Wiltse's critical bibliography reveals, it rests upon a thorough acquaintance with the voluminous and intricate secondary literature in his field. Broadly interpretive rather than merely factual, it is a synthesis of the political, social, intellectual, economic, and diplomatic history of the age. Falling chronologically between Esmond Wright's forthcoming study of the Revolutionary era, *The Fabrick of Freedom*, and Roy F. Nichols' analysis of the

Civil War period, *The Stakes of Power,* Mr. Wiltse's book provides simultaneously a panoramic view of some of the most crucial years of American history and a fresh interpretation of their significance.

DAVID DONALD

Contents

Maps

THE NEW NATION
1800 – 1845

1

Conceived in Liberty

THE ELECTION OF 1800 was a revolutionary turning point in American history. So thought the victors, who believed they had snatched the reins of government from the reckless and power-hungry grasp of a moneyed aristocracy. So also thought the vanquished, who believed their property now unsafe and saw before the still unfinished Capitol at Washington the elongated shadow of the guillotine. Between these two extravagances the President-elect, soft-spoken Thomas Jefferson of Virginia, was probably more nearly right than his defeated opponent and one-time friend, Federalist John Adams. But the man who above all others had engineered the Republican victory would prove a better prophet than either. To artful, ambitious Aaron Burr of New York the election was a party triumph which was to transfer the honors and perquisites of power from one set of partisans to another. The more far-reaching results of the election were foreseen by no one. It began the alliance of southern agrarians and northern big-city bosses that has dominated the Democratic party ever since; it gave impetus to the dogma of local sovereignty that would set the stage for the sectional conflict of the mid-century; it turned the direction of growth toward the limitless West, where the destiny of the nation would ultimately be determined; and it loosed in America the humanistic forces that would ultimately endow the common man with worth and dignity.

The common man of 1800, whatever his political inclinations, was restless, curious, acquisitive, jealous of his freedom and skeptical of authority. He was proud of his country but not quite sure whether his country was the United States or only that one of them in which he happened to live. He was optimistic, confident, self-reliant, with a strong sense of "mine" if not always of "thine" and a well-nourished hankering after this world's goods. His family was large, although every childbirth was a hazard and too many died in infancy. In person, save for the aristocratic few who might be nostalgic for the caste and privilege of Europe, the American was inclined to be ill-mannered, contemptuous of fine clothes and polished speech, quick to fight, ready to help a neighbor, eager to try anything that promised gain. He had a practical knowledge of geography and a physical hardiness that led him time and again to set out on foot or horseback, or by whatever conveyance was at hand, to better his fortune or to see some new portion of the world. He was a hard drinker, a gambler, a brawler. He was a fierce competitor who believed in progress as surely as he believed in sin.

Yet after a quarter-century of independence, the differences among Americans remained as apparent as those common qualities that had united them against the mother country. Handed down from diverse colonial origins, differences of heritage, of culture, of occupation early tended to assume a regional character that was nurtured by a local community of interest and in no way modified by a form of government that was itself a sectional compromise. In terms of broad cultural pattern and economy the country was almost evenly divided. Eight of the sixteen states that then comprised the Union accepted Negro slavery as a legitimate form of labor. In the other eight human bondage, never widespread, had already ceased to exist or was in process of gradual extinction. The old Northwest Territory, lying between the Ohio River and the Great Lakes, was free soil, while slavery existed unchallenged in the newly established Mississippi Territory, extending from Georgia and Tennessee to the Spanish possessions of Louisiana and West Florida. Although population was equally distributed between slave and free states, 893,602 of the 5,308,483 Americans counted by the census of 1800 were slaves.

In homogeneity of interests there were four rather than two regional groupings. The framers of the Constitution had distinguished the eastern or New England states, the middle states, and the South. Since the formation of the government, the West—where Tennessee and Kentucky had already been added to the Union and Ohio's statehood was assured—had also emerged as a distinct sectional entity. Boundaries, however, were fluid, with Maryland and Delaware sharing the pursuits of both their northern and their southern neighbors, while New York, Pennsylvania, and Virginia had each a western as well as an Atlantic interest.

In New England commerce ruled. The small farms between the port towns and the hills, and deep in the sheltered valleys farther inland, supplied those who worked them with food, and with clothing in the form of linen from home-grown flax and woolens carded, spun and woven in the home. But their more important function was to serve the needs of the merchant hierarchies whose far-flung trade knew no political bounds. Powerful families like the Cabots, the Derbys, the Crowninshields owned fleets of sturdy cargo vessels that carried American grain, salt fish and beef, tobacco and cotton, iron and leather and rum distilled from West Indian cane to Europe and returned in months or years with manufactured goods from England, wines from France and Portugal, or silks and spices from the Orient. Others, operating on a smaller scale, owned and captained a single vessel, or bought and sold the cargoes of those who did, on credit, commission or shares. Either way brought profits which financed new commercial ventures, increased the retinue of clerks and stevedores, built homes and warehouses, and filtered down at last to the support of churches, colleges and schools. It was not unusual to see four or five hundred sail tied up at Boston's "long wharf" or anchored in the bay, a pattern repeated on a lesser scale in Salem, Portsmouth and Providence.

New England ships and sailors engaged in other activities as well. Whalers out of Nantucket and New Bedford brought in a million gallons of oil a year to light the homes of the well-to-do from Maine to Georgia. Stout New England boats, and men as durable, fished the icy North Atlantic for cod, fighting off if need be French or British rivals, to earn the bounty paid by the Federal Government. And New England ships, though the trade was barred by every American state,* still risked the law for profit to bring their fellow men in chains from Africa—those same slaves whose children their own sons and grandsons would give their lives to free.

Less profitable as yet but of mighty portent were the textile mills that were beginning to appear along the rocky shelf where the streams from the mountains in their final plunge to the sea could be intercepted by water wheels. Typical was the mill of Almy, Brown and Slater in Pawtucket, Rhode Island. Samuel Slater had evaded the laws of his native England (which forbade the emigration of textile workers) and smuggled the plans of Arkwright's power loom to America in his head. By 1800 he and others had improved on the English model, creating new and superior machines, and setting in motion a textile industry that now dotted the fall-line from New Hampshire to Connecticut. New England was beginning other forms of manufacture, too. Such items as shoes at Lynn and hats at Danbury were still individually made by master craftsmen, journeymen, and their apprentices. But in Plymouth, Connecticut, Eli Terry was preparing to convert his clockmaking business into a mass-production enterprise; and in New Haven, Eli Whitney, whose cotton gin was being pirated on a scale in keeping with the fantastic demand for

---

* Georgia retained the slave trade until 1798; South Carolina would reopen it in 1804. By one of the sectional compromises that secured the adoption of the Constitution, Congress was forbidden to interfere with it prior to 1808.

textile fibers, had turned to the manufacture of firearms with parts so precisely tooled that they were interchangeable.

As befitted a dominantly business community, New England was conservative in thought and in politics. Her Representatives had most of them backed the suppression of free speech by the Alien and Sedition Acts of 1798, that had called forth Jefferson's Kentucky Resolutions, and she had voted solidly for Adams, who was one of her own. Yet even as her leaders were freely predicting a reign of terror on the French model and wondering out loud what benefit their mercantile constituents could possibly derive from the rule of this slaveholding Jacobin who believed in the virtue of man instead of the vengeance of God, a leaven of liberalism was at work. There were Republicans among the back-country farmers, among the artisans and small shopkeepers of the towns, and occasionally among the merchant princes themselves. The churches and colleges, long dominated by the stern Calvinist faith that was their heritage, were being challenged by the more intellectual Unitarianism that would soon win over Harvard and through that center of learning infiltrate pulpit and classroom to spread a new spirit of reform over all New England.

The ferment of change was actively at work in the middle states. New York, with her strong merchant class, her landed gentry, her growing financial power, should have been as conservative as New England. Until very recently that state had been a Federalist stronghold, a pocket borough for the brilliant Alexander Hamilton, whose administration of the Treasury in Washington's time had done so much to promote the moneyed ruling class that Jefferson had pledged himself to overthrow. While Hamilton had been content to plead the conservative cause with substantial citizens, who did not need persuasion, his arch-rival, Aaron Burr, had recruited behind Jefferson the artisans and mechanics of the city for whom the Tammany Society provided a social outlet. With their active aid and the grudging cooperation of the Clintons and the Livingstons, who only a generation ago had used their aggressive championship of the Revolution to shoulder aside the more reluctant descendants of the Dutch patroons, Burr had secured the election of enough New York City Republicans to the state legislature to give the party control. That control had been used to switch the state's twelve electoral votes from Adams to Jefferson, thus insuring the Virginian's triumph. It had also been the lever by which Burr had hoisted himself to second place on the ticket, despite the prior claims of George Clinton, already six times governor of New York, and of Chancellor Robert R. Livingston, who had served with Jefferson on the committee that drafted the Declaration of Independence.

New York by 1800 was the second largest city in America. Her 60,000 inhabitants more than doubled those of Boston or Baltimore, and were three times as many as Charleston could boast. Only Philadelphia, with close to 70,000, was larger, but would not be for long. In the bustling, hurrying, noisy, smelly city that sprawled across the tip of Manhattan Island, creeping northward to merge with open country a stone's throw beyond City Hall Park, one rubbed elbows with British or Yankee sailors (and who could tell one from the other?), with Irish and German laborers, Scotch traders, free Negroes and Negro slaves. Farmers who came into the city before dawn from Long Island or upper Manhattan to market potatoes or fruit or poultry gossiped with clerks and craftsmen; and if the language they spoke was Dutch, a good half of the city would understand.

These urban workers, like the farmers, toiled through the daylight hours, ten to fourteen according to the season, at bench or last or forge, in shop and counting house, but were never so busy they could not talk politics. The professional men such as the doctors and lawyers worked almost as long, and even the ministers, what with preaching, teaching, writing, presiding over marriages and funerals, visiting the ailing and keeping on friendly terms with the well-to-do, had little or no idle time. One class of busy men to be found in increasing numbers in New York were those who in one way or another had acquired a little money, and by hook or crook were bent upon multiplying it. Most successful but still typical of them all was German-born John Jacob Astor, who already dominated the American fur trade and was now investing heavily in New York real estate. Across the river in Hoboken, New Jersey, John Stevens was building steam engines with which his brother-in-law, Chancellor Livingston, still hoped to drive boats up the Hudson.

Outside New York City, with its diversified interests, the state was strictly agricultural. The Hudson Valley north to the head of navigation at Albany was still the feudal domain of the old Dutch families like the Schuylers and Van Rensselaers. From Albany a ribbon of cultivated land ran west along the Mohawk. To the north and east the tilled lands of New York merged with those of Vermont, and touched Quebec at the head of Lake Champlain. For the rest, there were outposts at Oswego and Niagara, but farmers were pushing into the Genesee Valley and on to the watershed of the Allegheny. Her lakes and rivers made New York a natural gateway to the West that would soon give her metropolis commercial advantage over every rival.

Chief among those rivals was Philadelphia, which served and drew tribute from an agricultural hinterland that included much of New Jersey and extended west to the Ohio Valley. Including Hamilton's Bank of the United States, almost half of all banking capital in America was in Philadelphia in 1800. The city boasted the most extensive and varied industry in the country and a foreign commerce of substantial proportions. Until this very year, Philadelphia had been the capital of the United States, and with her coterie of scientists, artists, and philosophers she was the intellectual capital still. Philadelphia was also conservative. Her merchants and shipowners, alarmed by French contempt for life and property and frightened by what seemed to them a similar lack of restraint on the part of the Republican press, gave their allegiance to Adams, and the state's electoral vote, which had been Jefferson's in 1796, was divided now between the two.

The people of Pennsylvania had none of the homogeneity that

persisted in New England. The original Quaker heritage had long since been diluted by successive waves of immigration including Germans from the Palatinate and Scotch-Irish from Ulster. The Germans, largely of Amish faith, found haven in the vicinity of Lancaster where their descendants live to this day. The Scotch-Irish were more restless. A few, like the Buchanans, remained in the vicinity of Lancaster. Others, like the Jacksons and Calhouns, turned south down the Valley of Virginia; and still others by 1800 had made their way across the mountains to Pittsburgh, which bestrode the Ohio as Philadelphia did the Delaware. Jefferson's strength lay chiefly in the farming country and in western Pennsylvania, where his principal lieutenant was Swiss-born, Geneva-educated Albert Gallatin, hero in the Whiskey Rebellion and, because of his comprehensive knowledge of finance, soon to be Secretary of the Treasury.

The coal of Pennsylvania was still largely unused, save for cooking and heating, but iron was being smelted with charcoal from native hardwoods up and down the Schuylkill Valley, and also in northern New Jersey. In both states were foundries and forges and the more pretentious "iron works" to temper the metal and convert it to articles of daily use—nails, horseshoes, guns, tools for the farmer and the artisan. Of still greater import were the steadily improving steam engines, which in addition to their original use in pumping water were now operating milling machinery and boats. Steamboats, indeed, had been plying the Delaware intermittently ever since John Fitch made his first successful run in 1787. By 1800 Oliver Evans, in Philadelphia, was developing the high-pressure engine that would immensely extend the usefulness of steam as a motive force.

Another Pennsylvania product was the rugged Conestoga wagon, which with its teams of four or six deep-chested, heavily muscled horses hauled loads weighing up to two tons across the Alleghenies and in regular freight service between town and country. These great wagons with their arched covers of gleaming homespun carried the corn and wheat and rye of the farmlands to the cities, as grain or flour or in the still more compact form of whiskey. Furniture, tools and other manufactured articles, household wares, even type and printing presses for the new communities beyond the mountains were cargo for the Conestoga wagons. Heavy keelboats, gliding with the current or laboriously poled upstream, and coastwise sailing vessels were their only rivals for an internal carrying trade that was more than enough for both. The only limit appeared to be the availability of roads and waterways.

Below Pennsylvania lay the South, set off from the free states by the Mason-Dixon line, which was in fact a cultural barrier as well as an economic one. The South had not yet transmuted a common interest and a common fear into political and social unity, but the forces were at work that would tend to concentrate her energies in a single direction. Delaware, which had industrial and commercial as well as agricultural interests, gave her electoral vote to Adams. Maryland, whose Catholic background set her apart from the other southern states and whose interests were divided between agriculture and the commerce of Baltimore, split her vote between Jefferson and Adams; even North Carolina gave the Federalist President a third of her strength. The Republican majority in the South as a whole represented an agrarian bias, and hostility to the concentration of power in the Federal Government lest that power be wielded by northern votes to her disadvantage. In Hamilton's assumption of state debts, and in the chartering of the United States Bank, many southerners believed their section had already been victimized, and they voted for Jefferson as much for the state rights formula he had advanced as for the fact that he was one of themselves.

The factors tending toward southern unity were slaves and cotton. The corn, small grains, and cattle raised for local consumption; the rice of South Carolina and Georgia; even the tobacco of Virginia and Maryland were beginning to pay tribute to King Cotton. The cotton output had catapulted from three million pounds in 1792, the last year before Whitney's gin had been introduced, to more than thirty-six million pounds in 1800; but the mills of England, with their constantly improving textile machinery, still hungered for more. Prices soared and men nursed visions of vast wealth. In the Carolinas and in Georgia the plantation system of the lowlands began to encroach upon the small farms of the piedmont region, introducing slavery where it had not been, or had been only nominal before.

Each new extension of the realm of cotton increased the dependence of the South upon her British market. Each new investment of capital in cotton lands and slaves left less for employment in other pursuits. Thus early was diversification inhibited. The South would grow more conservative as her destiny became more deeply involved with cotton and with the anachronistic system of labor that produced it. Long-standing political and religious differences between the tidewater aristocracy, dominantly of English ancestry and of Anglican faith, and the Presbyterian or Methodist Ulster-Scots who farmed the Appalachian foothills were being erased by 1800 in a conscious bid for internal unity.

Jefferson's campaign did not play overtly upon southern fears, but his lieutenants—especially the faithful James Madison, whose trenchant pen and encyclopedic knowledge of government were among the foremost assets of the party—dwelt incessantly upon checks and balances, the limits of federal authority, and the residual powers of the states. To men who only a dozen years earlier had felt it necessary to tie their system of labor to the Constitution itself, the implications were clear. So the South began her long fealty to what came to be the Democratic party; but then as later her understanding of the party's purposes was very different from that of its northern adherents. The Jeffersonians of the South in 1800 were a landed aristocracy that had drawn into its own orbit a rank and file forced by the very existence of slavery to make common cause with the master class. In the North the party was based on the aspirations and instincts of artisans, small tradesmen, small farmers. The measure of Jefferson's victory was the extent to which he had been able to bring southern planters and northern workers to support a common cause.

If the line of division between North and South was psychological and economic, the barrier between the Atlantic seaboard and the West was physical. The long mountain chain was pierced at intervals by natural passes that had been Indian trails only a generation before. Through these gaps now streamed the wagons and carts and pack animals of new settlers, from Virginia and the Carolinas into Kentucky and Tennessee, and from New England and the middle states into Ohio. Land-hungry pioneers were beginning to push the Indians from the pine barrens and cane-brakes below the Cumberland, and to barter or fight their way into the vaguely defined Illinois country between the Wabash and the Spanish settlement of St. Louis, where the western fur trade centered. By invitation of the Spanish authorities there were already more Americans there than there were Spaniards and Frenchmen combined. The beaver pelts and other furs bartered by Indians for knives, whiskey and trinkets still went by La Salle's old route from St. Louis up the Illinois River and through the Great Lakes to Montreal. The heavier buffalo hides, and lead from the mines at Potosi newly reopened by Moses Austin, floated down the Mississippi to mingle with the commerce of the Ohio Valley.

That commerce was growing mightily, with Cincinnati, Louisville, Nashville, and finally Natchez adding their boatloads of grain or flour or whiskey, cotton and hides, and a mounting variety of manufactured articles to those from Pittsburgh on the long journey to Europe or the Atlantic ports by way of New Orleans, where the right to unload and transship to ocean-going vessels was guaranteed by treaty with Spain. Few realized that the treaty had expired in 1798, but those who did thought little of it. It was enough for them that this ever-expanding western commerce was profitable to all concerned.

Thus it was clear by 1800 that whoever controlled the Mississippi would control the West, and almost as clear that the first

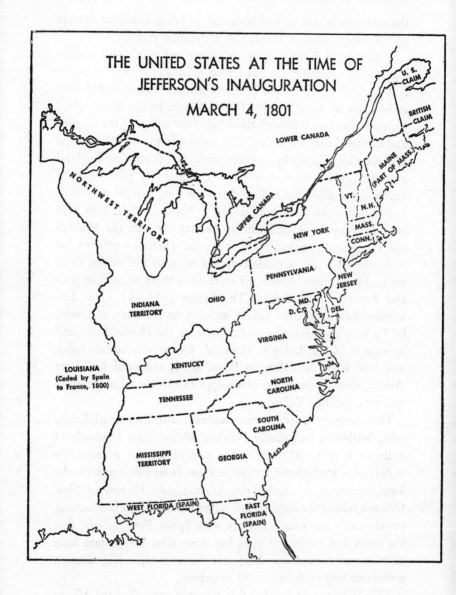

THE UNITED STATES AT THE TIME OF
JEFFERSON'S INAUGURATION
MARCH 4, 1801

U. S. CLAIM

BRITISH CLAIM

LOWER CANADA

MAINE (PART OF MASS.)

NORTHWEST TERRITORY

UPPER CANADA

VT.

N.H.

MASS.

CONN.

NEW YORK

PENNSYLVANIA

NEW JERSEY

INDIANA TERRITORY

OHIO

MD.

D.C.

DEL.

VIRGINIA

LOUISIANA (Ceded by Spain to France, 1800)

KENTUCKY

NORTH CAROLINA

TENNESSEE

SOUTH CAROLINA

MISSISSIPPI TERRITORY

GEORGIA

WEST FLORIDA (SPAIN)

EAST FLORIDA (SPAIN)

loyalty of the western people, however their representatives might declaim in Congress, was to the River. Except for a few sober ones among the Ohio Yankees, they were an emotional lot, boastful and quick-tempered and ready to fall in with any new project that might be offered, no matter how improbable. They were periodically "saved" by itinerant evangelists who preached in relays; but their redemption never kept them from gambling hugely at cards, or marred their pleasure in horse-racing, cockfighting, wrestling or carousing. If not completely self-sufficient yet, they were on the way to it, with newspapers, colleges, and even a colorful folklore of their own. They believed in easy credit and uncurbed expansion, both goals they found implicit in the Jeffersonian attack on Federalist financial policy.

The partisan bitterness of the campaign still lingered when Thomas Jefferson, just six weeks short of his fifty-eighth birthday, walked the two hundred yards from Conrad's boarding house to the Capitol at noon on March 4, 1801, to take the oath as third President of the United States. Tall, raw-boned, freckled, with sandy-red hair now turning gray, his garb careless or slovenly according to your point of view, and manners easy but without polish, he fitted naturally into the expanse of water, woods and open fields half circled by low hills that was Washington City. From the high ground to the west the small community of Georgetown looked across with a mixture of disdain and envy at the one completed wing of the Capitol that stood naked amidst a cluster of shops and boarding houses. Between the two lay the inhabitable but unfinished White House (called the "Palace" by some) with its entourage of homes and buildings. Most of the city's 3,200 inhabitants, 600 of them Negro slaves, lived near the President's house or on Capitol Hill. These two settled areas were joined by a muddy slash through swamp and woodland that was dignified by the name of Pennsylvania Avenue.

John Adams, who had lost the election and with it the office he had held tempestuously for the past four years, did not wait to witness the inauguration of his one-time friend. Neither was

Alexander Hamilton, the real leader of the defeated Federalists, in the city. Yet Hamilton a bare two weeks before had sent word from New York to elect Jefferson as the lesser evil when his followers in the House of Representatives would have thwarted the popular will and chosen the Republican vice-presidential candidate, Aaron Burr, instead. Small of stature but with magnetic charm, Burr was a manipulator of men, whose purposes were so well concealed and whose methods were so devious that none knew then or knows today how far he might have been willing to go in quest of glory or in search of gain. His electoral vote and Jefferson's had been the same, thanks to an oversight by those who wrote the Constitution,* and in the tie the Federalists who would control Congress for a few more days had seen the prospect of salvaging something of power and place. Intrigue and rumors of intrigue filled the snow-laden atmosphere of Washington. Some thought Adams would try to retain his office, others that Burr would perpetuate Federalist power in return for the Presidency. The Republican governors of Virginia and Pennsylvania were considering armed intervention by the state militia when Hamilton broke the tie in behalf of his intellectual adversary against his political foe. Now, as Vice-President, Burr presided in the small Senate chamber while Jefferson read his inaugural address.

An aristocrat by birth and taste, Jefferson's championship of the common man was impersonal, scientific, pragmatic. In a narrowly materialistic age, he brought to government idealism and breadth of vision, tempered by political shrewdness. An individualist who prized freedom more than order and placed human welfare above the rights of property, he had lately added

---

* Electors were originally required simply to vote for two persons, the one with the largest vote to be President and the second largest Vice-President. In case of a tie, the House of Representatives was to determine the outcome, each state casting one ballot. The system could hardly fail to result in a President of one party and Vice-President of another, as in 1796; or in a tie, as in 1800. The 12th Amendment, ratified before the election of 1804, provided for separate balloting for President and for Vice-President.

to his creed in the Kentucky Resolutions the dogma of the states as guardians of individual liberty. The Resolutions had been evoked by the subversion of the Bill of Rights in the Alien and Sedition Acts, which Hamilton's "high-Federalist" followers jammed through Congress early in 1798. These reprobated statutes pronounced it sedition to criticize the government or hold up to ridicule any of its officials and subjected the foreign-born to rigorous control under threat of deportation. To Thomas Jefferson all this was both tyrannical and unconstitutional, but argument proved no match for the fines and prison terms meted out by Federalist judges. So Jefferson drafted and the Kentucky legislature passed resolutions declaring that the remedy in such cases lay with the states. The Constitution was defined as a compact between sovereigns by which the contracting parties delegated certain powers to a general government created by them for that purpose. Should the government exceed its powers, "each party [i.e., each state] has an equal right to judge for itself, as well of infractions as of the mode and measure of redress." In other words the states might pass judgment on the Congress, and each was to decide for itself what to do about any law it pronounced to be unconstitutional.

Virginia followed Kentucky with similar resolutions from the pen of James Madison, and other states were soon embroiled in the controversy. It is notable that those controlled by the Republican party tended to concur in the state rights formula, while those whose legislatures showed Federalist majorities upheld the right of the central government to judge of its own powers. The debate quickly became general and merged with the more familiar issues of the presidential campaign. The principles of Federalism owed less to Adams than to the mercurial Hamilton, but both agreed in advocating government by a ruling class whose self-interest would be the best guarantee of solvency and stability; a government strong enough to protect property at home or at sea, to levy and collect taxes, to put down internal rebellion. Jefferson believed in the infinite perfectability of man, whose unalienable right to life, liberty and the pursuit of happiness it was the primary business of government to assure. He advanced the premise, seemingly borne out by the Alien and Sedition Acts themselves, that the kind of power the Federalists wanted could also be used to deprive of liberty, of livelihood, even of life itself all who dissented for whatever reason. At the end of the eighteenth century the fear of tyranny remained very real and there was nothing in the meteoric rise of Napoleon Bonaparte to indicate that times had changed. The state rights doctrine advanced by Jefferson in the Kentucky Resolutions was a defense of civil liberty against the arbitrary power of government, but it would soon be turned to support the most reactionary of vested interests.

What the new President hoped to accomplish as a long-range goal was to substitute a government by the mass of the people for the rule by a propertied few that characterized Federalism. But he knew well that the masses were far from agreed among themselves as to what they wanted their government to be and do. The Congress elected with Jefferson was dominated by the South, with her human chattels to secure and her growing dependence upon a foreign market for her staple crops, but at the same time he owed his own election to northern votes in New York and Pennsylvania, where the leading interests were a thriving commerce and a nursling industry, and where the dominant party—in spite of his election—was not his own. So in his inaugural statement of policy, Jefferson made his bid for all shades and complexions of opinion, even inviting the defeated Federalists to rally to his standard. The principles for which he stood, and the program he meant to follow were so broadly stated that it was difficult for friend or foe to take issue with him. Indeed, the nicely balanced elements of his creed would be mouthed by partisans for generations to come in support of positions as far apart as the poles.

Any hope there may have been for an end to party warfare in the new administration was quickly dissipated when the President set himself to eradicate Federalist control of public offices and to break the hold of the defeated party on the courts. In his last weeks of office, John Adams, convinced by his own partisans that anarchy was at hand, had become panicky. He had done his level best to stack the political deck in favor of the conservative side. The vacant Chief Justiceship went to formidable John Marshall of Virginia. Lesser offices, such as collectors of customs, postmasters, consuls, and departmental clerks also were filled by good and loyal Federalists, and new offices for more Federalists were made. The judiciary system was overhauled, reorganizing old courts and creating new, each with its judges, clerks and functionaries; and justices of the peace were named at the President's discretion, which appeared to be limited only by the speed with which he could sign his name to their commissions.

While Jefferson did not claim the appointive offices as spoils of victory, he meant much the same thing when he argued that a chief executive must be allowed to act through instruments of his own choice. When he found himself with no offices to fill below Cabinet level and saw no Federalist resignations passing over his desk, he undertook to create vacancies, beginning with those offices Adams had filled after the election returns were in. Marshall and the other judges he could not reach, but there were justices of the peace whose commissions had not yet been delivered, so recently had the appointments been made. These commissions Jefferson withheld. He then replaced the other of Adams' "midnight appointments" with men of his own choosing. After that Jefferson moved more slowly, but before his first term was over half of the offices filled by the President with the concurrence of the Senate had changed hands. In distributing the patronage in New York it was significant that Jefferson did not consult Burr, despite his own political debt to his Vice-President, but followed instead the advice of the Clinton and Livingston factions. It was a snub that turned Burr's never-too-scrupulous ambition to seeking other channels for its expression. Jefferson was preparing to attack the Federalist stronghold of the courts when public attention and his own were diverted to the Mississippi.

The West had suddenly burst into flame. After years of profitable acquiescence in the practice, the Spanish authorities at New Orleans now abruptly refused to allow American river boats to unload their cargoes for transfer to ocean-going vessels. The commerce of the Ohio Valley, amounting to a million dollars a year, was not to be surrendered so lightly. Always aggressive and, where her "honor" was concerned, impetuous, the West demanded war with Spain, and the Federalists, for no better reason than the discomfiture of the President, egged them on. When news reached Washington confirming the transfer of sovereignty over Louisiana from Spain to France, Jefferson prepared to intervene.

Louisiana had been ceded by France to Spain in 1763, but Napoleon, firmly in control by 1800, had decided to take it back. Spain had been too weak to resist. The treaty of retrocession had not been made public but rumors of the transfer reached the United States in 1801. Jefferson then sent Robert R. Livingston as Minister to France with instructions to prevent the retrocession if he could. If it was already too late for that, he was to make an offer for West Florida, which was understood to include both Mobile Bay and the east bank of the Mississippi south of latitude 31°. When the transfer of Louisiana to France was confirmed, James Monroe, whose term as Governor of Virginia had just expired, was hastily sent to join Livingston in Paris, and a secret appropriation of $2,000,000 to defray expenses was rushed through Congress by Jefferson's partisans. Monroe carried more detailed instructions than it had been possible to give to Livingston. The two negotiators were to offer up to $10,000,000 if need be for New Orleans and the Floridas, but the President would settle if he must for no more than a promise that American ships might navigate the river through what was now French territory and might unload and reship their goods at New Orleans. If even this much could not be secured, there was no alternative but to treat France thereafter as an enemy. In that event the Americans were to cross the Channel and make what terms they could with Britain against a common foe.

Napoleon, as usual, had considered all the angles. Without bases on Santo Domingo, which had already been lost, along with 35,000 French troops to rebellious slaves and yellow fever, he knew that he could not hold Louisiana against the British fleet. Once he had renewed his war with England, the territory would therefore be worthless, but if he acted quickly he might get for it badly needed cash from the Americans, who did not even know how rich they were. When Monroe's arrival at Le Havre was reported by heliograph, Talleyrand asked Livingston what his government would pay for all of Louisiana. In a matter of days the bargain was struck. Two months later, in July, 1803, news reached Washington that the United States had agreed to pay Bonaparte what would amount to some $15,000,000 in return for all the lands still claimed by France on the North American continent.

Jefferson, taken wholly unaware, first doubted the government's authority to purchase territory for which no appropriation had been made. Trapped by his own strict-construction arguments of 1798, he hastily discussed with his advisers a constitutional amendment to validate what his envoys had done. The mass of the people, save only an undertermined number in New England, brushed aside such niceties. They wanted Louisiana and that was enough authority for them. Their representatives in Congress quickly voted the necessary funds, and on December 20, 1803, the American flag was raised in New Orleans. The extent of the new territory was indefinite, but all sources agreed that it was vast, extending from the Mississippi to the fabled Rocky Mountains, so remote that only a handful of white men had ever seen those majestic peaks. Even without West Florida, which it was claimed had been excluded from the tract returned by Spain to France, the new acquisition was almost enough to double the land area of the United States.

But if Jefferson had been surprised that France would part so easily with Louisiana, he was not wholly unprepared. Young Meriwether Lewis, lately the President's private secretary, and Lewis' chosen companion, William Clark, had been dispatched with proper passports to find a land route across northern Louisiana to the Pacific before the purchase was known. The Oregon country had been for ten years already a favorite port of call for New England skippers who traded with the Indians for the furs which became in turn the currency of a highly profitable commerce with China. The Hudson's Bay Company was also interested in the fur trade of the Northwest, but a practical overland passage would help give the United States a competitive advantage. Lewis and Clark wintered in southern Illinois, across the river from the busy town of St. Louis, where they would help to raise the American flag before starting up the Missouri in the spring. While the more famous pair were spanning the continent by way of the Yellowstone and Columbia rivers, Captain Zebulon Pike traced the Mississippi to its source, then explored the headwaters of the Arkansas and Red rivers, and made contact with the Spanish settlements in New Mexico.

It was perhaps as well that these exploring expeditions were not generally known, for Jefferson's ideas as to the destiny of the continent were very different from those of the New England Federalists, led, since Adams' repudiation at the polls, by Senator Timothy Pickering of Massachusetts. Pickering, who had been Quartermaster General in the last years of the Revolution, yearned for military glory, but his real genius lay in agitation and intrigue. As Secretary of State in Adams' Cabinet, he had found no difficulty in stretching the Constitution to cover the Alien and Sedition Acts, but the purchase of Louisiana was another matter. He could find nothing in the document to authorize the purchase of any territory at all, much less a land peopled by slaveholding foreigners who would sire new states joined in interest to the West and South. The truth was that Pickering and the hard-core Federalists of the Essex Junto—a group of wealthy merchants identified by the name of the county from which most of them came—had never forgiven Jefferson for his victory in 1800. They had put their fears temporarily at rest, because the Republican President had retained the codfish bounty and had dealt decisively with the Barbary pirates to the advantage of New England shipping; but Louisiana sent them plunging headlong into a new and intensified form of opposition. They saw New England and her allies of the middle states as a permanent minority, defenseless against legalized plunder by the numerically stronger group, and they prepared to withdraw their own states while yet they might. The arguments Jefferson had used in the Kentucky Resolutions were ready-made to serve their purposes; for if the Constitution were indeed a compact between sovereign states, which alone might judge of infractions and determine remedies, then surely a state might legitimately decide that the remedy was to leave the Union. The theme would recur again and again in many guises until it would be put to rest at last by force of arms.

In the plans of the Essex Junto—freely communicated to Anthony Merry, the British Minister—the cornerstone of the northern confederacy they envisioned would be New York, where Hamilton controlled the party and might be counted on to give them his support. Hamilton pointedly condemned the secession rumors that were soon table talk in all the northern states, but Aaron Burr, repudiated by his party and dropped from the 1804 Republican ticket in favor of George Clinton, allowed his name to be put up by dissidents of both parties for Governor of New York. If all went well the Federalists might give him their support in return for his at the proper time. Again, as on earlier occasions, Hamilton loomed across his path, endorsing the candidacy of the man already backed for Governor by the Clintons, the Livingstons, and the President. With all factions against him, Burr's defeat was crushing, but he held Hamilton alone responsible. Behind the slanderous words that could not be withdrawn, behind the challenge and the acceptance, lay fifteen years of bitter rivalry. The two men met on the dueling ground at Weehawken, New Jersey, in the early morning of July 11, 1804. Hamilton fell, mortally wounded, and Burr fled to Philadelphia to keep a rendezvous with General James Wilkinson, fresh from New Orleans, where he had received the territory from France in the name of the United States. Wilkinson was still the ranking officer of the Army, but he would not have been had Burr not interceded for him in the early days of Jefferson's administration. He was also an accomplished scoundrel, who courted both intrigue and money, and had discovered many ways by which his two passions might feed upon each other. What passed between the General and the Vice-President we do not know; but before he reached Washington in December, 1804, Burr had solicited from the British Minister financial and military aid in a scheme to separate the western country from the Union, and Merry listened as dispassionately as he had listened to the proposals of the Essex Junto.

Thanks to Merry's indifference, Hamilton's loyalty, and perhaps most of all to Jefferson's wisdom, the New England secession movement had meanwhile collapsed. Though aware of the conspiracy, if such it may be called, the President had said and done nothing. The country was at peace and prosperous, taxes were low, the public debt was on the way to extinction; the Mississippi was open to unrestricted commerce, and beyond the great river American soil stretched westward endlessly. Could New England do better on her own, or in alliance with Great Britain? The voters agreed she could not, and Jefferson was reelected with only Connecticut and Delaware opposed. When the votes were counted, the President prepared once more to move against the courts where the last stronghold of Federalism lay.

He had already eliminated a handful of judges by persuading Congress to repeal the law that created their offices, and he might have been content with that had it not been for his kinsman, John Marshall. The cold intelligence and iron control of the Chief Justice concealed the talents of a master political strategist who more than any other single individual would transmute the loose federal structure created by the founding fathers into a nation strong enough to withstand even the shock of civil war. One of Adams' midnight appointees as justice of the peace had sued the Secretary of State for the commission Jefferson had withheld, and Marshall, though he refused to order the President to issue the commission, had used Marbury *v*. Madison to assert the power of the Supreme Court to overrule acts of Congress. In this power so subtly claimed but not yet put to use, Jefferson could hardly fail to see a tool by which the will of the people, expressed through their representatives in Congress and their President, could be thwarted by three judges (the Supreme Court then had only five members), holding office for life and therefore beyond the popular reach. The remedy was to make them responsible by making them insecure.

To establish precedent a United States District Judge, who was peculiarly vulnerable because his mind had given way, was quickly impeached. Then plans were laid to impeach Associate Justice Samuel Chase of the Supreme Court. It was, of course, John Marshall at whom Jefferson's ire was directed, but Chase, signer of the Declaration of Independence though he was, seemed more easily within reach. In the popular mind—and Jefferson's— Chase was identified with the Alien and Sedition Acts, those instruments of oppression that had become for the Republicans the very embodiment of ruthless and arbitrary power. He had presided over the most notorious of the trials, and still made no pretense of concealing his prejudices in long political harangues from the bench. The charges against him were brought in proper form by the House of Representatives, for which John Randolph of Roanoke, brilliant, capricious, sometimes prophetic and always implacable Virginia member served as prosecutor. The Senate, with Aaron Burr presiding, sat in judgment.

Jefferson had set his heart on a conviction, and so he received his Vice-President with unaccustomed warmth. There was no mention of the way Hamilton had died, or of the indictments against Burr for issuing a challenge in New York and for murder in New Jersey. Though he had little to gain and nothing more to lose, Burr's conduct of the Chase impeachment trial was a model of firm impartiality and decorum. It was Randolph who failed, or better, Jefferson; for though Chase's faults were many, they were not impeachable. His acquittal was a turning point for the Supreme Court, which under Marshall would ultimately make of these United States something greater than the sum of its parts.

In a way it was a turning point for all concerned. From this rebuff Jefferson turned his energies back to territorial expansion. The purchase of Louisiana had been popular, except with a few die-hard Federalists, and had strengthened his administration. Acquisition of the Floridas, he hoped, would make up in popularity what the court fight had cost him in prestige. But fearing to alienate Spain by revealing his purpose prematurely, he asked an appropriation in secret, without telling the Congress precisely how it was to be used. Randolph learned the purpose from Madison, who hinted also that, should Spain prove reluctant, Bonaparte might be willing for a price to repeat the Louisiana pattern. The Virginia congressman, inclined to take personally the administration's defeat in the Chase impeachment and suspicious of his collaborators in that ill-advised venture, probed deep for duplicity and deceit in this latest land speculation. He recalled an earlier real estate promotion in which corruption had tainted the sale of state lands along the Yazoo River by the Georgia legislature; repudiation had come only after resale to individual investors, and Jefferson had failed to discriminate between innocent and guilty. For Randolph there were no shades of gray but only black and white. He turned savagely against the President, to become the focus of an opposition that would shatter Jefferson's dream of infinite improvement and leave the dogs of faction baying at his heels.

For Burr also the die was cast, the Rubicon crossed, the bridges burned. To his vaulting ambition, territory was not to be pro-

cured by haggling like a peasant over price or title. The amplifying world of the nineteenth century belonged to the bold and
the daring, like the Corsican brigand who had made himself
master of half a continent. Burr knew that Hamilton, too, had
thought in some such terms when he had tricked Adams into
giving him command of an army, and he did not believe the
Essex Junto had meant to stop with New England and New
York. In the West, where not land alone but empire was ready
for the taking, Burr did not doubt he would find kindred spirits
for any venture he might fix upon. His friend General Wilkinson, adept at cozening money from the Spaniards, was one; and
he remembered Andrew Jackson of Tennessee, who had served
briefly with him in the Senate and had seemed sympathetic. In
the spring of 1805 Burr called once more on the British Minister,
with a concrete offer to separate the West from the Union for
half a million dollars and a British fleet in the Gulf of Mexico.
He then set out overland for Pittsburgh and a leisurely, almost a
triumphal journey down the Ohio and Mississippi to New
Orleans.

The notion of starting a new confederacy in the West would
not have seemed particularly treasonable to Burr, nor would the
private conquest of Mexico if that rather than a western empire
were his real intent. If, as Jefferson himself had said, the states
were sovereign, the Union was hardly more than a rope of sand.
As for Mexico, was it not part of every American's creed that
Indians must give way to the triumphant march of civilization?
And who would care if a handful of Spaniards were evicted
along with the savages? With Bonaparte at her back and the
British Navy never out of gunshot of her coasts, would Spain
go to war for Mexico? Neither scheme would have seemed
bizarre to Merry, either. From his vantage point also the American Union was a tenuous and impermanent thing, whose government was too weak or too indifferent to protect itself from
treasonable acts. Better than most, the British Minister knew how
far Pickering had been willing to go, yet the Massachusetts

Senator had lost nothing in prestige or place. When the time came for Britain to regain her lost colonies, there would be, he thought, no dearth of hirelings ready to pocket His Majesty's gold.

As Burr had calculated, he found volunteers more than ready to help him in whatever it was he meant to do. Everywhere in the West, where it was no disgrace but rather a mark of distinction to have killed one's rival in a duel, he was lionized by such as young Henry Clay in Lexington and accorded by Andrew Jackson in Tennessee all the honors due to one who has held the second office in the Republic. General Wilkinson, now military governor of Louisiana Territory with headquarters at St. Louis, was waiting at the mouth of the Ohio with boats for the remainder of the journey to New Orleans.

The following year, Burr returned to the West, still undaunted even though the British had ignored his schemes and Spain had deemed his potential services not worth the asking price. With a force of sixty men in nine boats and money raised by friends, Burr proceeded once more down the river, this time officially explaining his mission as one of colonization in the Red River country. Rumor had it otherwise, and twice he was arrested in Kentucky, charged with an intent to make war on Mexico. With Clay as his counsel, he was both times cleared, only to be picked up in Mississippi Territory and charged once more. Again he was acquitted but now he found himself friendless. Wilkinson, deciding Burr's was a losing cause, had betrayed certain "confidences" to the authorities. Burr sought to flee to Spanish Florida but was taken and brought to Richmond to stand trial for treason.

After weeks of delay he was brought before a grand jury. There were further delays for assembling witnesses, including General Wilkinson, whose testimony was so incriminating he narrowly missed being indicted himself, and Andrew Jackson, who was excused by the prosecution because he was too friendly toward the prisoner. Burr was eventually held for trial, which took place in an atmosphere charged with personal tensions, political rivalries, and public airing of private hostilities. The Richmond courtroom, in anticipation, had become a social mecca for the gentry from fifty miles around. John Marshall presided; George Hay, the United States Attorney in Richmond, was the prosecutor; defense counsel was Federalist Luther Martin of Maryland, who had also defended Chase. None could forget that Burr had so recently been only a heartbeat from the Presidency; or the manner of Hamilton's death. As the trial got under way the President, with unsuspected vindictiveness, virtually took over the prosecution from his White House study, acting through Hay and the United States Attorney General. It was no secret that Jefferson, after the failure of the Chase impeachment, would welcome any opportunity to discredit Marshall, or that Marshall would go to almost any length to uphold the independence of the courts, which he conceived the President to be attacking. At one point Marshall, at the request of Burr's counsel, issued a subpoena for Jefferson, who refused to honor it. As in his earlier bout with the judiciary, it was Jefferson whose knuckles were rapped. The Chief Justice ruled that treason must involve an overt act of war against the United States. Such an act was not proved, and Aaron Burr was set free.

The Burr conspiracy served to emphasize again the remoteness of the West, and the looseness of the cord that bound the Mississippi Valley to the Union, to say nothing of the boundless lands beyond, from which Lewis and Clark had so recently and so confidently returned. Let the West continue to grow and to develop in comparative isolation and some other adventurer would succeed where Burr had failed. The pressing need was for better communication and closer ties of commerce between East and West. A National Road, financed by the sale of public lands in Ohio and by congressional appropriation, already groped toward the Ohio River from Cumberland on the headwaters of the Potomac. The administration now proposed that this road should be only one of many routes across the mountains. The

others, as worked out by Gallatin, were to link the Hudson River
by canal with Lake Champlain and Lake Ontario, with a water
passage around Niagara Falls; and to connect the Atlantic watershed with that of the Ohio by highways joining three pairs of
rivers: the Susquehanna and the Allegheny in Pennsylvania;
the James and the Kanawha in Virginia; and farther south the
Santee and the Tennessee. North and South were to be similarly
brought closer by a coastal inland waterway, and by a turnpike
from Maine to Georgia.

The plan was shelved even before its details were put in place.
The Richmond grand jury was still hearing evidence in the case
of Aaron Burr when a British warship overhauled and fired upon
an American naval vessel within sight of the American coast,
and the position of the United States with respect to Europe was
suddenly the only question of importance before the country. The
West would prove its loyalty and reveal its power; but the peace-
loving philosopher-President who had stressed the rights of man
and the autonomy of the states as the guardians of liberty would
be faced with the necessity of curbing both in order to avoid a
war for which neither he nor the country was prepared.

2

There Are No Neutrals

THERE WAS NO reason why the United States frigate *Chesapeake* should have been stripped for action when she stood out to sea on June 22, 1807. There would be no action until she reached the Mediterranean, where she was to relieve her sister ship, the *Constitution,* and probably none even then. The Barbary pirates had made no trouble since the treaty of 1805 with Tripoli. Coils of rope, rolls of canvas, and unmounted rigging still cluttered her decks and encumbered her thirty-eight guns when she passed the Virginia capes, where a British squadron lay in wait for a handful of French warships to quit the Bay. The British frigate *Leopard* trailed the *Chesapeake* beyond the limit of national waters, then signaled "dispatches" but sent instead a demand for the surrender of deserters. When the American commander, veteran Commodore James Barron, refused, the *Leopard* opened fire at point-blank range. Minutes later, with three dead, his ship crippled, and himself among the eighteen wounded, Barron struck his flag. The British took four men who had indeed departed the King's service without leave (though three were Americans whose earlier British "enlistments" had been under similar compulsion) but they would not take Barron's sword, nor hold the *Chesapeake* as prize.

News of the outrage was received the country over with angry demands for vengeance. In Norfolk, nearest to the scene, mobs

roamed the streets in search of British sailors, and the town fathers
refused water and provisions to British ships. In port cities
from Charleston to New York and even in Federalist Boston, the
aggravated memory of similar occurrences swelled protest meetings and sharpened the tone of resolutions pledging men and
money. Then the West took up the cry and for a little time a loose,
uncertain confederation was a nation. War would have been the
logical and popular response, but Jefferson would not go that far.
His reluctance stemmed in part from the avowed hostility of the
Essex Junto, the dubious loyalty of Louisiana's Creoles, and in the
light of disclosures coming out of the trial of Aaron Burr, a possible disaffection of the West. But his best argument was national
interest, which seemed to dictate strict neutrality in the mighty
struggle then raging over land and sea between France and
Britain. Following his own judgment, the President called Congress to meet six weeks ahead of its regular December session and
met the *Chesapeake* outrage by excluding British vessels from
American waters.

In context, the *Chesapeake* affair was only a minor incident,
not really aimed at the United States at all. The sailors taken from
that luckless ship, and others like them, might even be written off
as partial satisfaction of a lien against Louisiana, for that rich territory could not have been so easily acquired, had it not been for
the pervading presence of the British fleet. It was a fleet whose
warships were perennially short of seamen and whose time-honored method of recruiting was by force. In less stringent times the
press gangs raided only British ships, but the long war with
France had increased the need for men even as it had limited the
supply. There were fewer British merchant ships to raid and there
were more deserters. It was to recover these deserters that British
boarding parties first visited American ships; then British nation-
als were taken indiscriminately, and finally as survival overrode
all other considerations, American citizens as well. It has been
estimated that 20,000 British seamen deserted to the United States
between the Revolution and the War of 1812, in return for which

about 9,000 were impressed from American vessels. That the men recovered were seldom the men who had been lost was immaterial. From the British point of view, the United States still had the better of the exchange.

Indeed, the United States stood to be the principal beneficiary of the war, in British eyes. American shipowners had taken advantage of their country's neutrality and of the skill and daring of their crews to seize the carrying trade of the world as Britain was forced by her own competing demands for men and ships to let it go. With prices adjusted to compensate for risk, American grain, cotton, and meat products found ready markets in England and at Continental ports. Trade between France and Spain and their respective West Indian colonies was likewise carried on in American ships, which evaded British restrictions by calling first at an American port and paying duty, most of which was later rebated. This profitable triangular trade was outlawed by Britain without warning in 1805, at the same time that impressments were being multiplied and British warships were becoming so numerous in American waters that no merchantman could enter or leave a harbor except under their guns. In this crisis, the President again called upon James Monroe, this time to go to London, where he and William Pinkney, the mildly Federalist attorney general of Maryland, were to persuade the British to give up impressment and to permit reopening of the West Indian trade. In return for these concessions, Jefferson could only promise that a retaliatory act of Congress prohibiting the importation of certain British goods would not be put into effect.

Monroe and Pinkney found the British conciliatory, but on the real points at issue immovable. Napoleon had forged from the debris of the French Revolution a military power the more dangerous because it no longer claimed any moral moorings. Bonaparte's ambition was without limit, his methods devious, his resources vast. Only the naval might of Great Britain lay between him and world conquest on a scale to dwarf the dreams of a Caesar or a Genghis Khan. The American envoys considered the tight blockade of the European coast from Brest to the Elbe, noted the grim mood of the British people, and decided to take the best treaty they could get regardless of their instructions. The only concession was that the three-cornered West Indian trade would be permitted provided that not more than 99 percent of the duty was rebated, and that neither destination nor point of origin was a blockaded port, but it was a meaningless gesture, since all French and Spanish ports were either already blockaded or could be declared so at any time. Nothing at all was said about impressment. On the whole the treaty was little if any better than the one John Jay had made in Washington's time, which also failed to end impressment or to deal effectively with the West Indian trade, and for which failure Jay had been roundly condemned by Monroe himself. Neither Jefferson nor Madison believed, when the Monroe-Pinkney Treaty reached Washington, that it could be ratified by the Senate, and so it was allowed to die quietly in the State Department. Monroe returned to Virginia to nurse his wounded pride while the thicker-skinned Pinkney remained as resident Minister in London.

The treaty was signed on December 31, 1806, simultaneously with the arrival of month-old news from France. To counter the British blockade, Napoleon had issued a decree from Berlin prohibiting all commerce with England and making all vessels sailing from England or her colonies subject to seizure. The American treaty was forthwith amended, Britain reserving the right to retaliate against the French decree in any way she saw fit unless the Americans resisted its enforcement. Retaliate she did immediately with another Order in Council on January 7, 1807, closing the coasting trade of France and French-occupied countries to neutral shipping. For the time being American commerce suffered no further ill effects, because Napoleon chose not to enforce the Berlin decree against Americans. He was waiting for an agreement with Czar Alexander that would close to Great Britain her last continental source of grain. This agreement he achieved in the summer of 1807. The Berlin decree was forthwith invoked and any vessel flying the United States flag was thereafter treated as a prize. If the ship had not been trading with the enemy, or carrying British goods, her crew spoke English, which was almost enough in itself for condemnation. The attack on the *Chesapeake,* coming as it did before the French shift of policy was known in Washington, played directly into Napoleon's hand by channeling American wrath toward his enemy rather than himself.

When Congress met in an atmosphere of sober second thought on October 26, America was still a pawn in the European game of war. The special British envoy who arrived in mid-November to discuss the *Chesapeake* was forbidden to negotiate at all until British vessels were readmitted to American waters. It scarcely mattered, for the same ship that brought the envoy brought also the text of a Royal Proclamation of October 17, directing the British Navy to impress "British subjects" to the fullest extent from neutral vessels, and the unofficial word of a forthcoming Order in Council that would prohibit all trade through ports from which the British flag was excluded, unless a British port had first been visited, duty paid, and a fresh clearance obtained. Napoleon would reply with another decree, promulgated from Milan in Italy on December 17, 1807, ordering confiscation of every ship that had complied with any provision of this latest British order.

Jefferson did not wait for Napoleon to move. He asked for and obtained an embargo that would prohibit the exportation of any goods whatever from the United States. Under British Orders in Council and French decrees, American ships were subject to seizure by one belligerent or the other no matter where they went or what they carried. Jefferson would "protect" them by seeing that they went nowhere and carried nothing.

More positively, he hoped to starve England into a change of policy. Though politically the early and staunch advocate of American independence, Jefferson in his economic thinking conceived the United States as a colonial hinterland of Britain still. He believed the best permanent relationship for all concerned was that by which the United States sent the products of her fields and forests to England in return for the fabricated articles whose manufacture at home would corrupt his fellow citizens. For half a century Britain had leaned heavily on America to feed and clothe her people. Now, with the European continent closed to her, she would need more than ever the things America had to sell. The embargo was to cut off the supply at the source and through privation bring the proud mistress of the seas to heel.

This happy outcome, even if it could be brought about, would necessarily take time. The reaction at home was immediate and vocal. The South tried spinning and weaving for herself the cotton she could no longer ship to Europe; then gave it up and sold to New England merchants for whatever they would pay. In New York, Republicans fell to quarreling among themselves, making Federalist voices sound the louder in protest. New England quickly forgot her indignant reaction to the *Chesapeake* outrage and accepted once more the leadership of the Essex Junto. Jefferson was quite unprepared for the reception accorded his carefully devised retort to foreign aggression by those whose interests he was most trying to protect. But the truth was that the President was more successful than either the British or the French in stopping American commerce, and the commercial classes, to a man, resented it. Neither Bonaparte nor the British fleet had succeeded in keeping American ships from trading with whom they pleased. Sleek and swift and as skillfully manned as any vessels afloat, the Americans had been running both blockades, at prices so high that the owners could afford to lose two cargoes out of three and still grow rich. A merchantman bound for England had only to show her papers to the first British warship that fired a shot across her bows, and she could enjoy the protection of the Royal Navy for the remainder of the voyage. If she were bound for a continental port she could outsail the blockading frigates or she could carry two sets of papers and slip away from her "protectors" when opportunity offered. The embargo would put an end to all this by keeping American ships at home. There would be no further losses to the belligerent powers and no further impressment, but neither would there be any trade or any profit.

In practice, American trade was not completely ended. Ships at sea were warned wherever communication was possible, and many of them did not again make home ports. Instead they piled up more profits for their owners in whatever trade came to hand; for any risk was better than the certainty of rotting at the wharves of Boston or Salem or New York. Merchantmen caught at home went into the coastal trade, picking up in southern ports cargoes of wheat and cotton, corn or tobacco or sugar, for New England states that never before consumed a fraction as much. Nor had the ships concerned ever suffered such ill luck before. There were mysterious storms, broken compasses, defective rudders, a dozen other "acts of God" and skippers would "swear through a nine-inch plank" that their unheralded appearance in Nova Scotia or the Bahamas was beyond their control. In an effort to plug the leak, Jefferson required certificates of necessity from the governors of states importing produce from other states by coasting vessels. The governors—even the Republican ones—correctly read the temper of their people and issued whatever certificates were requested. Smuggling across the Canadian and Florida borders became routine.

Fortunately for the party in power, most of the local elections that would determine the complexion of state legislatures and hence of presidential electors were held in the spring of 1808, before the embargo was felt with its full severity. Jefferson's handpicked successor, James Madison, won a grudging caucus nomination from party members in Congress, but Randolph and his dissident followers supported James Monroe, while anti-embargo Republicans put Clinton's name ahead of Madison's in New York. Though the Republican margin was substantial, the Federalists more than tripled their electoral vote of 1804. The whole of New England was back under Federalist control and ready to hearken once again to the subversive counsel of Timothy Pickering.

The old state rights arguments were now given new authority, with proposals coming out of New England for a convention to nullify the embargo, and if need be to take the maritime states out of the Union. As his administration drew to a close, Jefferson, alarmed for the fate of the country and able no longer to beguile the people with territorial accessions or high-sounding principles, gave in. He asked only for a modification of the embargo, but Congress repealed the hated act in its entirety. After March 1, 1809, only the nonimportation act which had gone into effect at the same time as the embargo, remained in force, and the effect of that, as Congress and the country were to learn in a few short years, was very different from the effect of its companion measure. The one prevented any kind of commerce. The other prevented only half of it, leaving idle funds to burn the pockets of the exporters.

The essential difference between Thomas Jefferson's first prosperous and popular term and his second term of retrenchment, bickering, and opposition carried to the verge of treason was the difference between peace and war in Europe. Jefferson had entered the Presidency committed to Washington's policy of isolation, not because he was insular in his thinking but because he believed that the old world had become too corrupt to survive and that the only hope for mankind lay with the new. National self-determination, uninfluenced by the forces that were dragging Europe to her doom, was his goal. Yet maritime New England was more closely tied to Europe by the nature of her livelihood than she was to the planting states; and even the South relied on Europe to buy the products of her fields, to give her credit, to supply her with manufactured goods.

In short, the United States and Europe in the early nineteenth century were inextricably dependent upon one another. It was therefore possible for Britain and France each to manipulate the American trade as a weapon against the other. Jefferson saw two clear choices: to take sides with one of the belligerents, or to withdraw from both. Since he reprobated the policies of England and of France alike, he chose to withdraw, never realizing that

every barrier to commerce he imposed was in fact an aid to Bonaparte. France could satisfy her basic needs on the continent, but
Britain was forced by French mastery of Europe to depend on the
Western Hemisphere to supplement her own resources. New
England conservatives, unhappy over Louisiana and deeply resent-
ful of commercial restrictions, could never be persuaded the embargo had not been dictated in Paris.

James Madison's administration began in an atmosphere of
faction and distrust that was only in part attributable to the
policies of his predecessor. When he proposed Gallatin for Secretary of State, he was bluntly informed by Senator Samuel Smith
of Maryland that no "foreigner" would ever be confirmed—least
of all Gallatin. As a Baltimore merchant, Smith was widely and
favorably known in America and abroad for honesty and fair dealing, but politics did not follow the rules of the commercial world.
By a species of polite blackmail he had procured appointment of
his brother Robert to Jefferson's Cabinet as Secretary of the
Navy. It had fallen to Gallatin to expose irregularities in the
accounts of that department, and for this he had not been, nor
ever would be, forgiven. Smith now "promoted" brother Robert
to the State Department in return for Gallatin's confirmation to
the Treasury.

This arrangement forced the President to handle foreign affairs
himself, with Gallatin's unofficial aid. Unfortunately there were
no ghosts to do the work of War or Navy Departments, where
Madison had again traded competence for political support that
neither secretary, William Eustis of Massachusetts and Paul
Hamilton of South Carolina, was able to deliver.

For the moment the weakness of Madison's cabinet did not
matter. Commerce was booming as it never had before. With the
embargo gone the impounded shipping of New England, New
York, Philadelphia put to sea with bursting holds. Farther south
the warehouses were emptied of cotton, and new acreage was
planted in anticipation of still larger trade. Shipbuilding revived,
and tonnage by 1810 had reached pre-embargo levels. Revenues

from custom houses and from the sale of public lands at two dollars an acre paid all the expenses of government and left a surplus to be applied to retirement of the national debt. Economically the United States was better off than either Britain or France. Only in Virginia, where tobacco and grain surpluses had already been sold at substantial discounts to northern brokers, was recovery slow. By 1810 Virginia planters had begun to sell their slaves, whose labor no longer paid for their subsistence, to eager speculators in the new cotton lands of the Mississippi delta.

For another two years, Madison continued to negotiate with Britain and France, playing one against the other and being victimized by both. The new British minister in Washington, David Erskine, was reasonable—too reasonable, as it turned out. He had no authority to deal with impressment, but he offered to exempt all American vessels from operation of the Orders in Council if the United States would only repeal non-importation against Great Britain and continue to impose it on France. The arrangement seemed to promise an unlimited market for American staples, manufactured goods in abundance in return, and practical protection at sea in exchange for the renunciation of a market that at best had been erratic and difficult to reach. Madison agreed to the terms and issued a proclamation restoring trade with Great Britain as of June 10, 1809, the day on which the Orders in Council were to be revoked. But Erskine had allowed his sympathies, or perhaps those of his American wife, to becloud his judgment. George Canning, the British Foreign Minister, disavowed the agreement and promptly recalled his erring envoy from the too-heady atmosphere of Washington.

Congress then proposed its own solution to the problem, but with no better success. Both Britain and France were invited to abolish all restrictions upon trade. Should either accept the offer before March 3, 1811, the other was to be given three months to do the same, after which time the President was empowered to invoke non-intercourse against her. Great Britain officially ignored the offer but began issuing licenses to American ships whereby they might freely enter British ports in defiance of their own government. With the risk thus minimized, New England's profits soared and with them the vigor of her opposition to the party in power. Characteristically, Napoleon's response was more subtle. What better way to enforce the blockade he had declared, but could not begin to make good against the superior naval power of his foe, than to let the Americans do it for him? He let it be known that as of November 1, 1810, the Berlin and Milan decrees would no longer be applied to American ships. John Quincy Adams, shrewd and experienced American minister at St. Petersburg, warned Madison of probable trickery, but the too-unworldly President was satisfied with Bonaparte's word. A proclamation was issued on November 2, 1810, imposing non-intercourse against Great Britain if the Orders in Council were not repealed in three months. At the designated time, the proclamation was validated by act of Congress, despite reliable reports that American ships were still being seized in French waters and sold as prizes. Madison had begun his administration by offering, in effect, to become an ally of Great Britain against France. Within two years he was in what amounted to alliance with France against Great Britain.

The Federalists reacted with an articulateness worthy of a better cause. France, in their opinion, had stood for murder, rapine, and violated faith since the days of Robespierre; and Bonaparte was as close as mortal man could come to Antichrist. How could an honest, God-fearing people ally themselves with this traducer of all human values? The blow was not made easier to bear by the passage of enabling legislation authorizing Louisiana to prepare for statehood. Had it not been this very Corsican vandal who had dealt off that province to America in the first place? And would not its French-speaking inhabitants be loyal to their mother country still? It was even suggested that Madison's loyalties also were to France. At least the President had adopted Bonaparte's methods in annexing and adding to Louisiana that portion of West Florida lying between the Mississippi and Pearl rivers. If he could annex one piece of territory, he could annex another, until the original thirteen states would be outvoted by "foreigners." There were sober New Englanders who held that admission of Louisiana to the Union absolved them of their own allegiance to it.

Less vocal but in the end more damaging to the nation was the personal vendetta still being waged against Gallatin by Senator Smith. The administration, at Gallatin's insistence, had asked Congress to recharter the Bank of the United States, though it had been Hamilton's creation and opposed at the time by Madison himself. With the aid of Vice-President George Clinton, who broke a tie on the final roll call, Smith engineered the defeat of the measure in the Senate, multiplying thereby the difficulties his enemy would soon encounter in financing an unpopular war.

Bonaparte was another solid contributor to Madison's discomfiture, freely granting licenses to American ships to prove that the reprobated decrees were dead. But if the licensed vessels, by superior speed or daring, managed to elude the cordon of British frigates that patrolled American waters, they still risked being claimed as prizes when they got to France. No one could even be certain that the decrees had been revoked, or if they had, whether they would remain so for the time required for a cargo of grain or cotton to cross the Atlantic. Faced with crises abroad and at home, Madison at last threw caution to the winds. As soon as Congress adjourned he named Monroe to the State Department and called the new Congress to meet in November, a month ahead of time. Meanwhile, in London, William Pinkney, unable to convince the British of Bonaparte's sincerity, asked for his passports and came home to join the Cabinet as Attorney General. When Congress met on November 8, 1811, American neutrality was visibly disintegrating and the Union itself seemed about to explode into the fragments from which it had been so imperfectly forged.

Neutrality was doomed, but the Union was never in less internal danger. With the meeting of this, the Twelfth Congress to assemble under the Constitution, the balance of power shifted from men who had made a revolution to men who would create a nation. The past gave way to the future. The new men, predominantly from the West and South, were young and impatient with the temporizing of the past few years. Each in his own home district had urged war with Great Britain over the *Chesapeake,* and nothing had happened since to lead any one of them to change his mind.

It is true their reasons for demanding war with England differed according to the interest of their sections. In Indiana and Illinois territories the frontier was pushing into Indian country, and men who felt crowded if they could see the smoke from a neighbor's chimney were growing restive. Since colonial days the story had been the same: new lands for settlement had been procured from the Indian tribes by purchase, or by conquest if the asking price were too high. The time-honored practice had been to ply the chiefs with whiskey and when they were drunk enough to present them with treaties to sign that conveyed more thousands of acres of their hunting grounds to the white farmers. There had been intermittent scalpings along the frontier, to be sure, but there was no organized resistance until the Shawnee brothers, Tecumseh and the Prophet, brought the western tribes together in a powerful confederacy, weaned the braves from fire-water, and effectively stopped the alienation of their land.

The western settlers had no doubt that Great Britain was goading Tecumseh on, as they had seen British hands behind every Indian uprising since the Revolution. They saw safety for themselves only in driving the British from the North American continent—all of it, including Canada. And the southern planters, who coveted the rich river bottoms of Mississippi Territory but who found the warlike Creeks in their way, felt much the same toward the Spaniards in Florida, which they were prepared to seize under cover of war, no matter who the official enemy might be. In general, the real grievances against Great Britain—impressment and interference with neutral shipping—

were important only to the maritime states, which were sturdily opposed to war. But the new leaders from the South and West took up the cry and made it a matter of national honor.

Foremost among the War Hawks, as they were soon called, was Henry Clay of Kentucky. Born in Virginia, he had studied law under the venerable Chancellor Wythe, friend and teacher of Jefferson. Clay had gone to Kentucky at the age of twenty, and now, at thirty-four, he was completely identified with his adopted state and with all the western country. Tall and turbulent, he turned his gambling, his drinking and conviviality to account; but there was no pretending in his role of consummate politician, sure, deft, confident and ambitious, for his country as well as for himself. Teamed with Clay were three South Carolinians: Langdon Cheves, thirty-five-year-old veteran of one congressional session, who knew the commercial world inside and out; lanky, golden-haired William Lowndes, whose soft speech was cover for a mind as quick and as penetrating as any of his generation; and most famous of the three, the bushy-haired, bright-eyed human dynamo from the back country, John C. Calhoun, who like Lowndes was only twenty-nine. There was chunky, beetle-browed Felix Grundy, a veteran of the rough-and-tumble politics of Kentucky and Tennessee; Peter B. Porter from the Niagara frontier in western New York, where Canada was looked upon as an erring sister who must be redeemed for the sake of her own soul; and Richard M. Johnson, like Clay a Kentuckian who believed that for the West the future was at hand. These and others of only slightly less renown dominated the Congress that was to decide the issue of peace or war. They met in private caucus before the session opened, and agreed on strategy. Then in defiance of seniority they chose Clay as their Speaker, and Clay, with a fine disregard for age or party services, named committees dominated by the will to war.

In the battle of Tippecanoe, fought as Congress organized, the War Hawks chose to see the opening clash of the war they advocated. The encounter sprang only from determined pressure on

the part of settlers alarmed by the new reluctance of the Indians
to sign away any more of their tribal lands, but its effects were
sweeping. It brought to a head all the old grievances of the West
against the British, turned covetous western eyes toward Canada,
and provided the spark that would touch off the powder keg of
war.

Key figure in dealing with the Indians was the territorial governor, General William Henry Harrison, who like
Clay was a Virginian now firmly identified with the West, and
who shared western suspicions of Great Britain. As delegate in
Congress from the Old Northwest Territory in 1800, Harrison
had drafted the land act of that year, which still guided the settlement of the West. He had intervened from time to time to the
extent of his authority to secure simple justice for the Indians
against unscrupulous settlers, but he could hold back the tide of
settlement no longer. As governor, for the good of all concerned,
it was his duty to persuade the Indians to give up more land.
If he failed it was his responsibility as military commander to
drive them out. Harrison caught up with the Indians on November 7, 1811, near the point where the Tippecanoe River flows into
the Wabash. Tecumseh was away, and without his restraining
hand the younger braves elected to attack. The Indians were
beaten and driven off, but the skirmish left the entire frontier
open to Indian war, with or without British incitements.

Back in Washington, the New England Federalists, bent on
avoiding a war that would end a most profitable trade, found an
unsought leader in John Randolph, who saw in war only illogic
and a threat to slavery; but at every turn they lost. Their arguments were brushed aside; their satirical thrusts were parried
in kind; their proposals designed to stem the tide were voted
down. The army numbered no more than five or six thousand
men spread over a territory so vast that months were required
to communicate with all the outposts. The navy consisted of
twenty frigates, only three of them with forty-four guns and
three with thirty-eight, plus sixty-odd gunboats, mounting one

or two cannon and designed for rapid maneuvering in coastal inlets and bays. The frigates were more heavily timbered and faster than the British, as had been demonstrated in May, 1811, when *The President* fought and captured the *Little Belt;* but numbers were bound to count most heavily in the end, and the British had two hundred fighting ships, including a dozen or more seventy-four-gun ships of the line, in American waters alone. The War Hawks voted a large army, but because of some defection by their western colleagues, failed to enlarge the navy to any great extent.

The opposition argued over and over again that the Berlin and Milan decrees were not revoked, and that Bonaparte—not Great Britain—was the real enemy. The War Hawks retorted with statistics of commercial losses and seamen impressed, and calmly proceeded with their plans, with the tacit and sometimes overt encouragement of Monroe, who had an old score of his own to settle with England. In April, 1812, they imposed a sixty-day embargo, specifically to give American shipowners time to get their vessels to port before they became prizes of war. On June 1, 1812, under hammering pressure from Congress and Cabinet alike, Madison sent in a war message. There were also pressures of another sort, for the spring elections had returned Federalist majorities to the legislatures of Massachusetts and New York. Indeed, there were those who believed the President's war message to be the price exacted by the War Hawks for a second term.

The declaration of war came on June 18, too early by the length of time it would take a fast sailing vessel to make the trip from England to America. Napoleon's power had attained its peak in the winter of 1811-12. All of Europe save only Russia was under his control, and Russia—as Great Britain soon learned—was all but isolated as far as commerce was concerned. The British people had already become restive when a crop failure raised the price of wheat beyond reach of workers made idle by the closing of both Continental and American markets for British manufactures. Riots were translated into political action; a new government came into power, and the Orders in Council were repealed in London even as the Congress in Washington declared their continued existence to be a cause for war.

With superannuated officers and home-loving militia, the anachronistic war got off to a dismal start. Major General William Hull was neatly finessed into pusillanimous surrender at Detroit without a fight. The garrison at Fort Dearborn, where Chicago now stands, was massacred as soon as news of the war reached that remote frontier. In October Major General Stephen Van Rensselaer crossed the Niagara River to seize Queenstown, but his New York militia refused to move from the soil of their own state, leaving the spearhead of regulars to be captured by the Canadians. A month later, Major General Henry Dearborn, who had been Jefferson's Secretary of War and was perhaps the army's most experienced officer, led a substantial force by way of the classic Lake Champlain invasion route to Canada, but they too were stopped at the border, returning to Plattsburgh without ever engaging the enemy.

This retreat coincided with the fall elections, which, though Madison won his second term, revealed a dangerous schism in the body politic. The Federalists had put up no candidate of their own but had backed a nominal Republican, De Witt Clinton of New York—whose uncle, George Clinton, was about to be replaced as Vice-President of the United States by Elbridge Gerry of Massachusetts. Clinton carried every state north of the Potomac except Pennsylvania and Vermont, to garner 89 electoral votes against Madison's 128. In Congress the Federalists, after March 4, 1813, would double their strength. Only at sea, where rugged American privateers were cutting deeply into British commerce, and American frigates had won a handful of individual engagements, was the story one to give heart to the administration, but even there the British blockade was slowly reducing the number of Americans afloat.

Changes early in 1813 that brought John Armstrong of the

New York Livingston clan to the War Department and gave
the Navy to William Jones, a Philadelphia shipowner without
other qualifications, neither materially strengthened the Cabinet
nor vitalized the flagging war effort. The ranks of the army could
not be filled because recruits could not be induced to join; and
the individual excellence of American warships and crews could
never outweigh Britain's overwhelming superiority in numbers.
When an offer from Czar Alexander, to mediate between the
United States and Great Britain was received in March, 1813,
Madison and Monroe seized upon it eagerly. Russia's interest—
since Napoleon had forced her into an alliance with Great Britain
by his ill-fated invasion—was to free her new partner from a
peripheral and disproportionately costly war with the United
States. American Commissioners hopefully appointed to the
mission were John Quincy Adams, minister at St. Petersburg;
James A. Bayard, Federalist Senator from Delaware; and Secretary of the Treasury Albert Gallatin. But it would be more than
a year before the commissioners ultimately met at Ghent on
August 8, 1814.

The war was almost a year old when Congress gathered in
special session May 24, 1813, but no single objective had been
gained. Victories at sea, however spectacular, had no bearing on
the final outcome of the struggle, and every land campaign thus
far had ended in disaster. The army was only up to one third of
its authorized strength and all through New England Federalist
governors refused to permit their militia to serve outside their own
states. The Treasury was empty, and worse—it was $5,500,000
overdrawn. The American coast was blockaded from Georgia to
Long Island, and the Federalist representation in Congress was
not only larger but abler than before, the chief newcomers and
critics being old Timothy Pickering himself, and young Daniel
Webster of New Hampshire, both in the House, where the
talent of the War Hawks was also concentrated. Perhaps most
ominous of all, Napoleon had been soundly beaten in Russia, and

there was every prospect that Great Britain would soon be free to deal more decisively with her American war.

Not the least of Britain's assets was her illicit commerce with New England. Almost from the beginning of hostilities, she played upon the cupidity of Yankee shipowners, issuing licenses under which their ships might pass the blockade and sail for Lisbon, where cargo could be reshipped to the British Isles. Or if the lure of profit were greater, the vessel once past the British cordon in the western Atlantic risked the dash to Sweden whence the markets of all Europe would be open. Licenses were bought and sold on the public exchange in Boston, where one with three months to run might bring as much as $1,000. So New England traded freely with the enemy, while the gold and silver that flowed into her banks from the country over in exchange for the goods brought home by her far-ranging merchant ships was denied the government, and her representatives in Congress hampered the war effort in every conceivable way. One of those ways was to reject Gallatin as peace commissioner, though he was already on his way abroad, because he had not formally resigned as Secretary of the Treasury. The Secretary had called for a $16,000,000 loan for the war effort, but with New York and New England bankers refusing to touch it, only $4,000,000 was subscribed. The rest was taken up by three personal friends of Gallatin's, who, like the Secretary himself had been born in Europe—John Jacob Astor of New York; and David Parish and Stephen Girard of Philadelphia.

The only good news came from the Canadian front, where the Navy had won control of Lake Ontario and Lake Erie. Early in October, General Harrison defeated a mixed force of Canadians and Indians at the battle of the Thames on the Ontario peninsula north-east of Detroit. In the engagement Tecumseh was killed, reportedly by Colonel Richard M. Johnson, who had left the House of Representatives for active duty at the head of a regiment of Kentucky riflemen. Neither these successes, nor the presence of British warships in the Potomac River within sight of Wash-

ington, moved New England. She remained obstinately opposed
to war, still withheld her troops and her money, and through her
spokesmen in Congress challenged every move of the administration.

The next move was a new embargo imposed in December and
again there was talk of secession or at best a separate peace, halted
only by the arrival of dispatches from abroad. Lord Castlereagh,
now British Foreign Minister, had rejected the Czar's offer of
mediation, but was willing to negotiate directly with the American commissioners. Madison named Henry Clay to take Gallatin's
place; then added Jonathan Russell, newly appointed United
States Minister to Sweden. Gallatin was subsequently restored to
the list as fifth member when his resignation as Secretary of the
Treasury was received, paving the way for his confirmation by
the Senate.

The task facing the commissioners was getting more difficult
with each passing day. In the early months of 1814, the British
blockade was extended to the New England coast itself, and New
Englanders began actually to experience some of the hardships of
which they had so ardently complained. Then came news of
Napoleon's abdication on April 6, and of British preparations at
long last to put a military end to the American stalemate. The
only hope for the United States now lay in the war-weariness
of the British people and in the skill of the peace commissioners
at Ghent.

The Americans had found commanders and learned the essen-
tials of war too late. On the Niagara frontier General Jacob
Brown captured Fort Erie July 4. One of his subordinates,
Virginia-born Winfield Scott, won the hard-fought battle of
Chippewa the following day, and the even more stubbornly con-
tested battle of Lundy's Lane three weeks later. In the south
General Andrew Jackson and his Tennessee militia had crushed
the Creek Indians and were moving on toward New Orleans.
The disgraceful battle of Bladensburg on the outskirts of Wash-
ington, where the Virginia militia fled without fighting on

August 24, 1814, was no longer typical. Commodore Joshua
Barney, with a handful of seamen from the gunboats he had been
forced to abandon in the Patuxent, fought valiantly but in vain
against an overwhelmingly superior force brought up by the
British fleet now operating as freely in Chesapeake Bay as in the
English Channel. The British swept on to Washington where
they burned the Capitol, the White House and other public
buildings, sparing only the Patent Office in response to the
emotional appeal of its director, Dr. William Thornton. The
Maryland militia, commanded by Senator Samuel Smith, redeemed American arms the following night, holding firm at
Fort McHenry to save Baltimore from the fate of Washington.
Francis Scott Key, watching the bombardment from a British
vessel to which he had gone under flag of truce with dispatches,
composed the "Star Spangled Banner," to give the United States,
belatedly, a national anthem. On September 11 Thomas Mc-
Donough destroyed a British fleet off Plattsburgh on Lake Champlain and compelled withdrawal of the enemy's land forces in
the vicinity.

None of these victories was enough to rescue what appeared a
hopelessly lost cause. When Congress met on September 19, 1814,
the Treasury was again empty and the secretary, now Alexander
J. Dallas of Philadelphia, could only propose the re-establishment
of Hamilton's Bank of the United States as offering any hope
of avoiding bankruptcy. In another Cabinet shift, Monroe took
over the War Department as well as the State Department after
the Bladensburg fiasco. The British fleet was now based at Cape
Cod, and land reinforcements—Wellington's veterans from Europe—were or soon would be on the way. Most discouraging of
all, on October 5, 1814, the Massachusetts legislature called a convention of the New England states "to lay the foundation for a
radical reform in the National compact." The call was accepted,
with December 15 chosen as the date. The place was to be Hartford,
Connecticut. The result, if Pickering's radicals gained the upper

hand, would probably be a dissolution of the Union—if indeed British arms had not already dissolved it by that time.

When the Hartford Convention met, the moderates, led by Harrison Gray Otis, were in control, and remained so through six weeks of wrangling. Instead of declaring their independence, the embattled New Englanders did no more than propose a series of constitutional amendments. They would require a two-thirds vote in both houses of Congress to admit new states, to impose commercial restrictions, or to declare war; they would abolish the so-called federal ratio whereby five slaves counted as three free men in apportioning representation; they would confine federal office-holding to the native born; and they would limit the Presidency to one term, at the same time forbidding any state to furnish two consecutive encumbents of that office. The Hartford protest, conservative and strictly according to the rules though it was, accomplished no more than a violent protest would have done; for the events that led up to it and gave it meaning were already past.

The Hartford Convention had not yet reached its mid-point when a treaty ending the war on honorable terms was signed at Ghent on Christmas Eve, 1814. The treaty re-established the pre-war boundaries between the United States and Canada, but left all other questions at issue to be resolved by later negotiation. The only positive gains were the virtual destruction of Indian power east of the Mississippi, and the seizure from Spain of that portion of West Florida lying between the Pearl and Perdido rivers and including Mobile Bay.

Ironically, the one decisive battle of the War of 1812 was fought at New Orleans on January 8, 1815, two weeks after the treaty was signed. In the Battle of New Orleans, Andrew Jackson, commanding a motley army of Tennessee and Kentucky militia, local volunteers, some Indians, Negroes, and Gulf pirates, crushed a larger force of British veterans from Europe. Fighting Indian and frontier style from behind barricades of cotton bales, the American sharpshooters all but wiped out their attackers while suffering only a handful of casualties themselves. The victory could hardly fail to enhance the fame and increase the popularity of the already colorful and controversial Jackson.

The proud news from New Orleans reached Washington just in time to make the Hartford proposals seem petulant and a little immature. Then both events were lost in the general relief that followed the simultaneous arrival of the Treaty of Ghent ending two and a half years of war.

3

Full Steam Ahead

OUT OF THE bungling, the ineptitude, the fortuitous accidents of the War of 1812 came a generation of Americans determined to assume at last among the powers of the earth the separate and equal station their fathers had so confidently declared to be their due. Europe they no longer feared, or envied; and so their energies were released to build their own nation on their own continent with materials of their own selection. Since Jefferson had cast the money-changers from the temple of government, his own followers had tasted the forbidden fruit and found it to their liking. So now they would refurbish the old political and economic concepts to serve the needs of the new, dynamic world that would be theirs.

Even before the war was over the changes had begun. Profits wrung from neutrality by elusive Yankee traders had been immobilized by the embargo and the war. For want of better employment they had been invested in manufacturing ventures to the tune of $40,000,000. Stimulated by wartime demands and with the customary sources of supply cut off, American industry reached out into new directions, and grew fat in proportion to the ingenuity of its votaries. At Waltham, Massachusetts, Francis Cabot Lowell built the world's first fully integrated cotton mill where with the aid of improved machinery raw fiber was converted to finished cloth under a single roof. William Jarvis, representing the United States in Lisbon, took advantage of Napoleon's sack of Spain to export thousands of the jealously guarded Merino sheep to his homeland where woolen mills now dotted the eastern states. The years of restriction enlarged the output of Pennsylvania's iron mines and foundries, and turned the skills of her artisans and engineers into new channels, such as the development of better engines for the steamboats that had multiplied since Fulton in 1807 hit upon the right combination of motive power and marine design. Wood-burning paddle-wheelers now churned the waters of the Hudson, the Delaware, the Potomac, and even the far-off Mississippi.

In the West and South the frontier was surging forward into the former hunting grounds of the Shawnees and the Creeks in the wake of military victories by Harrison and Jackson. More than a million acres were taken up in 1814 and each succeeding year would surpass the total of the year before. Few of those who pushed northwest from Ohio and Kentucky or followed the bone-shattering wagon routes across the mountains from the East had money to buy outright the minimum quarter section at the established price of two dollars an acre, but the government did not demand full payment all at once and the banks that were beginning to proliferate in the western towns were generous with credit. The land itself was acceptable as security, for its value could not fail to advance with the advancing tide of settlement. Differing only in the magnitude of his dream was the settler who erupted from Georgia and South Carolina and Tennessee into the rich river bottoms of Alabama and Mississippi. If lucky he could still find land at the government price, but if not he bought from a speculator at a figure deceptively geared to the rising price of cotton. He bought as many acres as he could and carried with him whatever slaves he owned or was able to acquire. Other than sheer availability of land and Negroes, the only limiting factor was credit, but southern bankers proved as accommodating as their western counterparts. With peace restored and British cotton mills insatiable, the risk was nothing in comparison to the anticipated gain.

As the widening fingers of cultivated land pushed up the broad river valleys, even those of the Missouri and the Arkansas, new villages sprang up, old villages became towns, and towns grew to the dignity of cities, providing a base of operations for the factors and commission merchants who would pass the harvest of farm and plantation along to the ultimate consumer. These urban centers imported or themselves produced the manufactured goods the farmer needed and such luxuries as he could afford to buy; they spawned the builders, the traders, the speculators, the business venturers of every kind. Pittsburgh and New Orleans, at the two extremes of the long river system that was the major avenue of commerce for the West were being challenged by Cincinnati, Louisville and Memphis. St. Louis, still the nerve center of the American fur trade, was the gateway to all the lands so alluringly described in the newly published account of the Lewis and Clark expedition. Smaller, but no less ambitious towns adorned the prairies of Indiana and Illinois, and commanded the watercourses of the deeper South. Indiana came into the Union in 1816. Mississippi, Illinois, and Alabama followed in successive years.

Everywhere men looked forward to a new and incredible age. Nothing seemed impossible. In the West land was unlimited, and so it could become collateral for unlimited credit. In the South notes of hand secured by cotton, actual or in prospect, passed for money and were accepted as such in Liverpool and London. New forms of corporate organization, not always fully understood by those who entered into them, contributed to the industrial growth of the North and East. The placid, agrarian world of Jefferson was being visibly if not yet articulately supplanted by a form of capitalism in which the emphasis would be on "enterprise." A man no longer needed a fortune of his own. If he had imagination, energy, and a good character in the community he could buy land or stock, become a merchant or a manufacturer, with money borrowed from a bank or supplied by some well-to-do individual willing to gamble on a share of a future profit. All he needed was access to markets and raw materials, a currency that would not eat up all returns by its tendency to decline in value, and some protection against the competitive dumping of British goods at prices he would not be able to meet for years to come. All these needs the young War Hawks of 1812, now turned to empire building, undertook to furnish.

With surprising unanimity, considering the violence of past differences, the Congress that met in December, 1815, consciously chose the direction of consolidation, of national self-sufficiency, of world power. Led by Clay, home from Ghent and back in the Speaker's chair, the tireless Calhoun and the self-effacing Lowndes, with occasional help from such as volatile Richard M. Johnson of Kentucky and methodical Samuel D. Ingham of Pennsylvania, they would tax freely, spend generously, and by the application of "plain good sense" would make the Constitution serve their needs. Those who, like Webster and Pickering, had been on the other side would sometimes hinder, sometimes be of aid. Only Randolph, waiting like an attenuated spider behind his web of "Virginia doctrines," would be consistently opposed, but even from Randolph the bitterness was gone.

The program offered in the name of Jefferson by these self-nominated spokesmen for the New America was one that Alexander Hamilton could have approved in whole and in detail. It comprised a subsidy to the manufacturers of New England and the middle states in the form of a protective tariff to keep alive their war-born industries and give them nurture until they could supply the basic needs of the nation; a subsidy to the farmers and planters of the West and South by way of an improved system of transportation at government expense to facilitate the marketing of their crops; and a national bank to provide the uniform currency so necessary to the exchange of goods, and to regulate business and commercial activity by regulating credit. Proponents of the measures that would be known collectively as the "Ameri-

can System" based their case on the imperative need for unity,
self-sufficiency, and strength if the nation was to survive and grow
in a hostile world. With the defection of New England still vivid
in their minds, they held national weakness more to be feared
than power and saw in division the prelude to extinction. Those
who opposed, with John Randolph as usual the most articulate,
argued in eighteenth-century terms that a government strong
enough to carry out the intended program would also be strong
enough to deprive the people of those liberties for which the
Revolution had been fought, and that such an outcome, given the
nature of man, was all but inevitable, whereas the threat of
foreign conquest was remote.

The second Bank of the United States was frankly patterned
on the first: the same bank that Jefferson and his followers had
opposed, but with diminishing degrees of assurance as over and
over again it proved its value to the Treasury. As we have seen,
it was not traditional fear of a "money power" but factional
hostility to Albert Gallatin that kept the Republicans from rechartering the first Bank in 1811. Now, with a second chance,
they raised the stakes. The United States Government would put
up 20 percent of the Bank's $35,000,000 capital (the old Bank's
had been only $10,000,000), own 20 percent of the stock, appoint
five of the twenty-five directors, and be the largest depositor. The
Bank was to be physically located in Philadelphia, still the financial center of the country, but the directors might establish
branches at will. Only Congress could suspend specie payments
—the redemption of the Bank's notes in gold and silver. A few
western Republicans refused to vote for the charter for fear the
Bank might curb the easy-money policy that was making their
constituents rich, but the losses were made up by Federalist votes
from the eastern commercial centers.

The tariff was another brain child of Alexander Hamilton,
who had shown in his celebrated Report on Manufactures that
industry could not be established without some form of subsidy
to compensate for the lower production costs of better intrenched

and therefore more efficient foreign competitors. The problem of those who framed the tariff of 1816 was to determine, item by item, the extent of the subsidy required, with due allowance for the fact that British manufacturers whose goods were already flooding the American market were probably selling below cost in the hope of destroying a potential rival. Three general categories were set up. Articles that could not be produced at home were to be admitted free of duty; and articles that could be produced in quantities sufficient to meet all domestic needs were to be protected by a tax prohibitively high. The third and largest category included all items that could be produced in the United States, but not yet in quantities large enough to meet the entire demand. On these articles the duties were adjusted to encourage the American producer without excluding the foreign. The manufacturers themselves were freely consulted but local self-interest generally governed votes, each individual congressman seeking maximum protection for the products manufactured by his constituents while attempting to get onto the free list everything they consumed.

It was agreed by all concerned that three years should be enough to put American industry on a competitive par with that of England, and a provision was therefore included reducing all duties in the year 1819 to the uniform 20 percent by value that was deemed adequate for purposes of revenue. As finally established, the average duty under the tariff of 1816 was not much above 25 percent, whch proved to be less than enough to enable American industry to compete with that of Britain. The coarse cotton cloth that made up the bulk of the New England textile output was the exception that more than proved the rule, for Lowell and a handful of others had succeeded in persuading Congress that the competition of similar fabrics imported from India at five or six cents a yard would be ruinous. In their behalf the minimum principle was adopted whereby all cotton textiles valued at less than twenty-five cents a yard were to be valued

at that figure for tax purposes, and would pay in consequence a
duty up to 100 percent.

The system of internal transportation that was to "bind the
Republic together" was essentially the system Gallatin had proposed in 1808, joining bays and estuaries by a series of canals to
create an inland waterway along the Atlantic coast; providing a
parallel but more extended coastal highway from Maine to Louisiana; making a water connection between the Hudson and Lake
Erie that would by-pass Niagara Falls; and linking by road or
canal the navigable reaches of streams on opposite sides of the
Appalachians. Although the West had done more than its share
to sustain the government during war, it was still closer to Europe by way of the Mississippi than to Washington or New York
by existing avenues of commerce. It was hardly realistic to believe the West could be held indefinitely in union with the East
unless western crops could find their way to eastern markets.
Now that British manufactures were to be made more costly or
excluded altogether, it had become equally imperative to make
the products of American industry accessible to all America. The
Cumberland Road, already clogged with traffic though it still
fell short of its Ohio River terminus, hinted at rich prospects for
the cheaper water routes proposed. The network of roads and
canals was to be financed by a bonus to be paid the government
by the Bank, and by the dividends from the government's Bank
stock.

These three measures that together constituted the American
System were conceived by their sponsors as a single economic
program, intended to benefit all sections of the country; yet to
each element there was a sectional opposition in Congress. The
West opposed the Bank; the South opposed the tariff; New England opposed internal improvements. Only the middle states—
New York, Pennsylvania, New Jersey—gave all three measures
uniform support, but that support proved decisive. However, the
interdependence of the three was also lost upon President Madison, who could not reconcile the internal improvement bill with

either the commerce clause or the general welfare clause of the Constitution. Of all men then living, Madison knew best what the framers had intended, and his veto, conscientious though it was, delayed for a generation an adequate system of internal transportation. When the scheme was revived a year or two later as a measure of national defense, Congress would have none of it, and the bold, nationalistic program that was to unify America collapsed the more thoroughly for being half carried out.

The chief gainer was New York, where the route of the Erie Canal had already been surveyed and construction awaited only the provision of necessary funds. Led, bullied, and cajoled by Governor De Witt Clinton, the state undertook to raise for herself the money that would not now be forthcoming from Washington. Clinton turned the first spadeful of earth for his "Big Ditch" at Albany on July 4, 1817, just four months after Madison's veto message had apparently destroyed the project.

The Erie Canal was only one of many ventures in expansion —solid evidence that the congressional leaders had gauged correctly the mood of the country. Americans everywhere were too busy digging, building, moving, making, experimenting, exploring to be hampered by events in Washington. Thus James Monroe's succession to the Presidency, though it seemed to stem from a species of primogeniture, was taken for granted. Federalist electors, what few there were, cast their ballots by courtesy for Senator Rufus King of New York, but the party had put up no candidate. With the Republicans now committed to the old Federalist philosophy of power, there was no reason why they should. Monroe was careful to do nothing by act or word to disturb this new-found harmony. Like Washington, whose aide he had once been and whom to the portrait painter's eye of Gilbert Stuart he somewhat resembled, Monroe regarded the presidential office as above all partisanship and sought in his policies and key appointments to reconcile sectional and class distinctions. For Secretary of State he selected rotund, balding, tenacious John Quincy Adams, whose name and birthplace were

assets almost as great as his long familiarity with European
courts, and the concessions he had lately won at Ghent. William
H. Crawford, the burly Georgian who had succeeded to the
Treasury for the last year of Madison's term, retained that post;
and the War Department, after both Clay and Andrew Jackson
had refused it, went to John C. Calhoun of South Carolina. Clay
felt that his party services were worth a higher price, and Jackson's political advisers would not risk their favorite in a post that
could add nothing to his fame. But Monroe's failure to persist
until he got a western representative in his cabinet would leave
him vulnerable. The Attorney General was William Wirt, best
known outside his native Virginia for his biography of Patrick
Henry; and a council of more than ordinary merit was rounded
out by Smith Thompson of New York in the Navy Department.

The Era of Good Feelings, as Monroe's administration is eu-
phemistically known, began with every outward evidence of prosperity. The western lands were being occupied with almost
frightening speed. New textile mills and other manufacturing
plants were springing up like mushrooms overnight in New
England, in the middle states, and in the Ohio Valley, their
owners bent on sharing the subsidy voted by their representatives
in Congress. In 1816, the South contributed 130 million pounds of
cotton, four times the output of 1800, and the average price at
Charleston was 27 cents and still going up. Shipping tonnage,
much of it carrying southern cotton to England, was the highest
it had ever been save only for the first post-embargo year of 1810.
Freed at last from the shackling grip of her colonial past, young
America with her tariff and her Bank was ready to take the
nineteenth century by storm.

The Bank, sometimes as villain and sometimes as victim, would
be engulfed in controversy for all the twenty years of its chartered
life. Its first president was William Jones, the Philadelphia shipowner whose brief service as Secretary of the Treasury in succession to Gallatin in no way qualified him for the job. He began
by cutting corners. The intent, if not the letter, of the charter had

prescribed that Bank stock should be paid for in part in gold and silver, thus supplying the specie that was to constitute 20 percent of the institution's capital. Instead, Jones sold the stock for promises and bought the necessary $7,000,000 in precious metals at a premium abroad, paying for it with the very notes it was supposed to secure. The ease with which Bank stock could be acquired worked to give control to a hungry group who saw in it an instrument for lining their own pockets. It was this same group that dictated the policy of expansion upon which Jones presently embarked. In addition to the main office in Philadelphia, there were eighteen branches in operation by the end of 1817, each merrily lending money as though it were the sole custodian of the collective funds. It soon became common practice for branches in the South and West, once they had exhausted their own reserves of specie, to issue notes against the parent Bank or one of the more solvent northern branches. Stephen Girard, who had helped to sustain the public credit in the darkest days of the war and was now both a government director and the largest single stockholder in the Bank, resigned in protest.

Girard's preponderance of stock gave him no greater power than many others, for no stockholder was allowed to cast more than thirty votes, no matter how large his holdings, and he disdained to use the device of a Baltimore stockholder, George Williams, who had each of his almost 1,200 shares registered in a different name, with himself as attorney to vote them all. This kind of chicanery went on at many branches, but Baltimore was the worst offender and soon to become the most notorious of them all. President of the Baltimore branch was James A. Buchanan (not be confused with the James Buchanan who would shortly enter Congress from Lancaster, Pennsylvania, and go on to be President of the United States). Buchanan was a partner of the politically powerful Samuel Smith in one of the best-known mercantile establishments in the country, a man of stature and influence in the business community as well as in the halls of government. The cashier was James W. McCulloch. The branch was hardly in effective operation before Buchanan, McCulloch and Williams began looting it. In two years time, their embezzlements would total some $3,000,000.

The first complaints against the Bank of the United States—the B.U.S., contemporaries called it—came from the state-chartered banks which did not care to share their lucrative businesses with what they termed a "foreign" corporation. The most immediately effective way to counterbalance the advantages enjoyed by the federally chartered institution was by taxation, and the device was resorted to in half a dozen states. The Baltimore branch refused to pay a $15,000 tax levied against it by the state legislature, and the state sued the cashier for the money. The case went on appeal to the Supreme Court, but before a decision was rendered in March, 1819, the whole financial structure of the country had become involved. The parent Bank, no wiser and little more honest than the branches, also lent money far too freely. Reserves of gold and silver were down to less than half the amount required by law, and dwindling fast before Jones finally became alarmed. Although the Bank began feverishly putting its house in order, it was already too late to forestall a congressional investigation. Jones resigned early in 1819, and conservative, widely respected Langdon Cheves of South Carolina, Speaker of the House during Clay's absence at Ghent and a tower of Republican strength in the war years, took his place. In a matter of weeks, with directors of his own choosing, with specie borrowed from the Barings and other European bankers, and by a sharp contraction of credit, Cheves restored the solvency of the United States Bank. But as their notes were presented for payment in the specie they no longer had, the state banks began to fail, carrying with them to destruction the farmers, the traders, the enterprisers of all descriptions who were over their heads in debt. The Baltimore bubble burst, engulfing in its collapse the house of Smith and Buchanan. Slowly at first, then with the accelerating speed of gravity depression settled over the land.

Undismayed by the almost universal clamor against the Bank,

John Marshall chose this time to reaffirm the doctrine of national power on which the whole American System rested. Since 1803, when he had first declared that the Supreme Court might overrule an act of Congress, Marshall had been refining and enlarging the old Federalist doctrine of a strong central government, supported by those with an economic stake in the community. He had upheld the inviolability of contracts, had made good the right of the Supreme Court to pass judgment in cases appealed from the state courts, and early in 1819 in the Dartmouth College case, he had held that corporate charters such as those under which banks as well as colleges operated were forms of contract. In McCulloch *v*. Maryland he went further still, explicitly affirming the supremacy of the Federal Government over the states. Counsel for the plaintiff, who was in reality the Bank, was Daniel Webster, assisted by Attorney General William Wirt, representing the government interest, and Senator William Pinkney of Maryland, who had been retained by the Baltimore branch. The Court accepted Webster's argument that the power to tax is the power to destroy, from which it followed that a state could not tax a corporation created by the Federal Government without placing that government in the unthinkable position of subordination to the state.

The Kentucky and Virginia legislatures replied to the doctrine of McCulloch *v*. Maryland by reaffirming their own resolutions of 1798 and '99; and Ohio endorsed them both, at the same time imposing a confiscatory tax of $50,000 on each of the Bank's two branches in that state. As in Maryland, the Bank refused to pay, this time citing the Supreme Court as its authority. The state treasurer seized the money by force, and agents of the Federal Circuit Court, at the instigation of the Bank, recovered it by the same means. The treasurer then sued the Bank, thereby giving John Marshall another opportunity to proclaim the supremacy of the Federal Government over the states.

What all this meant, in less legalistic terms, was that in the opinion of the Supreme Court, the Constitution of the United

States created a nation—not a confederacy—that the Federal Government had power to do anything not forbidden by the Constitution, including the chartering of a bank, the protection of industry, or the building of roads and canals; and that the Supreme Court—not the states, not the Congress, or even the President—would decide in the last resort what was and what was not forbidden. The compact theory of the Kentucky and Virginia Resolutions, with its southern corollary of state rights and all its New England glosses, was categorically denied.

The reaction, immediate and direct, was led by the authors of those resolutions themselves: Thomas Jefferson, now seventy-six and ten years in retirement, and James Madison, whose practical authorship of the Constitution was by 1819 a matter of public knowledge. The attack was shrewdly directed at Mc-Culloch *v.* Maryland, where the Court was most vulnerable and public sentiment more nearly unanimous. It was carried on in the press, by pamphlet and public address, in state legislatures, courts, college classrooms, and even in the pulpit. For Jefferson and those who aided the fight—Judge Spencer Roane of the Virginia Court of Appeals; John Taylor of Caroline, so called from the Virginia county of his birth, who even more than Jefferson himself was the philosopher of Jeffersonian Democracy; John Randolph of Roanoke; young John Tyler; and a host of lesser names—for these men the underlying issue was clear. They saw in the centralized national government proclaimed by John Marshall a government of potentially unlimited powers, no better than the monarchy of George III against which the Revolution had been fought. The checks and prohibitions of the Constitution, without power to enforce them, were meaningless paper; but if the states had not that power, it existed nowhere in the system. Such a government, they warned, could confiscate and redistribute the wealth of the country; it could silence its critics, make war on its enemies, and suitably reward its friends; it could free the slaves of the South. . . .

On the slave question southern nerves were exposed and raw,

giving an ominous turn to a controversy that quickly transcended the legal issue with which it had begun. The immediate stimulus was a bill authorizing Missouri to prepare for statehood, brought up in the House of Representatives in mid-February, 1819. James Tallmadge of New York offered an amendment that would have freed at the age of twenty-one all persons born into slavery in the new state after the effective date of its admission. The method proposed was essentially the same gradual procedure as that by which slavery had been or was being abolished in the northern states, and it reflected the common assumption of the North that slavery was eventually to be abolished everywhere. The amendment was debated briefly, adopted, and the bill that would admit Missouri as a free state was passed. In the Senate the slavery restriction was dropped and the bill was lost between the houses on the final day of the session.

When debate on the Missouri question was resumed nine months later, in December, 1819, it was no longer the routine admission of a new state but the permanence of the Union itself that was at stake, with the finest orators and keenest minds on both sides taking part. In the House, Clay, Lowndes, and Randolph spoke for the slaveholders, and John W. Taylor of New York—soon to replace Clay as Speaker—led those who sought to contain the institution. In the Senate, Pinkney of Maryland and James Barbour of Virginia argued the case for slavery against Rufus King of New York, and Harrison Gray Otis of Massachusetts, who had presided over the Hartford Convention. The ultimate outcome was the compromise by which Missouri was admitted with her slaves and Maine, with the consent of Massachusetts, was simultaneously brought into the Union as a free state. At the same time slavery was forbidden thereafter in all other territory acquired by the Louisiana Purchase lying north of 36° 30′ north latitude—the line between Missouri and Arkansas Territory. The two new states were the twenty-third and twenty-fourth, and their contemporaneous admissions maintained the even balance between free and slave states. Thereafter, until the annexation of Texas sharply posed the still more disrupting question of extending slavery to new areas, states were admitted in pairs and the North-South balance was scrupulously maintained.

The actual admission of Missouri was further delayed until a provision forbidding free Negroes to reside in the state was stricken from her constitution. This secondary contest, taking place largely within the presumptive state herself, is most revealing of the American character of that time. Missouri, with her small farmers, her lead mines, her salt deposits, and most of all her imperial trade in furs, boasted a population as heterogeneous as her economy was diversified. Her people were a mixture of old French and Spanish stock, Germans and a few Irish newly arrived from Europe, and migrants from the older states, for the most part the ambitious, driving breed that would halt only on the shores of the Pacific Ocean. Typical of them all was Thomas Hart Benton, who would serve Missouri in the Senate for thirty years. Benton had come from North Carolina by way of Tennessee. He had served as Jackson's aide in the Creek campaign but had quarreled with his former chief, who carried in his shoulder a bullet from Benton's pistol. With the aggressiveness so necessary to survival on the frontier, Benton combined a spongelike capacity for learning, a tenacious memory, and a more than ample measure of political shrewdness. Newspaper publisher, banker, lawyer, he became the very embodiment of the West, which meant to him not Missouri alone but also Oregon and all that lay between.

Missouri had relatively few slaves and an economy that, even by the standards of 1820, scarcely required their use. She could have destroyed the Compromise immediately after she entered the Union by abolishing slavery, as the northern states generally had done. But this she would not do because in a sense it had been demanded of her. She was no less sovereign than Tallmadge's New York or Clay's Kentucky, and she would stand upon her right to conduct her domestic affairs as she pleased.

The Compromise itself, whatever one may think of its wisdom in retrospect, was generally accepted by both sides. The unanticipated consequence was the extent of sectional difference and the depth of sectional hostility revealed by the Missouri debate. It was the specter of abolition in Missouri that led the South to take stock of her position and to admit to herself for the first time that she no longer had any intention of giving up her slaves. And it was this southern reaction that opened the way for the anti-slavery crusade that eventually dominated all the northern states. The attitude of each section toward human bondage had evolved almost imperceptibly with the development in each of its own characteristic economy.

The industrial revolution had brought both an enormous demand for cotton and the mechanical means of preparing it economically for the carding and spinning and weaving machines that would turn it into cloth. As the demand rose, new cotton lands were cleared in a deepening arc around the Gulf Coast and up the valley of the Mississippi. With each extension of the cotton lands came a new demand for Negro slaves, at prices high enough to encourage smuggling and to tempt tobacco planters and border-state farmers to part with some of their own human chattels. By 1820 a slave population that increased at the rate of about 30 percent in each decennium was producing a cotton crop that had more than doubled each ten years. This apparent increase in productivity per slave was owing in part to the higher fertility of the new lands planted to cotton, in part to better organization; but more than any other single factor it was a function of the diversion of slave labor from other pursuits to the cultivation of cotton. One effect was to concentrate a very large proportion of the slaves in a relatively few hands; another was to divert so great a share of southern capital into cotton as to render any thought of changing the system preposterous to those who lived under it. A concomitant was to increase the fear of the slaveholder in proportion to the number of slaves he held and to spur him to violent reaction against any suggestion of emancipa-

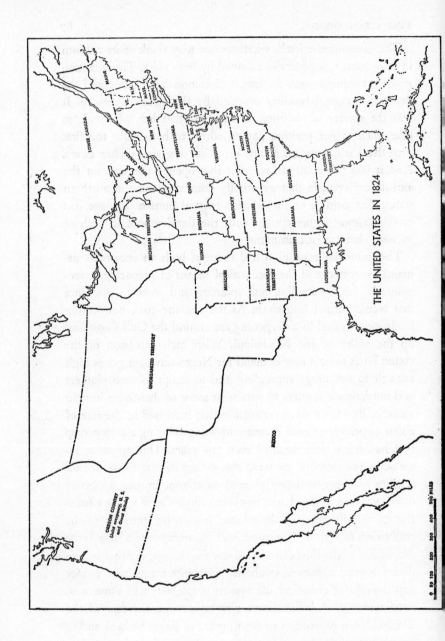

THE UNITED STATES IN 1824

tion. For the southern planter believed unshakeably that the cotton that produced his livelihood, and constituted one-third of the country's exports, could be grown only by Negro slaves. He believed that only the Negro could endure the relentless heat of the cotton fields; and he was equally sure that Caucasian and Negro could coexist in the South only in the relation of master and slave. Any other relationship, the average southerner of 1820 believed unalterably, would be an invitation to the blood-bath of internecine war. By such arguments the small up-country farmers who owned one or two slaves, or might own none at all, were driven to make common cause with the great planters of the tidewater shelf and the piedmont plateau.

The South had once regarded slavery in much the same way the North regarded it—as an inherited evil, but still an evil, to be got rid of as promptly as possible. As late as the end of 1816, when the American Colonization Society was founded to return freed slaves to Africa, southern leaders still looked to the ultimate extinction of the institution. Such national figures as Monroe, Crawford, and Clay helped found the Republic of Liberia, and the colonization idea was kept alive for years, but even at the time of its inception, it should have been clear that the project would have a negligible effect. The effect, indeed, may even have been to help perpetuate slavery by removing the potential danger of the free Negro from the sight of his fellows still in bondage.

When the Missouri debates forced thoughtful men the country over to take another and closer look at slavery, there were a million and a half Negro slaves in the southern states, representing a capital investment of about $300,000,000. This investment could not be transferred to any other form of enterprise, as New England's capital had been turned from shipping to manufacturing, because it could not be liquidated by sale of the property except within the same economic sphere; and it could be made to pay a reasonable return only if both the price of cotton and the volume of cotton production remained high. In a word, the South was too deeply committed to slavery by the date of the Missouri

Compromise to give it up. On the contrary, her spokesman regarded the institution as permanent where it was and held its further extension desirable to siphon off the uneconomically large slave populations of the southeastern states. They held bluntly that any attempt to restrict slavery, pointing as it must to ultimate abolition, was an attack on the whole economy of the South.

Northern spokesmen, shocked by what seemed to many both a breach of faith and a violation of morality, retorted that the slave representation clause of the Constitution had already given to the southern states twenty representatives in Congress not justified by the census—representatives whose votes had lately been used to attack the economy of New England. The South, with an equal sense of shock, realized her vulnerability and began to fashion both a moral and a political defense of her "peculiar institution." The moral defense was to present slavery as a positive good beneficial alike to master and to slave rather than as the crippling evil it was; the political defense was the compact theory of the Constitution with its correlatives of nullification and secession. With the intensified perceptions of those who live forever in the shadow of danger, the slaveholders heard their doom in Marshall's nationalism, for the free states already had the preponderance of population, and despite slave representation could outvote the South in the House of Representatives.

While the effect of her one-crop economy, her system of labor, her whole way of life was to solidify the South into a social and political unity that would not tolerate change, the free states, stimulated by industrial growth, were becoming increasingly diversified in economy and culture. The development of large urban centers brought demands for better means of transportation, lighting, water supply—for more efficient forms of power and speedier communications. The needs of the city were also stimulating the growth of a working class of artisans such as plumbers, tailors, bakers, brewers, locksmiths, and scores of others, as well as the beginnings of a proletariat in the persons of factory hands and common laborers, many of whom were newly arrived immigrants. The textile mills were still largely operated by women, like the "Lowell girls" of Massachusetts who came mostly from the farms and whose regimented lives were justified on moral grounds; but the building trades, transportation, metal working, and many, many more were the prerogatives of men, who were becoming politically articulate in the 1820's. The only northern counterparts of the southern planter-aristocracy were a merchant class whose power and prestige were definitely on the wane; and a rising class of industrial magnates who were inclined to be contemptuous of the planter and his fine manners, elegant clothes and cultured speech. Political leadership in the free states was tending more and more to fall to men who had risen from the ranks and would be guided by the wants of the new middle class.

North and South were far apart when Congress met in December, 1820. Clay was not present at the opening session, and the choice of a Speaker to succeed the tall Kentuckian was made along strictly sectional lines. The popular and universally respected William Lowndes was the choice of the slave states, but the winner was John W. Taylor of New York, who had led the fight to restrict slavery in Missouri. The sectional breach was further widened in June, 1822, when a free Negro, Denmark Vesey, led a slave revolt in Charleston. Divulged by a faithful retainer, the conspiracy collapsed. Vesey and thirty-five other Negroes were hanged; thirty-four were exiled; and sixty-one acquitted. Behind the revolt was a pamphlet copy of Rufus King's speech in the Senate on the Missouri Compromise, which had led the too-literal-minded Vesey to conclude that the slaves of the South were held in bondage in defiance of the law. The episode served to underline all the anxieties and tensions of the South, while it led well-intentioned southern men to question the justice of their northern brethren. The South already felt aggrieved by the northern assault on her system of labor when the tariff of 1824 seemed to carry the battle to the product of that labor, and to threaten her source of income as well as her social structure.

The tariff controversy arose out of the economic collapse of 1819. The tariff of 1816 had been a direct, uncomplicated attempt to encourage the growth of manufactures in the United States by means of import duties that would raise the cost of foreign products to an equality with the cost of producing the same goods at home. Except for the coarse cottons that came within the scope of the minimum principle, the duties were not in fact high enough to serve their avowed purposes, yet they were to be lowered in 1819 to a uniform 20 percent by the terms of the 1816 act itself. Agitation for higher tariff schedules had begun almost at once, gaining in volume and authority as the manufacturers of coarse cottons visibly prospered. Under the easy-credit policies of the Bank of the United States, new manufacturing ventures sprang up throughout New England, the middle states, Ohio and Kentucky, adding weight to the growing appeal for more protection. In 1818, Congress heeded the appeal to the extent of holding the duties at the original level while more experience with the problem was gained.

Then came the depression, with all its attendant hardships and cross-purposes. Men who had lost their jobs or their savings or their land all looked to government to help them, though there was little agreement as to what should be done, and less on the explosive question of whether, whatever it was, it should be done by the Federal Government or by the states. In 1820, Congress revised the land laws, making 80 rather than 160 acres the minimum unit, lowering the price from two dollars to a dollar and a quarter an acre, but requiring payment in cash. Anyone who could raise a hundred dollars could have a farm with title free and clear. But those who could not—and there were many— settled upon the land anyway, defying the authorities to put them off and calling loudly upon their congressmen to aid their cause. The acquisition of land, however, was only part of the problem, of little concern to those who already had land for which they could not pay, or a business whose physical assets were pledged to a bank as security for a loan long since used up.

The Bank of the United States fitted easily into the scapegoat role—the villain of the depression, responsible for every loss and deprivation. The tariff, in the hands of skillful publicists like Hezekiah Niles whose *Weekly Register* probably reached more readers than any other periodical in America, became the panacea —the simple formula that would automatically restore prosperity. Instigated by a growing lobby of manufacturers, a move had been made in each Congress since 1816 to increase the duties, but except for the extension of time in 1818, without success. The depression, which the tariff was supposed to cure, was already lifting in the northeastern states, though it still persisted in the West, before an upward revision of the duties was assured in 1823.

By that date the sectional pattern had been significantly changed by the reapportionment under the census of 1820. Those states that had opposed the tariff of 1816, or had been evenly divided, showed in the aggregate neither loss nor gain. Those states that had supported the earlier measure had gained an aggregate of twenty-two seats. Nine congressional seats were added from states that had not been members of the Union in 1816, but a majority of them were on the tariff side. In sectional terms, the slave states had gained eleven seats to a gain of twenty for the free states. The balance in the Senate, thanks to the Missouri Compromise, was even; but Kentucky, at least, could be counted among the tariff states. It was, therefore, with good prospects of success that a bill to increase the import duties on various items was introduced into the House early in January, 1824.

Like the bill of 1816 and every tariff bill since, the 1824 measure was argued primarily in terms of local self-interest, with each Representative, each Senator, seeking the maximum gain for his own constituents. Each wanted high duties on the articles his people produced, low duties or none at all on the things they bought. Only after the individual duties had been established was the bill debated in terms of broad national policy, but it was this phase of the debate that was most significant.

Clay, though himself a slaveholder, defended the economic nationalism of the immediate postwar years, and coined for it the name by which it became known—the American System. Daniel Webster, whose $15,000-a-year private law practice was the least of his assets, had queried the leading businessmen of his newly adopted Boston and found them opposed. The powerful argument he delivered for free trade was one he never quite refuted after his constituents changed their minds. But the southern phalanx looked beyond economics. Led in the House by George McDuffie, spare, lantern-jawed protégé of Calhoun, and by the ever-formidable Randolph; in the Senate by handsome, eloquent Robert Y. Hayne of South Carolina and by old John Taylor of Caroline, for whom Virginia had made a vacancy for the purpose —they concerned themselves with first principles. Taylor had not wavered in his political faith since he introduced into the state legislature the Virginia Resolutions of 1799, and he did not waver now. That a tariff high enough to reduce substantially the dollar volume of British goods sold in the United States would automatically reduce in proportion the dollar volume of American cotton sold in England, the free-trade spokesmen took for granted. To them the only real point at issue was the point of power. They found no authority in the Constitution to subsidize one economic interest, or class of citizens, at the expense of another, and they wanted none. The state rights argument against Marshall's doctrine of the strong central government was applied once more, and once more in vain. Among those who followed the debate from the floor of the Senate but took little part in it were Benton of Missouri; Martin Van Buren of New York, whose control of the "Albany Regency" had raised machine politics to a new level of effectiveness; and Andrew Jackson, serving briefly as an adjunct to his unhurried campaign for the Presidency.

The tariff of 1824 passed the House by five votes, the Senate by four. In each case the voting was strictly sectional, with the

West, New York, and Pennsylvania favoring, the South opposed, and New England still divided. The bill was signed into law by President Monroe on May 22, 1824.

In this tariff the average duty was raised from 25 to 37 percent by value. It proved just enough to stimulate substantially the spread of industry, and to whet the appetite for more. Manufacturing ventures, already growing in number, would also in time increase in size as the corporate form of organization became better understood. The Supreme Court had already stimulated the growth of the corporation in decisions upholding the inviolability of contracts and legislative charters. In Gibbons v. Ogden, decided in March, 1824, while the tariff bill was pending, John Marshall cleared another obstruction from the pathway to business expansion. He ruled that the monopoly of steamship navigation on the Hudson granted by the state of New York and still enjoyed by the heirs of Fulton and Robert Livingston, was invalid. The lower reaches of the river, and the bay into which it emptied, were declared interstate waters subject to commercial regulation by the Federal Government alone. Since Congress would be most reluctant to act in such matters, the ruling meant in effect that interstate commerce for many years to come would go unregulated.

Industrial growth was already solidifying protectionist sentiments in the northern and western states into an interest too powerful to be ignored by seekers of public office. The South, by the same token, achieved increasing unity in opposition. Her investment in land and slaves was too great, her capital too immobilized, to permit any significant change in her own economy, even had an industry operated by slave labor proved more feasible than southern slaveholders almost universally believed. So the nation's wealth continued to move toward the North and East, as it had since Alexander Hamilton's time, but at an accelerated pace as the profits of tariff-fostered industry continued to outstrip the returns from agriculture. The Erie Canal, opened throughout its 363-mile length from Albany to Buffalo on July 4, 1825, brought the Northwest into the commercial orbit of New York, to further increase the preponderance of the free states.

The heady nationalism of the immediate postwar years had broken down in less than a decade into sectional contention. The idealism of Jefferson had now become a self-interested struggle for wealth; the old dependence upon Europe, a new and aggressive form of isolation.

4

Expansion and Isolation

PARALLEL IN TIME with the rise of nationalism and its breakdown into sectional hostility was the development of a foreign policy isolationist toward Europe but expansionist toward the Western Hemisphere. Even before the unprogrammed purchase of Louisiana set imaginations soaring, planters in Georgia and settlers moving into Mississippi Territory demanded Florida as necessary to their own protection. With all her energies absorbed by the struggle raging in Europe, Spain was in no position to police her American possessions. The warlike Seminole Indians, who had never accepted any sovereignty but their own or any condition save that of independence, were more than a match for the handful of troops Spain could afford to keep in the Floridas, and they asserted their dissatisfaction with the role allotted to them by periodic raids across the border. They also welcomed and encouraged runaway slaves, which was another reason for the active animosity of their Georgia neighbors. After the purchase of Louisiana, Jefferson sought to buy the Floridas from Spain, or from Bonaparte if he saw fit to act as middleman; but John Randolph's opposition brought this Machiavellian scheme to nothing. A small piece of West Florida—the area between the Mississippi and Pearl rivers—had revolted in 1810, had been annexed to the United States, and was now a part of Louisiana. Another portion of West Florida, lying between the Pearl River and the Perdido and including Mobile Bay, had been seized in 1813 and was divided between Alabama and Mississippi territories at the time James Monroe took office in 1817. The remainder of Florida was still Spanish soil at that time—still the starting point for Seminole raids on Georgia and Alabama plantations, still the sanctuary beneath a foreign flag to which the Indians withdrew, secure in their knowledge that the white man's peculiar respect for national boundaries would provide them immunity from pursuit.

Elsewhere in the Western Hemisphere, Spain's position was even more precarious than in Florida. During the years that Spain herself was a battleground, she lost all effective control over her New World possessions. Spanish governors in Chile, Venezuela, the Argentine continued to fly the Spanish flag and to sanction their edicts in the name of the mother country, but by 1812 the colonies were in fact autonomous. They were, moreover, building for themselves a place in world affairs that had nothing to do with Spain. Orders in Council and French decrees had sent Yankee skippers to the South Atlantic in search of markets and the embargo had sent British merchantmen and British investors on a similar quest. So important had the South American trade become by 1810 that Madison had sent Joel Roberts Poinsett as special agent to Río de la Plata (Argentina) and Chile. Poinsett was a South Carolina Huguenot, widely traveled and multilingual, whose secret yearning for military glory was probably not known to the President. Before he was recalled home in 1814, Poinsett had encouraged revolutionary movements in the countries to which he was accredited, but he had also made himself an "authority" on Latin American affairs.

When Napoleon's power finally came to an end, and the Bourbon monarchy was restored in Spain, the principal Spanish-American colonies were too well established in their independent ways to take kindly to any return of the old autocracy. They were promptly beaten into line, but the South American continent was vast, with a difficult terrain of jungle, mountains, and endless plains, and Spain was weak. Revolt broke out once more, and under the leadership of Simón Bolívar and José de San Martín, Venezuela, Chile, and Argentina made good their independence.

These fledgling nations now looked to the United States for aid—moral, economic, if need be military—just as the revolting British colonials of 1776 had looked to France. But the United States had no Lafayette or Rochambeau. Monroe, new in his office and cautious now he had attained the summit of his dreams, withheld both aid and recognition, and took what steps he could to close the ports of the United States to Argentine privateers. In all of this the President's principal adviser on foreign affairs, John Quincy Adams, was in full accord.

Henry Clay, from his seat in the House, made himself the champion of the new republics, seeking congressional action to force the President's hand. Clay's motives were twofold. If thereby he could discomfit Adams, who as Secretary of State held the post that had come to mean the succession, so much the better. It would not be the first time these two had gotten on each other's nerves. There had been times at Ghent, with Adams rising for his scholar's day before Clay finished with his night of cards, that Gallatin had had to mediate. In the still unacknowledged rivalry between the pair, Clay required a popular issue to balance Adams' advantage of position. He judged rightly that the residues of Spanish dominion in the hemisphere were obnoxious to a large majority of Americans, who were inclined to mix sentiment with cupidity and would back any underdog who showed a disposition to fight.

The first round went more or less to Adams, who would not budge until he knew how far the British meant to go in support of their South American investments, and whether the Holy Alliance intended to intervene in behalf of Spain. Another reason for Adams' counsel of delay in recognizing the new republics was that in his European-nurtured, book-cultivated wisdom he did not believe the peoples of Latin America capable of self-government. He saw only arbitrary power, both military and ecclesiastical, "stamped upon their education, upon their habits, and upon their institutions," and he had "little expectation of any beneficial results to this country from any future connection with them, political or commercial." He was prepared to subordinate the needs of the revolutionaries to what seemed the more immediate problem of Florida, still coveted by the United States but unattainable, so Adams thought, should Spain be offended by a premature recognition of her rebellious colonies. The administration asked for and got from Congress a declaration of neutrality. It was a long step away from hemispheric solidarity, and one calculated to help make suspicious onlookers of those who might have been good neighbors.

In another sphere, Monroe was less reluctant to take advantage of Spanish weakness. Late in 1817 the administration ordered Andrew Jackson, then commanding the southern department of the Army, to pursue a band of marauding Seminoles into Florida. If the Indians took refuge in a Spanish fort, Jackson was to communicate with the Secretary of War. Otherwise he was to destroy them wherever he found them. The episode was the culmination of a long series of border depredations which had southern Georgia and Alabama Territory up in arms. A similar situation existed on Amelia Island, in the mouth of the St. Mary's River, between Georgia and Florida, where the sovereignty that Spain was too weak to exercise served to cloak the activities of a crew of pirates. Monroe, secure in the magnitude of his victory at the polls and confident the country would back him up, ordered the Navy to occupy Amelia Island at the same time he sent Jackson in pursuit of the Seminoles into Spanish territory.

The American flag was flying over Amelia Island before Christmas, but Jackson's task proved more difficult. It took him until March, 1818, to track the Indians through the swamps and jungles of the West Florida neck. He caught up with them at the Spanish fort of St. Marks, which he seized before the Indians could take cover there. Inside the fort he found two British subjects, one an elderly Scotch trader named Alexander Arbuthnot, the other a British officer named Robert Ambrister.

Ambrister's own testimony and papers found on Arbuthnot's trading schooner convinced Jackson that his prisoners, with the connivance of their government, had deliberately stirred up the Seminoles and had even been leading their raids. In short order he court-martialed and executed both, then moved in the wake of the fleeing Indians to Pensacola, where he stormed and seized Fort Barancas.

When the news of Jackson's exploits reached Washington, the President was away on one of his barnstorming good-will tours, but Adams held the Spanish and British Ministers at bay until Monroe returned. Jackson's peremptory action in Spanish territory was thrashed out in the Cabinet, where Calhoun, whose direct orders the general had disobeyed, favored a court of inquiry. William H. Crawford and Monroe, both former War Secretaries themselves, were inclined to agree. But Adams, who had gotten nowhere at all in his efforts to acquire Florida, defended Jackson, who had unwittingly shown the Spanish government (and Adams) that there might be other ways of acquiring the Floridas than by treaty. The Secretary of State finally convinced his colleagues that to punish or even to disavow the general would be to throw away a bargaining advantage. The Spanish forts were courteously returned but no apologies were made.

Nor were apologies made to Britain for the execution of Arbuthnot and Ambrister. During the war, Britain had used the Floridas as a base for harassing the United States. From this neutral ground her agents stirred up Indian depredations, raided American shipping, and finally prepared a landing for the army that met disaster at New Orleans. The activities of the pair had been a carryover of such raids. There had even been rumors during the South American revolutions that Florida was destined to pass into British hands, and indeed, by 1816 the "inspired" hit-and-run tactics of the Seminoles had assumed such proportions as to lead later historians to classify them as a "war"—the first Seminole War, which Jackson terminated at Pensacola.

British protests, vigorous though they were, were not allowed by either side to jeopardize the discussions then going on in London between Richard Rush, the American Minister; Gallatin, who was still accredited to France; and the friendly Lord Castlereagh, who was looking toward a settlement of many of the issues left unresolved at Ghent. The treaty signed in October, 1818, followed that of a year earlier under which each country agreed to a virtual naval disarmament on the Great Lakes. The new agreement clarified the right of access to the North Atlantic fisheries and drew the boundary between the United States and Canada westward along the 49th parallel from the Lake of the Woods in what is now Minnesota to the crest of the Rockies. The vaguely defined Oregon country lying between Spanish claims to the south and Russian claims to the north was opened to joint settlement by Americans and British for ten years. American claims to the territory rested on the first navigation of the Columbia River by Captain Robert Gray in 1792 and on the explorations of Lewis and Clark in 1805–1806. Great Britain's claims were based on the activities of the Hudson's Bay Company and on her treaty of 1790 with Spain.

Americans, by the 1820's, had already staked a claim to half the continent. Yankee skippers who had been trading with the Indians on the lower Columbia since the 1790's had been calling more or less regularly at California ports almost as long. Agents of the American Fur Company roamed the plains and the eastern slopes of the Rockies. In 1823 Fort Bent was established on the upper Arkansas River, about where Pueblo, Colorado, stands today. But the area had been explored in 1806 and 1807 by Captain Zebulon Pike, who had also visited the Spanish settlements at Taos and Santa Fe. In 1822 William Becknell made the first trip with wagons and trading goods from Missouri to New Mexico over what came to be known as the Santa Fe Trail. Backing up these far-flung outposts was a line of forts and Indian trading posts from Little Rock to Council Bluffs. Army engineers were systematically exploring and mapping the country, promoting trade and settlement. When the first steamboat breasted the treacherous Missouri current from St. Louis to Council Bluffs in 1819, the way west was open. Only Indians, a handful of Spaniards, and a few Englishmen stood between young America and the pot of gold which was indeed at the end of the western rainbow.

Jackson's activities in Florida, as well as United States relations with both Latin America and Canada, can be properly evaluated only in the context of this continental explosion that would be recognized in the next generation as "manifest destiny." For the immediate time and place, however, rival presidential candidates saw in Monroe's willingness to vindicate Jackson a potential danger to their political future. Partisans of William H. Crawford took the lead, appealing to the people through their Representatives in Congress with resolutions condemning by indirection everything Jackson had done. Clay joined the attack with a fiery speech filled with allusions to classical generals who had overthrown classical republics. Then Jackson himself arrived in Washington, to receive a hero's welcome, and after weeks of alternate eulogy and stricture, a triumphant vindication. There was a species of vindication for Adams' judgment, too. Dispatches had made their slow crossing of the Atlantic, instructions had returned, and on February 22, 1819, just ten days after Jackson's triumph, the Spanish Minister signed the treaty yielding the Floridas to the United States. In return the United States paid $5,000,000 and gave up any pretensions she may have had to Texas or California or to any lands between.

The treaty barely escaped defeat in the Senate. Many believed that Texas had been part of the Louisiana Purchase, and others felt—as indeed did Adams himself—that eventually the Bay of San Francisco must belong to the United States. And in Spain a new government, at once fearful and dilatory, let the treaty lie unratified for two years. In the interval, the Missouri Compromise fixed the line between slave and free soil at 36° 30′ north latitude for all territory included in the Louisiana Purchase, and by implication for all territory that might still be acquired. Florida would eventually enter the Union as a slave state but the renunciation of Texas appeared to close the door to any subsequent extension of slavery. Also in the two-year period of waiting, Mexico followed the example of other Spanish colonies and declared her own independence, but Monroe and Adams dared not acknowledge the accomplished fact lest Spain be angered and the Florida treaty fail. It was not until 1822 that the Latin American republics were officially welcomed by the United States into the family of nations, and diplomatic relations were established.

Such caution was unnecessary, as John Quincy Adams of all people should have known. Spain was clearly too weak and, save for her pride, too indifferent to intervene without the active help of England or France—both war-weary and hardly disposed to tackle the young colossus across the sea to salvage an empire for a historic rival. Had the revolutionary governments of Argentina, Chile, and Venezuela been recognized at once and given whatever aid and counsel they then required, Spain might never have signed and ratified a treaty yielding Florida; but Florida, Texas, and perhaps California as well would have fallen to the United States of their own weight, and leadership of the hemisphere would have been earned. Only because Britain too, for reasons of her own, was reluctant to recognize the rebellious Spanish colonies, did the cautious Monroe-Adams policy succeed at all.

Perhaps Europe realized the inherent strength of the Americans no more clearly than they did themselves, but she was given ample opportunity to see what manner of men they were. The South American revolutions aroused sympathy throughout the country, whether government-sanctioned or no; and the long struggle of the Greeks to win their freedom from centuries of Turkish domination became something of a national cause. Some showed their sentiments by fronting their homes with hurriedly-carved Greek colonnades; others built ships and sent food, clothing, medical supplies, and weapons. Several, like the young physicians Samuel Gridley Howe and John Dennison Russ, sailed for Greece themselves. European travelers surveyed American institutions and probed the American character with increasing frequency and sometimes with admirable objectivity. And American tourists were becoming familiar if not always welcome sights all over Europe and in the Middle East. They had not yet become the ill-mannered critics of their hosts that more opulent generations grew to be, but they were on the way. Undiscerning they were, and often unsympathetic toward the strange ways of others, yet they seldom failed to impress all they encountered by their vigor, their earnestness, their almost mystical conviction that they were a people of destiny.

This sense of mission was often combined with an impatient indifference to the rights or prior claims of others—an impatience nowhere better revealed than in the history of Texas. The broad, fertile plains stretching west and south from the Sabine River were already a magnet for Americans when Burr was indulging in his imperial fantasies. The Army had sent observant, if unofficial, scouts as far as the Rio Grande before American claims to any part of Texas were renounced in the Florida treaty. When the treaty was first published, even before its ratification by Spain, there were grumblings from western men such as Thomas Hart Benton who argued—if they did not wholly believe—that all of Texas was already American soil; and the depression of 1819 started a trickle of emigrants moving in that direction. One of those who visited Texas at this time was Moses Austin, who had mined lead in Missouri under a Spanish grant before the Louisiana Purchase. He now secured permission of the Spanish authorities to colonize a number of families in Texas.

Austin died before he could carry out his ambitious plans, but his son, Stephen F. Austin, secured new grants of land from the revolutionary Mexican Government and in 1825 began settling the first three hundred families. No one seems to have balked at conditions requiring the settlers to accept Mexican citizenship and to become Roman Catholics. To all intents and purposes the goal of the settlers was no more than to farm their land. As warring factions in the new Mexican Government claimed the attention of Austin, he cautiously advised his people to "play the turtle, head and feet within your own shell," but differences soon arose over the extent of Texan autonomy and laid a basis for future conflicts with the Mexican authorities. In addition, Joel Poinsett, back in diplomatic harness as first United States Minister to the new Republic of Mexico, helped things along as he had in his earlier missions to Chile and Argentina, by meddling. He dabbled, not subtly, in Mexico's local politics, managed to set aristocrat and peasant at one another's throats over the relative merits of Scottish Rite and York Rite Masonry, and was finally sent packing by the Mexican Government. Poinsett's "indiscretion" together with the growing recalcitrance of Texas settlers whose loyalties to the United States had never left home were added reasons for suspicion and distrust of the United States below the border.

Both in Texas and in Oregon, American expansion extended beyond the limits of the Louisiana Purchase and was parallel in time with the belated recognition of Latin American independence and with European moves in the direction of intervention in the Western Hemisphere. These factors combined to force from the United States a definitive expression of foreign policy. It was a policy isolationist toward Europe, expansionist toward the North American continent, and toward South America a combination of the two. The spark was provided in the summer of 1822 by the death of Lord Castlereagh, who had come to the British Foreign Office just too late to prevent the War of 1812. George Canning, who succeeded Castlereagh, had been more responsible than any other individual for the Orders in Council and for the resultant crisis in Anglo-American relations. During the period while the United States was virtually immobilized by the delicacy of her negotiations with Spain over Florida, Britain had been steadily improving her position in South America. The manufactures she could no longer sell profitably in the United States because of the new tariff policy, she now sold to Brazil and to Argentina. By 1822, her exports to Latin America exceeded those to the United States. British subjects were exploiting the rich mineral deposits of Mexico, Brazil, and other areas. Her bankers extended generous credits to governments still regarded by Spain and her European allies as colonies in revolt. Canning saw in American recognition a future threat to Britain's economic position in those countries, but he made no move toward official recognition of them himself until the summer of 1823, when France intervened with arms to restore the lost prerogatives of the Spanish king and it seemed likely she might seek to restore the lost Spanish colonies as well.

Canning then suggested that the United States and Great Britain issue a joint declaration of policy toward Latin America, each disavowing territorial ambitions while warning against interference by others. Before notes could be exchanged across the Atlantic, France repudiated any designs on the former Spanish colonies, and Canning dropped the subject. Not so President Monroe, who first saw the correspondence early in October. The President consulted his two predecessors, Madison and Jefferson, as he was accustomed to do with knotty problems, and both approved. John Quincy Adams did not, arguing that any warning against intervention in the hemisphere should be strictly American, directed at Britain herself as much as at the Holy Alliance. Already concerned over Russian penetration on the Pacific coast, not only into Oregon but as far south as San Francisco Bay, the Secretary of State had earlier taken the position that the New World was no longer open to colonization by any European power. Monroe's interest in the British suggestion offered an opportunity to combine nonintervention with this noncolonization principle in a single statement of national policy, which would in effect be a reassertion and an enlargement of the credo of Washington's Farewell Address. The resulting statement was the declaration we still know as the Monroe Doctrine, included in the President's annual message to Congress of December 2, 1823.

The relevant passage declared that the Americas, "by the free and independent condition which they have assumed and maintain," were thenceforward closed to any further colonization by any European power. Britain, France and Spain alike were warned that any attempt to establish or regain control over any American state would be considered an unfriendly act toward the United States; and to make the declaration reciprocal, the world was informed that the United States would thenceforth take no part in the affairs of Europe unless her rights were "invaded, or seriously menaced."

In the heat of an increasingly bitter presidential campaign, this declaration of isolation went almost unnoticed, yet its implications were enormous. The United States, in the 1820's, was already far too completely a part of the world to withdraw to a hemisphere. The carrying trade she had taken from Britain during the Napoleonic wars she had never relinquished. American sailing ships had steadily improved in design and now outclassed their British rivals at every point. The British, as befitted the world's most advanced industrial nation, would answer superior sail with steam, which Americans were slow to apply successfully to ocean use. Over the next two decades the British need for markets for the products of her industry would become acute, and so would her need for the agricultural products of the United States, now grown in increasing abundance. The Monroe Doctrine would not keep Britain from wooing Texas, nor prevent the United States from interfering in Canadian affairs, but the economic needs of both countries would ultimately transcend their differences and bring them closer together, as we shall see in a later chapter.

The Monroe Doctrine had still another effect. Along with its warning to imperialistic squatters to stay out of the Western Hemisphere, it carried an implied pledge of friendship, aid, and encouragement to Latin America at least to the extent that European powers might be supplying these things. In thus arrogating to herself the prerogatives of leadership, the United States was obligated to assume the correlative responsibility. It was an obligation slow of recognition and slower still in honoring. Monroe's declaration was followed by no specific treaty pledges to Latin American nations, nor by any promises that the United States herself would not encroach upon their sovereignty.

The United States was still not prepared to offer positive leadership or to enter into partnership with her southern neighbors when the first crisis came early in 1825. At that time Britain formally recognized the independence of the Latin American countries and simultaneously took steps to extend British influence in that area, not so much in defiance of the Monroe Doctrine as in complete indifference to it. A Congress of American States was then being projected to meet in Panama in 1826, and at the instance of Simón Bolívar himself, Great Britain was invited to send delegates. Pointedly not invited was the United States, which had rebuffed advances from the southern continent to enter into working treaties of alliance in accordance with the plain invitation of Monroe's famous message. The snub was rectified by Mexico and Colombia, whose diplomats inquired circumspectly if the United States would participate if invited. Perhaps Adams saw in this belated bid to make common cause with the other independent powers of the hemisphere a second chance to undo the damage that had already been done. If so, the revision of policy was not permitted to take place. The Panama Mission became a political football, as we shall soon see, and eventually the vehicle around which an opposition party would be formed.

In any event, it was probably already too late. The restless, forward surge of American settlers, who had in a mere two decades extended their boundaries from the Mississippi to the Pacific, had absorbed Florida, had made no secret of their wish to possess Canada, had claimed and still claimed Texas in spite of their pledged faith to let her go, and who were now casting covetous eyes at Cuba—how was this drive to be stopped short of the Strait of Magellan? Who could blame the proud, sensitive Latin Americans for preferring Britain, on her record of supplying capital, technicians, and unlimited markets, with never a question of territory being raised? Perhaps the British themselves did not fully understand the consequences of their activity, for few indeed were then aware that in an industrial age the control of raw materials, of the tools of production, of the means of transportation, is more important than mere geographical sovereignty. For an economy based on mass production, customers are always more important than territory. What Britain was doing in Latin America in the 1820's is a technique better known in the twentieth century than it was in the nineteenth. She was in effect lending money to underdeveloped countries, with which they were expected to buy her goods, and with the aid of her technicians develop the raw materials of which she was desperately in need.

As for Russian penetration on the Pacific coast—it was halted by treaty between Russia and Great Britain in 1825, fixing the boundary between their respective claims at 54° 40′ north latitude. No threat to the hemisphere developed from either Spain or France. Toward Great Britain the Monroe Doctrine was never applied, nor could it be, until the two countries were prepared to drop the barriers imposed by American tariff and British Corn Laws and resume a mutually beneficial trade with each other.

5

Old Republicans, New Democrats

IF WE MAY conceive of property, real or intangible, as the basis of political divisions, then one party may be said to represent wealth, the other numbers. One party will fear, the other will seek, majority rule, for the majority can always vote wealth into its own hands. Even the modern advocate of the Welfare State is not immune, for when he seeks to have government do for him what he would otherwise have to do for himself, he is redistributing property as surely as was his ancestor who wanted a protective tariff or free land or access to markets at public expense. The history of party is one of mass appeal to eject those in power, "reforms" that will benefit primarily the new group of partisans, a new conservatism to "consolidate" the reforms, and finally the overthrow of the current "ins" by the current "outs," with the same motives and the same future.

The cycle was completed in the middle 1820's, though party distinctions had been minimized under the Virginia Dynasty with its intellectual tendency to confuse principles and issues. The differences between Jefferson and Hamilton had been clear-cut reflections of two distinct philosophies of government, the one authoritarian, the other grounded in human rights. In terms of doctrinal antecedents, Hamilton followed Hobbes and the Leviathan state; Jefferson stemmed from Harrington and Locke. The Federalists, under Hamilton's leadership, had encouraged the growth of a propertied class, bound by ties of self-interest to the government, and had ultimately resorted to the abridgment of free speech and free assembly in a vain attempt to maintain themselves in power. The Republicans, under Jefferson, had invoked the states as guardians of civil liberties; but those who had been rescued in the name of liberty from the clutches of an all-powerful government soon discovered how to use that power to their own advantage. First it was Louisiana, then the embargo, and in Madison's time the very bank and protective tariff that had been the key policies of Federalism. When the Federalists countered with the same doctrine of state sovereignty that had served the Jeffersonians in their day of protest, the last ideological difference between the parties was gone. Half Federalist and half Republican, Monroe faced only local opposition in 1816 and in 1820 had been unopposed.

Jefferson, watching from his retirement the nonpartisan course of the Era of Good Feelings, though he did not criticize or openly interfere, must have realized that Monroe, like Madison, was a mistake. Madison was too weak to lead the party whose younger members, in consequence, led him; Monroe did not even perceive the need for party leadership. As the dynasty approached the end of its too-long tenure, faction displaced party and public service was subordinated to personality. To succeed Monroe there were almost as many candidates as there were issues, and an issue was any question on which two politicians disagreed. The tariff, the bank, public lands, internal improvements, Latin America, all offered opportunity to exploit the heritage of discontent left by the depression of 1818–1821, and with the franchise no longer the exclusive possession of a planter and merchant ruling class, discontent had become a formidable asset. Eighteen of the twenty-four states would choose presidential electors by popular vote in 1824,* and in those eighteen states 250,000 ballots would be cast. After

---

* All but Vermont, New York, Delaware, South Carolina, Georgia, and Louisiana. Delaware held out for one more election. South Carolina did not change until the Civil War.

Madison and Monroe the voters were ready for an aggressive, vigorous administration—one that would talk less about the Constitution and do more for the individual, such as subsidizing his business, staking him to a farm, providing him with cheaper transportation or easier credit or lower taxes. Among those who promised some or all of these benefits, four stood out: John Quincy Adams, the Secretary of State; William Harris Crawford, the Secretary of the Treasury; Henry Clay, the Speaker of the House; and Andrew Jackson, the Hero of New Orleans. In these four candidates the interests and pressures that would recombine into two major parties came together.

The front-runner as the campaign got off to an early start was Crawford. A man of large physical stature, impressive presence, and unsurpassed political acumen, Crawford had entered the Senate from Georgia in 1807 to find the party weak and divided. He had given it strength and leadership, culminating in a bruising but hopeless battle against Republican dissidents to recharter the first Bank of the United States. His reward had been the mission to France, which he had yielded to Gallatin after the Treaty of Ghent; the War Department; and finally the Treasury. He had used both the influence and the patronage of the Treasury Department to rebuild and refine the party organization that had first carried Jefferson to power, and he was now the true inheritor of the Jefferson-Burr flirtation and the legitimate heir of the Republican party. He had established his claim as early as 1816, when he had allowed his name to go before a Republican caucus and had lost out to Monroe by only a handful of votes. Since then he had reforged the old political alliance of New York and Virginia, anchoring his northern flank on the well-organized and smoothly functioning Albany Regency, which was controlled by Senator Martin Van Buren, and appealing to the South on the basis of his own consistent state rights, anti-tariff record. In both these articles of southern faith, the more intellectual Calhoun was being pushed into the leadership, but this was not yet apparent, even to Calhoun, who gave up his own premature bid for the Presidency in return for support from both Adams and Jackson factions for the second office.

The caucus of 1824—the last ever held for this purpose—gave Crawford a virtually unanimous nomination. Albert Gallatin, home at last from Europe, was named as the party candidate for Vice-President, where he would serve as a living link between the old and the new Republicanism. The caucus was in reality no more than an unofficial gathering of the party's Senators and Representatives in Congress, whose acts were not even binding upon themselves, but with the weight of precedent behind it, its choices were accepted long after the extension of the franchise made it an anachronism. The system was under such crossfire of criticism by 1824 that no more than a third of those eligible were present, but this sparse attendance reflected the inadequacy of the method rather than the weakness of the candidate. Crawford's grip on the party machinery was not to be shaken by such defections. Despite the formidable nature of the opposition, the Georgian would probably have won with relative ease had he not suffered a stroke in the fall of 1823 that kept him bedridden for months and left him still in precarious health on election day itself.

Adams' assets included integrity, ability, an impressive record, and the advantage, after three successive Virginians, of northern birth. An apostate Federalist, he had offered his services to Jefferson in 1808 when his own party and section had made opposition to the embargo the test of loyalty, and he had served his adopted party faithfully since that day. Expansionist in America but isolationist toward Europe, Adams was on the way back to the Federalism of his father. On any issue between state rights and national supremacy, he would always be on the side of the Nation. As counsel for those to whom Georgia had illegally sold the Yazoo lands, he had identified himself with business and had given John Marshall his first opportunity to uphold the sacredness of contracts when that matter came before the Supreme Court by way of Fletcher *v.* Peck (1810). He was not yet committed, either to tariff or to federally financed public works, but both were implicit in his concept of nationalism; and he was already a partisan of the Bank.

Henry Clay, dynamic and resourceful, spoke for the first generation born after the Declaration of Independence. He was the prime architect of the American System, which had somehow managed to survive both Madison's internal-improvements veto and Jones' mismanagement of the Bank. He was almost a personification of the West, which had not yet been represented in the White House, yet his Virginia birth and legal training under the venerable George Wythe, Jefferson's own mentor, gave him special appeal in what was still the second most populous state in the Union. He was not yet the Great Compromiser he was to become, but he had already shown the qualities that would make him so, in the Speaker's chair and at the council table at Ghent.

It was inevitable that Clay, whose views on domestic affairs did not differ essentially from those of Adams, would offer his support to the New Englander when his own prospects failed. It was equally certain that Adams, anticipating the further growth of industry and more conscious than any other candidate of the danger inherent in an isolated West, would endorse the American System. Though each clung to his own fragment of Jeffersonian heritage, Adams and Clay recognized their own departure from the true faith when they called their joint party National Republican. In another ten years, as Whigs, they would repudiate that faith entirely.

Less experienced in public affairs, and from any logical point of view, less well-equipped for the Presidential office, than any of the others, Andrew Jackson was by all odds the peoples' choice. By some special magic of his own, Jackson seemed to embody in his own person the aspirations of most Americans of his day. Since the Battle of New Orleans he had been of presidential stature, if popularity with the rank and file could vest a man with heroic proportions. His exploits in Florida had only enhanced his appeal, and the vindication he had wrung from Congress against the united forces of Crawford and Clay had been more like an apotheosis. He came before the people now as a latter-day Joshua who would at last lead the people into the promised land that Jefferson, for his political sins, had only glimpsed from the mountain top.

The Jackson following was both intensely emotional and detached. It included long-time friends who used every art known to politics to advance his cause; those who admired the energy and decisiveness of his military career and his brief but equally decisive term as first civil governor of Florida Territory; and those who believed it was time to break the pattern of Cabinet succession. Unhampered by political promises, untroubled by the fetish of consistency, untainted by old partisan associations, Jackson could be and was all things to all people. Himself a slaveholder and cotton planter, he yet voted as Senator from Tennessee in favor of the tariff of 1824. He was against the caucus system, yet his own name had first been placed in nomination by a caucus of the Tennessee legislature. He had been outspoken enough in his denunciation of banks and stockjobbers to endear himself to the victims of the depression, yet vague enough to avoid alarming the business community, of which he himself was a quondam member. He was a self-made citizen-soldier, whose tastes were aristocratic, whose economic and social ties were with a ruling oligarchy, and whose following, thanks to an inborn gift of leadership, included men of all types and conditions. He was a gambler, a duelist, sometimes a romantic but always a fighter— the raw material alike of frontier folk tale and national hero. The potency of his popular appeal had been long recognized by his rivals, but so far he had not shown himself to be a party man and so the politicians remained distrustful and aloof.

The campaign was one of paradox, prejudice, and personality. Gallatin withdrew from the Crawford ticket because of vicious attacks on his "foreign" birth (as if all Americans approaching fifty had not been born to the sovereignty of a "foreign" state). Crawford himself was denounced because he had once suggested intermarriage as a means of amalgamating the Indians into the white society. Adams was accused of "giving" American soil to Spain in Texas; Jackson was belittled as a mere military chieftain and decried as a potential Caesar; Clay was held up as dissolute and untrustworthy. Yet Clay alone had a consistent following in the manufacturing and commerical interests of Kentucky, Ohio and the farther West. Adams was supported at once by the anti-tariff merchants of Boston, the pro-tariff textile manufacturers of Lowell and Pawtucket, and the small farmers of upstate New York. Crawford was both the state rights candidate of the South and the candidate of a northern urban machine that cared nothing for state rights, but much for the perquisites of power. Jackson was simultaneously the favorite of small farmers in the South and West, of small businessmen who hoped to grow larger in the northern and middle states, and of large manufacturers in Pennsylvania.

When the ballots were counted, Jackson was out in front with ninety-nine electoral votes that cut sharply across sectional lines, but he was still short by thirty-two of the majority he needed. Adams had eighty-four electoral votes, Crawford had forty-one, and Clay only thirty-seven. As provided by the Constitution, the three highest names were then placed before the House of Representatives for a final choice, each state casting one ballot determined by a majority of the delegation. In the House it was Adams—not Jackson—who carried off the prize. Clay, out of the running himself, threw his strength to Adams, adding the votes of Ohio, Kentucky and Missouri to those of New York and the six New England states. The three additional votes Adams needed to make a majority came from Maryland, Louisiana and Illinois—all states in which he had run second to Jackson at the polls. In addition North Carolina, which Jackson also carried, voted for Crawford in the House. The politicians were still reluctant to accept the popular hero.

Adams' appointment of Clay as Secretary of State gave a semblance of truth to the charge of Jackson's partisans that a deal had been made between Clay and Adams, though it is difficult to see with the perspective of time how Clay could have supported either of the other candidates and still have remained consistent with his own views, or where Adams could have found anyone else as well qualified for the State Department. The cry of "corrupt bargain" soon became a rallying point for the opposition, helping to that extent to prepare the ground for the restoration of the two-party system. Another factor was the strongly nationalistic position taken by the President with respect to the powers of the Federal Government, which he held to embrace not only the elements of Clay's American System but higher education and the encouragement of science as well. The administration's maladroit handling of the solicited invitation to send delegates to the Congress of American States soon to meet in Panama gave the opposition the peg it needed on which to hang a policy.

The moving force behind a union in opposition of all factions save those immediately loyal to Adams and Clay came fittingly from Martin Van Buren. Small of stature, with round, balding head, yellow mutton-chop whiskers, and a disarming smile, Van Buren was deceptively unobtrusive. Affable and direct in personal intercourse, his political methods were devious and obscure. His starting point, like that of Aaron Burr before him, was the Tammany Society, strengthened since Burr's time by an influx of Irish immigrants who were enfranchised for their votes by De Witt Clinton but seduced from their Clintonian allegiance by the "little magician." Perhaps with Burr's fate in mind, Van Buren skipped no step on his way to the top, but parlayed his city organization into the powerful Albany Regency. The Regency, in turn, had been fitted into Crawford's national political machine. With Crawford broken in health and out of public life, Van Buren moved up to the higher echelon in Washington.

Looking four years ahead, it was clear to the New York Senator that the Radicals, as Crawford's followers were inappropriately called, could offer no candidate with a chance of winning against the strongly centralized party Adams and Clay were molding out of their disparate followings; but Jackson, with his tremendous appeal, could win against anyone. Van Buren lost no time in placing the Radicals at Jackson's disposal, and with the Panama Mission as a lever, he brought Vice-President Calhoun also into the Jackson camp. It could not have been difficult to convince the ambitious South Carolinian that Adams had overstepped his powers, or that it would be impolitic to say the least to ask delegates from the slaveholding states to sit down in amity with the revolted slaves of Haiti. Calhoun's nationalism was crumbling with the price of cotton, which had been halved since the tariff of 1824.

Commissioners to attend the Panama Congress were finally confirmed by the Senate in March of 1826, but not before Clay's tactics had drawn biting words from Randolph and the two had exchanged shots in consequence. The Panama Mission was the first and last congressional victory of the Adams administration, and one that, ironically, gained nothing, for neither commissioner ever got to Panama.*

In the off-year elections of 1826, the only issue before the country was Andrew Jackson, who his managers alleged had been the overwhelming choice of the people in 1824 but had been defeated by a combination of self-seeking politicians. When the sheep and the goats were parted on the Panama issue, the Jackson banner was raised by the opposition and "the Democracy," as the Democratic party was generally called in Jackson's time, was born; or rather, was conjured full-grown from whatever of antique republicanism had survived the cycle of Madison and Monroe. At the polls the country over, the people responded as they will always respond to decisive leadership. The Democrats won control of both houses of Congress and of a majority of the state governments; the two-party system of Jefferson and Hamilton was restored, and the election of Jackson in 1828 was assured.

* Richard C. Anderson of Kentucky, United States Minister to Colombia, died of a tropical fever on his way to Panama, and John Sergeant, former Pennsylvania congressman, refused to go at all in the fever season. The United States was represented at a second session held in Mexico in 1827, but this meeting broke up before it ever got started.

Jackson's appeal to the common people was sounder than Jefferson's had been, if only because there were now more of them qualified to vote and because they came closer to a common level; but the Democracy of 1828 was a "popular" party in only a limited sense. It was the same combination of interests that had elected Jefferson in 1800—a coalition, in Van Buren's phrase, of "the planters of the South and the plain Republicans of the North"; but the plain Republicans tended to be the hand workers, the artisans, and the tradesmen of the cities, with a sprinkling of northern farmers and a leaven in every section of the rising middle class. More broadly still, the Democracy of Jackson's day was very like the combination of northern and western liberals, southern conservatives, and big-city bosses that elected Wilson, Roosevelt, and Truman.* The real issues were often masked, and did not emerge until later, because these various elements wanted different and sometimes irreconcilable things.

Over the next two years the well-oiled Crawford machine became, with the blessing of Crawford himself, the Jackson machine, powerful enough to win all but two national elections between 1828 and 1860. That the machine had remained in working order to compass his own defeat was largely Adams' fault, for he, like Monroe, had so little appreciated the role of the President as party leader that he had not only refused to remove political opponents from office, he had even reappointed most of those who served fixed terms. Yet these officeholders, most important of whom were the collectors of customs, were Crawford partisans who were key figures in state political organizations. Their services to the Jackson cause were to prove invaluable.

So, too, were the services of the newspaper editors who brought the most highly developed skills of a profession just coming into its own to the support of the Democratic coalition. Most immediately influential of these were Isaac Hill, pro-Crawford edi-

* Even the southern bolt of 1948 did not destroy the pattern. Truman still won 117 electoral votes from southern and border states, which was more than his 114-vote margin of victory.

tor of the *New Hampshire Patriot,* whose Republicanism had
survived both the embargo and the Hartford Convention; Mor-
decai Noah, who had edited a Tammany organ for a decade before he founded the New York *Enquirer* in the interest of the
new Democracy, and fiery James Watson Webb, whose New
York *Courier* would be merged with the *Enquirer* when Noah
accepted a political appointment at Jackson's hands. Amos
Kendall, New England-born Kentuckian, switched the potent
Argus of Western America from Clay to Jackson; Thomas
Ritchie brought over the Richmond *Enquirer,* house organ of the
Radicals and most effective paper in the South; and Duff Green
gave up the St. Louis *Enquirer* to edit the newly established
United States' Telegraph, which was to represent the party in
Washington. In broad terms, Noah and Webb represented the
Van Buren wing of the party, Ritchie the Crawford faction,
Green the Calhoun interest, while Hill and Kendall gave their
undivided allegiance to Andrew Jackson. There would be defec-
tions and new recruits as policies and partisans changed, but the
Democracy would always be served by a vigorous and imagi-
native press.

The birth of the party was not, of course, quite so simple as it
sounds. The divergent elements that went into the making of
the Democracy had only yesterday been at bitter enmity with
each other, and had scant reason to trust each other now. The
National Republicans of Adams and Clay had made their own
the whole range of Hamiltonian doctrine—a strong central
government whose powers transcended those of the states; sub-
sidized industry; transportation and other forms of public works
at the expense of the Federal Government; a national bank. But
these were precisely the issues on which the still unassimilated
components of the Democratic party were themselves hopelessly
divided along sectional and class lines. If, therefore, the party
was to succeed, it had to be convincingly on both sides of every
important issue before the country.

The first demonstration of this Democratic ambivalence came

early in 1827 when the administration undertook to raise the
tariff on woolens to a prohibitive level before its slim majority
was lost in the succeeding Congress. The bill Webster drove
through the House was primarily for the benefit of New England. Reflecting improvements in textile machinery, it was designed to do for the woolen manufacturers what the minimum
principle of 1816 had already done for those of cotton. In the
Senate the bill was tabled by Calhoun's casting vote, after Van
Buren had manipulated a tie. The maneuver served to put the
party as well as Calhoun on record against tariff increases, for
the Vice-President had already been endorsed for a second term
by Jackson himself. Next time the question of protection arose—
as it was certain to do again before the election—the northern
members of the party could vote "aye," and Jackson, by saying
nothing at all, could stand with Calhoun in the South with Van
Buren in the North.

The tariff was an issue becoming increasingly difficult to evade.
The obvious prosperity of those interests protected by the duties
of 1824 inspired a convention in Harrisburg, Pennsylvania, in
the summer of 1827 to plan a new assault on Congress for an
upward revision of the duties. At the same time the falling price
of cotton, down from thirty cents in June, 1825, to nine cents two
years later, brought sober men in the cotton states to wonder if
a Union whose members fared so unequally at the hands of a
government they had themselves created was worth preserving.
Calhoun's vote to kill the woolens bill had some effect in quieting
the turbulence in the South, but it was not easy to keep in check
men who saw profits vanish into a mountain of debt and who
held legislation imposed by a sectional majority to be responsible
—no easier than it had been in 1804 or 1808 or 1814. Only the
implied promise of relief from Jackson, whose own cotton
brought no more than any other's, prevented an outburst.

When Congress met again in December, 1827, an impressive
delegation of manufacturers, chaperoned by Hezekiah Niles, was
on hand to deliver personally and with appropriate emphasis the

report of the Harrisburg Convention. Tariff legislation again became the first order of business in a Congress dominated by members from the northern and middle states, and controlled by the uneasy coalition of North and South that was the new Democratic party. Jackson's partisans undertook to escape the horns of their dilemma by deliberately concocting a bill that would hurt New England. The duty on raw wool was high, on finished woolen, low. There were heavy duties on the iron and hemp required by New England shipbuilders, and on the molasses so profitably distilled into rum in many a New England town. The reasoning was that on such a tariff, Democrats would be free to vote according to the interest of their sections. Administration supporters from New England would be forced to defeat the measure to save their own constituents. The South would be quieted, the Adams-Clay coalition hurt, and Jackson would still be on both sides of the tariff issue, uncommitted but somehow "right." Unfortunately for the success of this cunning scheme, Democrats from the western and middle states wanted the duties increased, regardless of what their southern colleagues thought, and did not propose to support a bill for the sole purpose of compassing its defeat.

New England also wanted the duties raised. Stimulated by the tariff of 1824, the northeastern states had completed the transition from a dominantly commercial to a dominantly manufacturing economy, and were prepared to gamble to increase their profits. Damaging as the bill in its original form would be to their interests, it passed the House by the votes of administration members from that section. The Democrats realized suddenly that they might well be saddled with the paternity of a monster; or perhaps their northern leaders had so planned it from the start. The bill was hastily modified in the Senate to conform to the Harrisburg proposals and was passed by Democratic votes, among them those of Missouri's Benton; John H. Eaton of Tennessee, close friend and campaign biographer of Jackson; and

Martin Van Buren who had been so "instructed" by a state legislature under his own political control.

The tariff of 1828, known to the free-trade men as the "tariff of abominations," raised the average level of duties from the 37 percent of 1824 to 45 percent by value. The outcry from the cotton states was ominous. In South Carolina, with the largest per capita slave population and the highest production costs, there were those who favored forcible resistance, and in Washington the South Carolina delegation in Congress soberly considered the military strength of their state. With the presidential election only months away, however, the Democratic leaders in the South kept a tight rein on the hotheads and bided their time. The election of Andrew Jackson—they hoped—would make everything right again.

The campaign was one of unparalleled bitterness that left its mark on all concerned. No real principle was at stake—only an office from which one man was to be turned out and another put in. Jackson's margin in the electoral college was more than two to one, but in most states the contest was close, giving the Democratic candidate a popular majority of only 40,000 out of more than a million votes cast. The electorate had been enlarged since 1824, reaching both outward and down to a lower economic level. In every state except Rhode Island and Virginia, where there were property qualifications, and Louisiana, where the voter was required to be a taxpayer, the electorate was substantially equivalent to the adult white male population. Only Delaware and South Carolina still chose presidential electors by their legislatures. In the western states, property qualifications were negligible, and in the populous eastern states the qualifications had been relaxed or were easily evaded. In each state and section the Jackson managers made their appeal in terms of local self-interest, but in all sections the methods, and in large measure the men who applied them, were carried over from the old Crawford machine. They were the methods of Aaron Burr and the Essex Junto, carried to new levels of efficiency by the Albany Regency and projected on a national scale. They were effective to the precise degree that the party leaders recognized and sought to fulfill the aspirations of the common man, who was—and is—the basic element in the political machine.

In its first victory the party was too large to be manageable, and its purposes too diverse to be encompassed within a single organization. The South had voted for Jackson in the belief he would use his influence to reduce the tariff. The middle states had voted for him for the opposite reason. The West expected cheap credit and land reform. So the Democracy came to power with many tacit promises but no commitments. The direction it would take would be determined by Jackson himself, who despite Jefferson's personal misgivings was the inevitable product of the egalitarian side of the Jeffersonian faith. He represented the majority and he would carry out what he conceived to be the majority will.

Minority interests would appeal to the conservative side of the Jeffersonian tradition, already identified with state rights, and the conservative leadership before Jackson's first term was over would pass to Calhoun. The ground was prepared immediately after the election when the South Carolina legislature approved and printed the most searching state rights argument yet to appear. Widely known to be Calhoun's, though not yet openly avowed, the *South Carolina Exposition* was designed to remind the incoming President that the Union itself could not ultimately survive a policy operating to enrich one section or class at the expense of another. The same document charted a course for the South should protest fail—a course ingeniously derived by logical analysis and extension from the compact theory of the Constitution and sanctified in the Kentucky Resolutions by Jefferson himself. Should the Constitution be violated by a sectional majority in Congress, Calhoun reasoned, then a single aggrieved state might interpose her sovereignty and as one of the parties to the compact by which Congress itself came into being, might "nullify" or arrest the action of the law in question within her boundaries.

Van Buren, who served a brief two months as governor of New York before becoming Jackson's Secretary of State, understood if Calhoun did not that the choice the party must ultimately make would have to be in the direction of greater political strength. Between these two men, the one Vice-President, the other in the key Cabinet post, there was from the start an underground struggle for control of the administration and an unacknowledged rivalry for the presidential succession. Jackson had already declared himself in favor of a single term and men still in their forties could afford to wait. Events favored Van Buren, but had they not he would have devised others that did; for there was more at stake than personal ambition. Van Buren represented and himself exemplified the Jeffersonian conviction that free men may be—nay, must be—trusted with their own government. The son of an innkeeper, Van Buren's strength lay in his ability to anticipate the majority and to guide the popular will in the direction it was destined to take in the end. Calhoun, on the other hand, did not believe in majority rule at all; but rather in a system so hedged by checks and balances that the more powerful could not exploit the weaker interests. It was a philosophy essentially conservative, defensive, static—and so, in a fluid, dynamic world, anachronistic. Van Buren, however amoral his methods, was an authentic product of the nineteenth century with all its conflicts and ambitions. Calhoun's political fortunes were linked to the defense of an archaic social structure resting upon an obsolete system of labor. Van Buren's were based on the rise of the common man to political power.

Speeded to an issue by unforeseen and largely irrelevant circumstances, the behind-the-scenes struggle between Van Buren and Calhoun was over almost before it began. A few weeks prior to Jackson's inauguration his close friend, Senator John H. Eaton, already destined for the War Department in the new administration, married Mrs. Margaret O'Neale Timberlake, daughter of a Washington tavernkeeper and widow of a Navy purser. Peggy O'Neale, by all accounts including her own, was beautiful, vivacious and intelligent; but her morals were open to question and her marriage to Eaton was a distinct shock to Washington society. The new Mrs. Eaton was pointedly snubbed by the aristocratic Floride Calhoun, who thereby established a popular but for her husband unfortunate precedent. Secretary of the Treasury Samuel D. Ingham, John P. Branch, the Secretary of the Navy, and John M. Berrien, the Attorney General all had wives or daughters who shared Mrs. Calhoun's feelings. Van Buren was a widower without daughters and could safely offer his arm to the wife of the President's friend, thus receiving for reward the eternal gratitude of his chief.

Chivalrous and sentimental, Jackson identified Peggy Eaton's cause with that of his own beloved Rachel, who had been cruelly traduced in the campaign and had not lived to be mistress of the White House. He was furious with all concerned, but especially with Calhoun. He held his Vice-President responsible for the disaffection of his Cabinet, which did not meet for months at a time because its members were not on speaking terms. Perforce, Jackson learned to seek advice elsewhere. He became increasingly intimate with Van Buren and consulted with growing frequency various unofficial counselors who soon came to be called the "kitchen cabinet." This group included former editors Amos Kendall and Isaac Hill, and Major William B. Lewis, a Tennessee intimate who took credit for originating the Jackson boom—each of whom held a minor Treasury job to keep him in Washington. The "Eaton Malaria" was significant only because it gave Van Buren ready and sympathetic access to the President in the early days of the administration and tended to cut off those who might have pressed for different policies. It only hastened a process that was, in any event, inevitable.

Martin Van Buren made the most of his advantages. The party had been swept into office, according to its own pretensions, to reform a government "corrupted" by its predecessors. The people had every right to anticipate the kind of prompt, decisive action they had learned to associate with their hero; but there was in fact very little that could be changed and nothing at all that could be undone until Congress met toward the end of the year. Only the officeholders were immediately vulnerable. Following a pattern long familiar to local politics, and introduced on the national scene by Jefferson, the President instigated a process that he called "rotation in office." In no time at all he was overwhelmed, and the town was cluttered, with deserving Democrats. As the pressure mounted, the ailing President was only too glad to let his Secretary of State relieve him of the burden. He was even grateful to Van Buren for making the sacrifice. Van Buren filled key positions to his own satisfaction; then stopped the wholesale dismissals to avoid replacing old Crawford men already disposed toward his interest. He did not need a clean sweep. It was enough that he strengthened the party organization and his own grip on it, while virtually freezing out both the Calhoun faction and the hard-core Jackson men from the West. Outside of the armed forces and the postal service (then largely under contract), only about 10 percent of the public offices changed hands, but they were the positions of power. The men appointed to these positions were, moreover, added to the large number of Jackson men already in the Federal service who owed their original appointments to Crawford and had survived the Adams regime. The people were satisfied because the changes seemed to bring them closer to the government, but the politicians were the primary gainers. Appointments to public office were tangible rewards to men who had served the party well, more readily identifiable than the slower if more valuable perquisites embodied in class legislation.

By December, 1829, when Calhoun returned to Washington with the members of the new Congress, Jackson had already decided upon his course of action. In his first annual message the President declined to make tariff reform an administration policy. He proposed instead to distribute among the states any proceeds from that source not needed for current expenses after retirement of the public debt—an event anticipated in about four years' time. The states might then use it to build the roads and canals that Madison had pronounced to be beyond the powers of the Federal Government. All but buried near the end of the message was a paragraph questioning both the expediency and the constitutionality of renewing the charter of the Bank of the United States, though the charter still had seven more years to run. New York stood to profit by the growth of manufactures which her merchants could send to the West by way of the Erie Canal in exchange for grain, wool and timber; but the Philadelphia-based Bank of the United States had not been generous enough with credit. So the New York business community had come to rely instead on its own banks, whose liabilities were now insured under a safety-fund law sponsored by Van Buren in his brief career as governor. Having thus publicly committed himself to Van Buren's policy, Jackson went on to endorse the New Yorker's presidential claims in a "private" letter to an old friend, but not so private it could not be publicly used when the time came. Nor did he challenge the proposal of the New York *Courier and Enquirer* that he himself accept a second term.

6

The Great Debate

ONE OF THE most far-reaching episodes of Jackson's Presidency—and for the nation's future, one of the most significant—was the renewal and ultimate resolution of the long-standing controversy over the respective powers of state and Federal Governments. Under Jackson an ideological dispute going back to the framing and ratification of the Constitution itself was carried beyond the realm of logic and precedent into the realm of power, where once and for all it was settled in the only way that could have assured the continuance of the Union.

The three-year contest was touched off by the President's first annual message to Congress in December, 1829, with its acceptance of Van Buren's program and its pointed omission of any reference to tariff reform. Southern leaders, who had kept their fingers crossed since Jackson partisans passed the tariff of 1828, responded with a quick offer to the West: unrestricted and virtually free public lands in return for tariff reduction. This proffer of an alliance of South and West to supplant the old Jeffersonian coalition of New York, Pennsylvania and the South became the springboard for a debate in which the well-known exchange between Webster and Hayne was the high point but by no means the conclusion—a debate that ranged far beyond the halls of Congress and the barriers of time.

The debate was innocently touched off by Senator Samuel

A. Foote of Connecticut, who offered a resolution proposing to restrict the sale of public lands for the time being to those previously offered at the established minimum price of a dollar and a quarter an acre. It would, in a word, force settlers to take up the less desirable farm sites passed over by the pioneers, and to pay as much for this inferior land as they would have to pay for better homesteads beyond the current line of settlement. If adopted, the measure would eventually bring about a more compact settlement of the public-land states, but it would also delay indefinitely the westward advance of the agrarian frontier.

Before the full-scale debate got under way in mid-January 1830, the stakes were raised. A pre-emption act that would give "squatters" on the public domain first option to buy the lands on which they had settled without benefit of title was passed by a combination of western and southern votes. With this majority behind him, Senator Thomas Hart Benton of Missouri charged that Foote's proposal was intended to delay the settlement of the West in order to retain a supply of cheap labor for factories artificially stimulated by excessive tariffs. Benton was followed by Robert Y. Hayne of South Carolina, who placed his section completely at the disposal of the West on the land question, with an offer to sell the public lands for a token to the states in which they lay. In all this Daniel Webster smelled danger to his own section. His manufacturing constituents would be hurt, both by tariff reduction and by western lands cheap enough to entice settlers from the mill towns of New England. In his own inimitable way he made untenable the nascent union of South and West before the marriage vows were said. Webster gained the floor to reply to Hayne, then adroitly turned all his oratorical gifts to a deliberate attack on South Carolina and state rights. Under the Senate rules this personal attack gave Hayne a right of immediate rejoinder, which he was bound by his own pride and his duty to his constituents to make. Hayne fell bodily into Webster's trap, defending the compact theory of the Constitution, the sovereignty of the states, and the right to nullify, just as Webster had intended that he should. Hayne's rejoinder gave Webster his right to the second reply, for which he had been waiting. This time the New England champion took Calhoun's *South Carolina Exposition* as his text. Brick by brick he tore down the careful structure that had justified the doctrine of "state interposition" or "nullification," and made it appear that those who held such doctrines were very close to treason.

The debate dragged on in the Senate for another four months, but for all practical purposes it ended with Webster's second reply to Hayne on January 27, 1830. The arguments differed not at all from those Webster had used a dozen times already before the Supreme Court—arguments that had been transmuted by John Marshall into the law of the land—but this time they were stated in thrilling words that the common man could understand, and understanding, heed. Hayne's case, too, was long familiar to the Senate and to Americans generally with their prodigious memory for the spoken word. Whatever new twist the ingenious Calhoun gave it in his *Exposition,* it was still basically the argument of the Kentucky Resolutions, of the Hartford Convention, of old John Taylor of Caroline against the tariff of 1824. But Taylor, like Jefferson, had been concerned primarily with the defense of liberty against tyrants, be they kings or presidents, parliaments or congresses or courts. A generation that remembered the War of 1812 but not the Revolution had little fear of tyranny but much of weakness. Only the South with her human chattels to protect against the chronic moral misgivings of the free states had any fear of a government strong enough to impose a tariff, and everywhere but in the Senate of the United States the South was in the minority.

By newspaper, pamphlet and word of mouth Webster's triumphant nationalism went out to the American people and a majority of them found it good. They might, and did, differ at a thousand points but that liberty and union were inseparably joined they could agree. Whatever the Constitution may have meant to its framers, or to those who ratified it in state conven-

tions, it was to a growing body of Americans after 1830 no longer
a treaty between sovereigns but the organic charter of a Nation.
Van Buren, securely in the driver's seat, moved quickly to take
the administration into Webster's ideological camp. The South-
West alliance was stillborn, those tainted with the poison of nullification were read out of the party, and the fortunes of the West
were linked to those of the northern and middle states. Benton
and those who had followed his lead in dickering with the South
scurried back to the administration. In the election of 1832 Jackson would count in his support the same sectional interests that
had elected Adams in 1824.

The first fruit of the realignment came swiftly with the elimi-
nation of Calhoun as a by-product of the celebration of Jefferson's birthday. Democrats from the slaveholding states, in a
series of toasts prepared and printed in advance according to
custom, sought to commit the party to the doctrines of the
Kentucky Resolutions. The toasts were all quotations from Jefferson, and in themselves innocent enough, but the "old Republican doctrine of '98" which they sustained had already received
a mortal blow. With Webster's identification of nullification
with disunion still vivid in his mind, Jackson offered his own
toast: "Our Federal Union—It must be preserved!" and Calhoun,
with none of the President's feeling for the quotable phrase, replied: "The Union—next to our liberty most dear. May we always remember that it can only be preserved by distributing
equally the benefits and the burdens of the Union." Removed
from the mythology that surrounds this famous dinner, two clear
statements of position emerge. Jackson was saying with Webster
and Marshall that the nation was superior to the states. Calhoun
was saying with all those before and since who have felt themselves ill used by the majority that a government that deprived
men of their livelihood and failed to protect their property was
not worth preserving. Only in the perspective of later events did
Jackson's toast become a challenge to the Nullifiers and Calhoun's

reply a declaration of war: but those later events were fore-ordained.

Over the next few months both Jackson's views and his inten-tions crystallized. Late in May he vetoed a bill that would have financed a road from Maysville to Lexington, Kentucky, and would incidentally have put the government back in the public works business; he did this not to appease the strict construc-tionists of the South but in Van Buren's interest to preserve for a little longer the trade monopoly of the Erie Canal. He told Congress in December that the tariff was not a violation of the Constitution, then went on to uphold the rule of the majority and to deny categorically that any state might lawfully refuse obedience to any act of the general government. Simultaneously a new administration paper, the Washington *Globe,* made its ap-pearance, with Francis Preston Blair, onetime editorial associate of Amos Kendall of the kitchen cabinet, as its editor. The *Globe* superseded Duff Green's *United States' Telegraph,* which had leaned toward the South-West alliance and toward Calhoun. The Vice-President's critical attitude at the time of Jackson's un-authorized seizure of the Spanish forts in Florida a dozen years earlier was now pointedly called to Jackson's attention by Senator John Forsyth of Georgia, friend of Crawford and one day to be Secretary of State, and the breach between Calhoun and Jackson became personal as well as political. A Cabinet reorganization followed, precipitated by Van Buren, who preferred to be in the wings rather than the center of the stage in this time of party crisis. Edward Livingston, brother of the late New York Chancel-lor, replaced Van Buren in the State Department. Though he had moved to New Orleans in 1804 and now represented Louisiana in the Senate, Livingston in sentiment and thought processes was a New Yorker still. Louis McLane, a former Craw-ford Radical from Delaware, was recalled from London to take the Treasury; the War Department went to Governor Lewis Cass of Michigan Territory, a future presidential nominee; and the Attorney General was Roger B. Taney of Maryland, who would succeed John Marshall as Chief Justice of the United States. It was a strong Cabinet, to a man nationalistic in sentiment, and with no leaning toward tariff reform.

That long and bitterly debated question was rapidly reaching crisis proportions. Cotton exported in 1831 brought an average price of 9.1 cents a pound and on the Charleston market dropped to 8.3 cents. The singularly articulate South Carolinians prepared to take matters into their own hands after Jackson's failure to make tariff reform an administration measure. How far the import duties were indeed the source of their distress cannot be measured. There were factors of soil erosion, wasteful cropping methods, overproduction, the competition of better lands in the Southwest; and there was the burden of what was over-all the costliest and least efficient labor system ever devised by the wit of man for his own degradation. But the tariff alone, by raising the cost of the manufactured products the planter had to buy, would have been enough to produce distress, wholly aside from the declining price of the staple itself. The falling price in turn was a compound of many factors, chief among them competition for the British market and the operation of the tariff in restricting British exports to the United States. Economists of the day—including southern economists—knew all this, but the tariff had become an emotional issue, not to be resolved by facts or figures.

The case that had been building for a generation and more was a case against central power, which the warped brilliance of a Randolph and the cold, amoral logic of a Calhoun could agree would ultimately be turned against the institution of slavery if it were allowed to stand. The question was no longer whether the tariff wrought more harm than good, but whether the Federal Government had the power to impose it. The only division of opinion in South Carolina was between those who wanted to nullify the tariff in accordance with the formula Calhoun had derived from Jefferson, and those who believed that good sense and justice would eventually prevail in Washington if no provocative steps were taken. This latter group, called Unionists, was led by Joel Roberts Poinsett, lately returned from Mexico, where he had discovered the Poinsettia, but could boast little in the way of diplomatic success.

Although Calhoun had hitherto avoided identifying himself with either party, he could do so no longer. The leadership of the Nullifiers was being seized by young fire-eaters who had been reared in a society consciously patterned on the feudal world of Sir Walter Scott. To men who exalted the violence of the duel as the honorable way of solving problems, rebellion held more attractions than any long-drawn battle in the courts. The situation was getting out of hand when the Vice-President placed himself at the head of the movement he had created with a signed elaboration of nullification. He had already been expelled from the Jackson party and had nothing further to lose. On the other hand, if Calhoun could prevent an outburst in his native state and at the same time exert enough pressure on the administration to force a change in its tariff policy, he had much to gain. His long public letter stressed the peaceful nature of his remedy, as well as its historical validity, but his language was too chilling to wean any followers from Webster. For the time being he had put a brake on the South Carolina hotheads, but he convinced no one who was not already a believer.

When the principal protagonists gathered in Washington for another session of Congress, there was no longer any doubt where each man stood. With unrivaled tactical skill, the President sought to cut the ground from under the malcontents. The public debt, Old Hickory reminded the legislators, would be paid off in another year, and it would therefore be desirable to begin reduction of the revenue to the needs of the government by modifying the tariff. But the duties proposed by the Treasury were not calculated to relieve the tumult in South Carolina. While new items were placed on the free list, prohibitive duties were retained on others, including the wool and woolens, the iron and hemp, so essential to the southern economy and so profitable, at tariff-inflated prices, to one or another of the northern states.

The anti-tariff forces saw behind these unacceptable Treasury proposals the will of Martin Van Buren, and so they joined with Clay and his National Republican following to chastise the New Yorker by rejecting his nomination to the British mission, though he had already been three months at his post in London. Calhoun himself gave the casting vote that, as Benton—now firmly allied with the Jacksonians—jubilantly observed, would break a minister but make a Vice-President. At the other end of the Capitol an equally formidable opposition was joined by ex-President John Quincy Adams, who would serve the House as its gadfly and its conscience for almost two decades.

Jackson's leadership was more than a match for the combined opposition of National Republicans and Nullifiers. After months of wrangling, an administration-sponsored tariff was passed by substantial majorities in both houses, and was signed by Jackson on July 14, 1832. From the standpoint of the South it was no better than the reprobated bill of abominations. In its implications, indeed, it was worse; for it embodied in its own language a tacit acceptance of protection as a permanent policy of the government, and it commanded majorities large enough to destroy any immediate prospect of a change of heart. National Republicans and Democrats alike hailed the tariff of 1832 as a final settlement of a long-standing sectional dispute; but the state rights men could accept neither the bill nor the principles on which it rested. Faced as they were in the North and West with a rising clamor against slavery, they could no longer assent to any law that rested even by implication on the legal supremacy of a majority in Congress. So their reasoning led to the foreordained conclusion of every state rights argument advanced between 1798 and the ratification of the 13th Amendment in 1865. If a majority in Congress could pass laws, for whatever purpose, against the convictions and interests of a substantial portion of the Union, it could also pass laws for the destruction of slavery. . . .

The uncompromising nationalism of the tariff of 1832 was uppermost in the collective mind of South Carolina when Union-

ists and Nullifiers opposed one another at the polls. The Nullifiers won a close victory in the Charleston city elections, but
swept all before them in the state at large. Governor James
Hamilton, Jr., himself a Nullifier, immediately called a special
session of the legislature and the newly elected majority authorized the calling of a state convention. After a brief, explosive
campaign delegates were chosen who were overwhelmingly in
favor of nullifying the tariff of 1832. The Convention met at
Columbia on November 19, by which date South Carolinians
knew that Andrew Jackson—one of themselves, however they
might disavow him now—would be President of the United
States for another four years.

The tariff cost Jackson no votes he would not have lost without
it, nor did his veto of a bill rechartering the Bank of the United
States—a matter that belongs more properly in another chapter.
The issues were various and often confused, but chief among
them was Andrew Jackson, who remained what he had been in
1824 and in 1828—all things to all people. Though his policies
followed no consistent pattern, he had uniformly championed
what he called "the people" and the Democracy had become the
political instrument of the common man. More than any other
partisan creed of the day, Jacksonian Democracy was sensitive to
a world-wide spirit of change, and in turn gave hope and purpose to European crusades for social and political reform. In
France the July Revolution of 1830 had brought Louis Philippe
to a throne stripped of much of its power; in Britain the long-
contested Reform Act of 1832 extended the franchise, eliminated
glaring abuses, and gave new authority to the popular will represented in the House of Commons. Throughout the western
world a brew of liberalism was fermenting that would bring
peaceful change in Britain but would result in violent upheaval on
the Continent and in America. Everywhere the common man was
reaching out for a more substantial share in his own government
and for greater freedom in pursuit of his own interests.

One reflection of this new impulse toward popular control was the substitution in America of the convention for the caucus as a device for naming party candidates for President and Vice-President of the United States, and for drafting party platforms. The caucus had disappeared after 1824, and the nominations for 1828 had come about by a sort of common consent that needed no other prompting. The convention with delegates chosen from among party members in each state quickly became a useful political tool, extending clear back to the grass roots where local conventions fed county gatherings and so up to the national level. Only the most deserving politicians could expect to make their way through the whole hierarchy to the top. By the same token issues of only local significance were likely to be eliminated before the party took a final stand on policy.

Popular movements in America also included the appearance of a Workingmen's party in Philadelphia in 1828, and a similar party in New York the following year. (The rise of labor as a factor in politics will be treated in more detail in another connection.) So far as the re-election of Jackson was concerned, it was of little or no significance, for Jackson had made his appeal to Pennsylvania and New Jersey on the tariff of 1832 and his appeal to New York on his opposition to federally financed transportation and to the Philadelphia-based Bank of the United States. In each case the Democracy stood squarely for individual initiative and freedom of enterprise, with a minimum of interference but all needful encouragement from government.

Another popular movement of a sort was that represented by the short-lived Antimasonic party, which flirted with Adams and Calhoun before naming former Attorney General William Wirt as its presidential nominee in the fall of 1831. The Antimasons were the direct political fruit of a reaction against the Masonic order which had come into ill repute through the disappearance and probable murder in upstate New York of one William Morgan, who was charged with betraying the secrets of his lodge. The Morgan case was seized upon by shrewd politicians such as Thurlow Weed, the Albany editor who had helped carry

New York for Adams in 1824, as a vehicle for channeling all the discontents of the time into a single political engine. After five years of existence the Antimasonic party included Democrats who opposed the tight control of the Albany Regency, and National Republicans who disagreed with their party's policy on bank or tariff or internal improvements. It included men afraid of too strong a government and others who wanted more rather than less activity in Washington. And it included in the northern states many who felt that slaveholding interests were too strong in both major parties. But Jackson's was still the authentic voice of liberalism, not to be set aside for any form of special pleading.

In New England and in the middle states, Jackson made his appeal on his championship of the tariff; in the West and South on his veto of the Bank recharter and on his removal of the Indians. This last was a settled policy, long advocated and finally enacted into law in 1830. The Indians were by 1832 in process of resettlement west of the Mississippi, most of them in what came to be known as Oklahoma Territory. The great bulk of the Indians affected were the Cherokees and Creeks of Georgia, Alabama and Mississippi, and these tribes were moving peaceably—however reluctantly—to their new homes, thus offering to the South new land for expanding the output of cotton. The Sac and Fox Indians of Illinois and Wisconsin, under Black Hawk, put up a show of resistance, but were quickly subdued by military forces that included Lieutenant Jefferson Davis of the regular army and Captain Abraham Lincoln of the Illinois militia.

Jackson's re-election in 1832 proved very little except that the President's political judgment was sound. With Van Buren his hand-picked choice for Vice-President, the Jackson ticket showed a popular plurality of 150,000 over Clay, the National Republican choice, and Wirt together. In the West, Jackson carried every state but Kentucky; in the South all but Maryland, Delaware, and South Carolina. Still voting by her legislature, South Carolina threw away her vote on Governor John Floyd of Virginia. The middle states were solidly for Jackson and even in New

England he carried Maine and New Hampshire. Wirt carried only Vermont, but as an indication of political restlessness with things as they were the vote was significant. Vermont would soon be in the antislavery camp. Jackson's 219 electoral votes included the entire net gain of 27 under the reapportionment following the census of 1830.* In sectional terms, New England lost one seat in the House of Representatives, the middle states and the South each gained eight seats, and the West gained twelve. More significantly for the state rights controversy, then coming to its dramatic climax, the eight seats gained by the slave states were more than doubled by the nineteen new seats going to free soil.

The presidential election was overshadowed in South Carolina by the state rights controversy, of which the tariff was only the immediate case in point. The state convention, by a vote of almost six to one, declared the tariffs of 1828 and 1832 to be unsanctioned by the Constitution and forbade the collection within the state of any duties levied under them. The single loophole in this tightly woven fabric that appeared to so many Americans to be rebellion was the effective date. The Ordinance of Nullification was not to be operative until February 1, 1833 (and was later further postponed), thus giving Congress ample time to act on the objectionable laws. The legislature then chose the tactful and conservative Hayne for governor and elected Calhoun to the seat thus vacated in the Senate. To accept the seat, Calhoun resigned the Vice-Presidency of the United States.

Jackson's reaction was typical and sure. On December 10, 1832, he issued a proclamation that aligned him unequivocally with Marshall and Webster. In terse, marching phrases he declared that the Constitution had created a nation, not a league. The nation, not the states, was sovereign and supreme. No state could refuse obedience to the law. No state could secede from the Union. The South Carolinians were bidden to give up the dangerous heresy

* Kentucky, in the Clay column, gained one seat, but this was offset by the loss of one in Maryland, which also voted for Clay.

they had embraced, and were bluntly warned that the duties they had repudiated would be collected by force if necessary. Virginia's Governor Floyd spoke for the old Jeffersonians who had so bitterly opposed the decision in McCulloch *v*. Maryland, when he pronounced the President to be a "tyrant who acknowledges no law but his own will"; but the common people listened and approved. In popular meetings across the land—even in South Carolina itself—the doctrine of nullification had been condemned, and from this condemnation it was but a step to the ringing nationalism of the proclamation. Jackson waited for this evidence of popular support, then asked Congress for legislation authorizing him to collect the duties by force.

A compromise tariff that reduced the duties of 1832 by annual decrements over a ten-year period to a uniform 20 percent was proposed by Clay, accepted by Calhoun, and passed by both houses of Congress; but the Force Bill was also passed as a grim reminder that the sovereignty lay in fact with the national government. The President signed both bills on March 2, 1833, as his first term of office was coming to its stormy close.

This state rights controversy, with its hair-splitting logic and its forced analogies, seems remote to us, but to those who took part and who lived with it, it was of immense importance. It was this debate, starting with Marshall's decision in McCulloch *v*. Maryland and ending with the publication in 1833 of Justice Joseph Story's *Commentaries on the Constitution of the United States,* that more than anything else fixed the lines of cleavage between North and South, and prepared the ideological basis both for the ultimate withdrawal of the South from the Union and for the coercion of the seceding states.

For Jackson's proclamation against the Nullifiers destroyed not nullification alone, but the whole state rights dogma from which it was derived. It meant in effect that a majority in Congress large enough to override a presidential veto might do whatever it pleased, restrained only by the consciences of its members. The third co-ordinate branch of the government—the Supreme Court

—might protest to high Heaven in opposition; it could do no more than lay down rules which only the President with the co-operation of Congress could enforce. In Worcester *v.* Georgia, as recently as 1831, the Court had held that Georgia had no jurisdiction or authority over the Cherokee Indians; but the state had ignored the decree and Jackson was said to have commented "John Marshall has made his decision. Let him enforce it."

In the practical destruction of the whole state rights doctrine by the proclamation and the Force Act, many who had no sympathy with nullification read their own doom, for the right to tax one interest out of existence is the right to tax any, and the power to coerce one state is the power to coerce them all. The southern states drew closer together, taking the road that would lead in another generation to a nationalism of their own; and all those in North and West who feared the power of a consolidated government began to look with greater tolerance on the obstinacy of the South. For the immediate future there would be new and still more dangerous manifestations of sectionalism; but for the long run the Great Debate was over. "United States" became a singular rather than a plural noun, and the entity for which it stood was well on the road to becoming a nation. The omnipotent state of the twentieth century was in germ if not yet in being.

*States rights
wiped out*

7

Toward the Millennium

THE NATIONALISM that found expression in Jackson's triumph over state rights was itself only one facet of a social revolution, rooted in the Declaration of Independence but actively released only when America weaned herself from Europe after the War of 1812. Stimulated by winds of doctrine blowing across the Atlantic from a continent in post-Napoleonic turmoil, driven by a sublimated need for self-expression and by the dictates of a Calvinist heritage, the American of the 1820's and 1830's emerged as idealist, reformer, experimenter, intellectual. In art and literature he strove consciously to free himself from his old dependence upon European culture; education became the key to the more abundant life, and hence a public rather than a private responsibility. He needed too many everyday things to concern himself deeply with pure science, although John James Audubon published his pioneer *Birds of America* in 1827 and Joseph Henry at about the same time worked out the principle of electrical induction that would make possible not only Morse's telegraph but future applications of electricity as a source of power. The American tended to become inventor and engineer rather than abstract scientist—to seek a practical solution rather than a logical explanation. Only where morals were concerned did he prove inflexible. There he was his brother's keeper, determined to raise his fellow man to the level he had himself attained by pulling on his own bootstraps.

By the 1830's the restraints of Calvinism were being progressively weakened. The perfection of man seemed not only possible but relatively near at hand. It was as though the same dynamic drive that set man to seeking new lands, to creating new machines, to making new products, to building, exploring, acquiring in a thousand physical ways, set him also to searching his own soul and to probing the souls of his fellows. There were few social evils that were not challenged by some inspired St. George or well-meaning Don Quixote. The evils of drinking, pauperism, ignorance; the abuses of the penal system and the inhumanity meted out to the handicapped and the mentally ill were exposed and remedies were vigorously advocated. The thick skin of tolerance that had developed through years of preoccupation with politics and with amassing wealth was punctured again and again by women demanding the right to be heard, and then the right of active participation; by workingmen seeking to improve the conditions of labor; by mothers who thought their children worked too long in the factories, often at tasks beyond their strength.

It has become a truism with a later age that as governments grow in power they are compelled for their own preservation to extend their functions into spheres not previously recognized as theirs. The 1830's were transitional years in which no group or body had clear responsibility for the welfare of all those whom humanitarians liked to call their "brethren." With the separation of church and state the activities of the church in these areas steadily declined but government was not yet ready to assume the welfare burden. There was still a fairly general belief that human suffering of whatever kind or degree was the punishment of God for some secret sin and it was not man's place to thwart the Divine retribution.

It was probably in literature, and perhaps to a somewhat lesser degree in art and architecture, that nationalistic forces were most clearly in evidence, but in the '30's and for two more decades Americans were divided in their allegiance between the familiar and the new. With no international copyright laws to be observed, it was less risky and certainly cheaper for American publishers to pirate British novels than to pay for local talent that might not prove salable. Inevitably the enormously popular Sir Walter Scott was imitated, along with more classic models, but competition with the original was at first unsuccessful. In poetry, Byron and Wordsworth were favorites, but in this area the early work of William Cullen Bryant was impressive and Edgar Allen Poe had contributed poems of first-rate quality by the beginning of the decade. Both Washington Irving, with his tales of Dutch New York, and James Fenimore Cooper with his use of Indian characters and frontier settings, recognized the need for an American literature, but though the materials were indigenous, the forms were as English as the mother tongue in which they were presented. The first half-century under the Constitution produced nothing in literature as typically American as Benjamin Franklin's *Autobiography* or *Poor Richard's Almanac.*

The American past and its heroic figures served as one of the early nationalistic forces. Painters like Gilbert Stuart and Charles Willson Peale preserved likenesses of the founding fathers and their immediate successors, and a whole host of portrait painters moved in on the post-Jeffersonian generation. Trumbull contributed larger-than-life idealizations of great moments in the young nation's history, while Benjamin West and John Singleton Copley added Indian figures to the American gallery. George Catlin, living with the Indians on the upper Missouri from 1832 to 1840, did even better, adding to his Indian paintings a realism born of understanding and appreciation beyond anything known to his predecessors. Others, like Thomas Cole, painted the "wilder image" of America's granite peaks and solitary lakes. Yet, like the work of their literary fellows, only the subjects were peculiar to the United States. The forms were those made popular by successful painters abroad.

Among leading architects, Jefferson himself had popularized classic forms, but he had also shown at Monticello a flair for incorporating useful devices and clever gadgets. Both as builder and as statesman, Jefferson knew how to blend the old and the new, how to prepare a foundation for the future from the building blocks of the past. Like Jefferson, Benjamin Latrobe, architect of the Capitol, was as much engineer as architect, obsessed with the practical and the utilitarian. Charles Bullfinch, who followed Latrobe in Washington after a long and successful architectural apprenticeship in Boston, worked both the functional and the eye-catching into his numerous and enduring creations.

With the exception of that early poetry of Bryant and Poe, American literature remained imitative, reportorial, or polemic until the appearance of major works by Ralph Waldo Emerson and Poe in the middle 1830's. Thoreau and Hawthorne followed closely, but all these would be surpassed by Herman Melville and Walt Whitman. Until these greater talents emerged to challenge the national conscience, literature was escapist or propagandistic. One could tread wilderness trails with Cooper's Uncas and Natty Bumppo, spend leisurely hours at Irving's *Bracebridge Hall* or among the frescoed courtyards of Moorish Spain, or race through the romanticized Middle Ages with Scott. In the South, Scott was preferred. The Waverly novels undoubtedly stimulated the creation of the southern myth of a cavalier ancestry, which made them all aristocrats, descended from second sons of British nobles and consequently born to rule over their feudal domains. To support the pretensions if not the myth, South Carolina's William Gilmore Simms channeled a promising talent to the defense of slavery, and Judge Beverley Tucker of Virginia, half-brother of John Randolph, wrote *The Partisan Leader* to forecast in fiction a South freed by force of arms from Yankee domination. But where men like Simms and Tucker had only local appeal, the nationalism of the age of Jackson was spread far and wide in the work of the first major American historian. George Bancroft, collector of customs in Boston under Van Buren and Polk's Secretary of the Navy, published the first volume of a ten-volume *History of the United States* in 1834. He was still dealing with the colonial period in the third volume, which appeared in 1840;

but even to that alien time he managed to bring a Jacksonian sense of destiny and of unity.

If one preferred the literary potpourri of the journals, Irving's *Knickerbocker Magazine* was available from 1833 on; and the *Southern Literary Messenger* from 1834, edited by Poe for three of its first four years. The *North American Review* and its short-lived Charleston counterpart, the *Southern Review,* dealt exclusively in criticism and polemics; but the *Democratic Review,* founded in 1837, included early stories by Whitman and Hawthorne, among many lesser contributors. If he read nothing at all but the newspapers, the American of the 1830's could hardly avoid imbibing something of the restless, questing spirit of Jacksonian Democracy. Outstanding in the 1830's and early 1840's were the New York *Evening Post,* edited by Bryant from 1829; the New York *Herald* of James Gordon Bennett, founded in 1835; and Horace Greeley's New York *Tribune,* started in 1841. The New York *Sun,* first appearing in 1833, was the first paper to sell for a penny, but was not yet of other journalistic significance.

For political controversy, none surpassed the Washington *Globe* under Francis Preston Blair and the Richmond *Enquirer* of Thomas Ritchie; but in the 1830's newspapers were beginning to serve more varied functions. Bryant made of the *Post* a Jackson organ, but also advocated free trade and leaned toward the various reforming movements of the day. The *Post* editor's principal assistant, William Leggett, was even more radical than his chief. Between them, they early made the *Post* a spokesman for the Van Buren wing of the Democracy. Another *Post* assistant editor —Parke Godwin—did much to propagate various socialistic doctrines imported from France.

If Bryant was the last true man of letters to edit a daily paper, Bennett was the first true journalist in the modern sense—a man concerned primarily with reporting the news, quickly, entertainingly, with fullness and originality. Mass circulation and advertising were merely means of financing the *Herald's* true purpose. Sensational he often was, and the truth was often stretched a little, but Bennett initiated many entries and techniques no paper today would be without. He was among the first to establish correspondents in Washington, and the first (1838) to employ regular correspondents abroad. It was he who personally persuaded Congress to admit reporters to the House and Senate galleries on a regular basis; he who began putting his most startling news instead of his best-paying ads on the front page; he who first made regular use of the telegraph, and developed the technique of meeting incoming vessels at sea with small, fast boats for the "scoops" not then known by the term. Though Bennett provided a step into the future, he was also a man of the present. He fathomed what people wanted to read from what they gossiped about. His crime news and other sensational reporting brought in readers by the tens of thousands, and gave matter to fiction writers, even as similar reporting does today. Poe's "Mystery of Marie Roget," for example, was the case of Mary Rogers, straight from the columns of Bennett's *Herald*. Only the solution—which proved to be the right one—was added by Poe.

The New York *Tribune* was a Whig version of the *Post,* with many of the features of the nonpartisan *Herald.* But Greeley, unlike Bennett, was concerned with causes, and his became the first great crusading daily. The cultured and fiery Margaret Fuller worked for a time on the *Tribune,* and its columns were open to reformers of all varieties and degrees. The free press in the 1830's and 40's was indeed becoming in fact the powerful engine of democracy Jefferson had insisted it must be—the fourth estate without which free government itself could not survive.

Neither could free government survive, the Founding Fathers had agreed, without a system of universal public education, but the agreement did not extend to means. Half the states had recognized their responsibilities by 1800, but except in the larger cities there was little tangible evidence of it. Education in the eighteenth century had been regarded as primarily a function of the family, church, private enterprise, philanthropy—by no means ever to be controlled or influenced by government at any level. No state—not even Massachusetts, advanced though she was in such matters—had a comprehensive school system before 1815. Ohio and the newer states of the West had grants of public land the proceeds from which were to be spent for education, but the money—what there was of it—was largely dissipated in hit-or-miss efforts. In the country districts that were still 90 percent of America the "field school" with its itinerant teacher, the local minister, and the home were the primary educational institutions, and the Bible the most widely used text. To be sure, there were also such well-appreciated works as Noah Webster's spellers, the sprightly biographies of Parson Weems (the original propagator if not the inventor of Washington's cherry tree), and the geographies of the Reverend Jedediah Morse; but the principal educational advance of the 1830's was made through more systematic and more dedicated teachers.

In the same decade a generation of scholars who traveled to Germany for their college education brought back first-class professionalism in their trade. In Germany an intellectual rebirth comparable to that of the Italian Renaissance was under way and Americans came home brimming with ideas, enthusiasm, and drive. But there were also Americans aplenty who had never left the genial soil of their homeland who were equally sure that the times demanded change. Among those who carried the torch from Germany were historian George Bancroft; George Ticknor and Edward Everett, who gravitated automatically to Harvard; and Thomas R. Dew, who became professor of political economy and then president of William and Mary College in Virginia. At the forefront of the home-grown teachers were William McGuffey, who was president of Cincinnati College when his first *Reader* appeared in 1836; and Horace Mann, who put ten years of experience in the Massachusetts legislature into the creation of a system of public education that became a pattern for all other states. McGuffey's readers, before they finally went out of print, sold something like 120 million copies. The educational ideas of Horace Mann have never become obsolete. Mann himself left the state senate to become secretary of the board of education set up by his own legislation. Then with borrowed Teutonic thoroughness, he adapted the Prussian system as analyzed by Victor Cousin to the needs of his own country as he saw them. One permanent feature was the establishment of normal schools (now expanded into teachers colleges) for the training of teachers who would in turn impart knowledge, and possibly wisdom, to the young. Another element of lasting worth was Mann's successful resistance to any restoration of sectarian instruction (barred by law in Massachusetts in 1827) in the public schools.

The universities, slowly emerging from the theological preoccupations of the past, were enlarging their scope and deepening the content of their teaching. Science, since Benjamin Silliman had begun offering such courses at Yale in 1802, was by 1830 quite generally included in college curricula. Jefferson's University of Virginia, opening its doors in 1825, gave new impetus to liberal education, but had less influence than it would have had if its launching had been closer in time to its founder's conception of it.

The impulse to teach had in it something of missionary zeal, so the teacher, like the evangelist searching out the greatest sinners, was apt to seek the most difficult and stubborn challenges. Thomas Gallaudet, for example, had founded his school for the deaf in 1817. Located in Washington, the school was supported by private contributions. A dozen years later Massachusetts, inspired by the fervor of John D. Fisher, set up a school for the blind. For the handicapped there was tolerance, even some sympathy. Prudence Crandall found neither when she admitted a Negro to the Connecticut girls' school she was operating in 1831. She met the vehement outcry of her neighbors by converting the school into one for Negro girls only, but even the Connecticut abolitionists were not prepared for this! The school was closed by act of the legislature in 1833, and its closing ultimately upheld by the state supreme court.

Education in America, like the American nation itself, was at a parting of the ways. One road—the old one of parochial schools or none at all for the poor, private schools and tutors for the rich—led like the particularism and provincialism of state rights to a divided country, stratified by class if it survived the impact of geographical difference. The other road led to education at public expense for every child, to a genuine democracy, and to a united nation. That choice, like the political choice, was made in the 1830's, by Americans who were themselves developing a thirst for knowledge at the adult level, who were attending lectures, reading and listening carefully, observing minutely. An informed and intelligent people, Jefferson had insisted, could govern themselves, and these Americans were bent upon fulfilling at least the minimum requirements. The educational choice, like that in government, was in favor of the democratic ideal and ultimately on the side of unity.

Americans differed sharply, of course, on what constituted an education. On the western frontier there was a positive prejudice against book learning, despite such examples of erudition as Senator Benton; and even in the eastern cities there was a strong feeling that education should be useful—that children should be taught the rudiments of making a living. In many minds there was a question as to whether the English chemist James Smithson's substantial bequest to found an institution at Washington "for the increase and diffusion of knowledge among men" ought to be accepted on practical grounds, or indeed could constitutionally be accepted at all. By 1838, when Congress decided the Smithson legacy would do no harm and might do good, the turning point had been passed. The yeast of change was working visibly, but no man could yet tell how heady would be the brew.

It had in it as many different strains as Jacksonian Democracy itself, but perhaps the strongest single element in young America's march toward the millennium was religion. Soul-searching came first, and came with relative ease to the descendants of men who first crossed an unfriendly ocean in search of religious freedom. Quakers in Pennsylvania, Catholics in Maryland traditionally felt some responsibility for the welfare of their fellow men, but the dominant Calvinistic strain in New England was more inclined to believe that God helped those who helped themselves. The change came almost at once, as Oliver Wendell Holmes showed in the "Wonderful One-Hoss Shay," but the collapse was not quite as complete as Dr. Holmes implied. A better analogy would be with a version of the Cinderella story, in which the overripe pumpkin of Calvinism would be transformed at the touch of a good fairy's wand into a dashing coach. For once the doctrine of free will supplanted the determinism of the New England theology, everybody became responsible for his own salvation, and by simple transference for the salvation of his fellows. In the concept of a universal God man found his own self-realization and in turn realized God in nature and in himself.

Out of this softening and broadening of the old Calvinistic faith came the true flowering of New England, with its arms wide to receive the best of German rationalism, of French humanism, of Jacksonian Democracy. The way had been prepared in America's own pioneering past; for surely Daniel Boone, making his way cautiously through the Cumberland Gap; Lewis and Clark descending the Columbia; or Jefferson contemplating the confluence of the Shenandoah and Potomac rivers from a jutting rock understood as well as Emerson that nature is "the dress God wears, the shadow he casts upon our senses." Emerson published his essay on nature in 1836, but he had already ceased to preach and begun to lecture—or, better, he had stopped calling his ethical and moral discourses "sermons" just because they were usually delivered in a church.

Through Emerson and the circle of New England intellectuals whose leader he was, the best of European thought found its way into the main stream of American development. The absurdities and deliberate obfuscations of heavy-handed German philosophers came out in simple English, graced by homely examples and everyday figures of speech. In Emerson the intellectual and cultural outpourings of revolutionary Europe were blended with the compulsive drive of the American toward perfection. In New

England transcendentalism America found a spiritual liberation comparable to the political liberation she had received from Jefferson and to the psychological release of her powers that Jackson forced upon her almost against her will.

Like Jacksonian Democracy, with its extremes of individualism and group activity, New England transcendentalism displayed the extremes of man in isolation with no intermediary between himself and God, and man as a selfless, almost will-less cog in a machine. But fundamentalist Thoreau left his self-imposed exile at Walden Pond having rapturously discovered himself to be no wiser than he had been at birth; and Brook Farm, as a communal enterprise, collapsed because the intellectuals who had thought to find there self-realization and perfect adjustment to life, here and hereafter, found only discontent with irksome tasks and annoyance at wasted time.

Brook Farm did not differ greatly from other Utopian experiments of the day, except in the intellectual quality of its people and their essential inability to do practical things. The movement had deep roots in religious communities like the Shakers and Mennonites, and had been given a social and economic cast as early as 1824 by Robert Owen, the widely known English reformer, whose doctrines foreshadowed Fabian socialism. Owen had established model villages for the workers at his Lanark, Scotland, textile mills, which were objects of study by manufacturers and social reformers alike. At New Harmony, Indiana, where he had purchased the land from a disillusioned group of Shakers, Owen undertook to rehabilitate 2,400 souls—"the dregs of the dregs of society"—by a work-rest-play-study-meditate regime. As he explained it in Washington to a fascinated audience that included James Monroe and John Quincy Adams, it sounded as though, perhaps, the millennium were at hand; but the experiment was wrecked on the rock of human nature within two years. A similar scheme, parallel in time, by which Miss Frances Wright undertook to colonize slaves who would earn their freedom by their labor in five years at Nashoba, Tennessee, failed similarly.

The Utopian idea reappeared in America in the 1830's and early 40's, again with European inspiration. This time it was the doctrine of association developed by the French socialist, François Marie Charles Fourier; brought to the United States in 1834 by Albert Brisbane, and propagated by Horace Greeley, among others. Altogether more than forty such Utopian communities—including Brook Farm and its distinguished group of literati—were established, but none of them lasted long. The doctrine itself was too static, its appeal too transitory, for the American taste. As a resident of a Fourierist "phalanx" one worked in the fields or shops, did intellectual or creative work if the body were not so weary as to have blunted the mind, and meditated. It was, perhaps, a splendid means of reforming oneself, but the American reformer could never be content with this myopic approach. To reform society in all its ills and evils, one had to mingle with and be a part of it, and be prepared to carry the fight through legislatures, courts, and the less conspicuous anterooms of power. Each reformer sought his own segment of perfection, but he sought it, chin outthrust and sleeves rolled up, in all the places where abuses were to be found.

Of such places there appeared to the newly awakened conscience of America to be an infinite number. The missionaries, the traveling evangelists, and the stay-at-home ministers with their congregations habituated to listening and predisposed to accept their moral leadership, were earliest in the reform movement. The Reverend Lyman Beecher's perennial crusade against Sabbath-breaking, tippling, and "ruff scruff" were to bear rewarding fruits in the next generation through the more pointedly directed efforts of his children, Henry Ward and Harriet. Emerson, to be sure, found the lecture platform and the pen better suited to his message than the pulpit, but there were others who took God into partnership and delivered their thunders as though from Heaven itself—enough to make of the early 1830's a period of mass repentance and spiritual rebirth. The phenomenon of hysteria and the uncanny cures that had been wrought a half century earlier by Dr. Franz Mesmer were being reconsidered, in America as abroad, and Dr. Holmes, in his engaging literary fashion, would soon be anticipating some of the principles of psychiatry; but for the 1830's it all went under the names of conversion and reform.

In western New York the great revival even took the form of a new religion, delivered on tablets by an angel to young Joseph Smith. Smith would lead his Latter-day Saints to Missouri, and back across the river to Nauvoo, Illinois, where in 1844 at the age of 39 he would find martyrdom. But his successor, Brigham Young, would become one of the most successful colonizers of modern times. Another who grew to manhood in that same New York state region that Smith claimed as home was Charles Grandison Finney, whose converts, as we shall see in another chapter, would successfully challenge the Quakers for the leadership of the antislavery movement.

The antislavery crusade, by the middle 1830's, had absorbed much of the energy and zeal of the reformers, but there was enough left over to keep temperance societies busy, and to keep women like Frances Wright and Margaret Fuller fully involved with the "rights" of their sex, and with all the reforms they meant to initiate when their rights were recognized. Cities were being cleaned up literally, by methods that were a distinct improvement over the old one of pigs roaming the streets to eat the garbage householders tossed out indiscriminately. Imprisonment for debt seemed so clearly to defeat its own purpose that many a debtor was allowed to leave his jail and work during the day, only returning at night to maintain residence. At best the prisons of the day were dirty and squalid; at worst they were unspeakable. And the asylums for the insane were worse, as Dorothea Dix would soon be arguing, by the degree to which their inmates were not able to care for themselves.

Everywhere one turned was evidence of something that could be improved, examples not in Calvinist phrase of God's will, but of man's debasement. The conditions of the poor, and of the criminal, the mentally ill, the merely unfortunate were conditions that man could change, and if man would not, then woman would— as soon as she achieved the status necessary to make herself heard. If Jefferson were correct—if man was indeed capable of self-government—then it should only be necessary to demonstrate the evil and to explain the remedy. But the reformer of the 1830's had also learned the essential lesson of Jacksonian Democracy, that God is on the side of the largest number.

8

Sow the Wind

WHEN JACKSON questioned the utility and constitutionality of the Bank of the United States in his first annual message
to Congress, he was launching what was to be no skirmish, or
even a battle, but a full-scale war with long-range effects on the
American economy that can never be accurately measured. The
President had shared the general resentment of the West over the
retrenchment of 1819, with its concomitant of local bank failures,
but he had apparently accepted the reorganized B.U.S. and had
made no issue of it in either of his presidential campaigns. Then,
during Van Buren's brief two months as governor of New York
in 1829, the state legislature set up a Safety Fund which was in
effect a device for insuring the deposits of all New York State
banks and linking them into a single system. By means of the
Safety Fund the New York banks achieved a degree of security
that permitted expansion with negligible risk and made them a
more responsive instrument of the New York business community than the Bank of the United States had ever been. It also
made them collectively a powerful competitor of the B.U.S. for
the banking business of the largest and most rapidly growing
commercial center in the country.

The implications of Jackson's message were not lost upon the
Bank's able and perceptive president, Nicholas Biddle of Philadelphia. Successively, and sometimes simultaneously, scholar,

lawyer, man of letters, politician, and financier, Biddle was no stranger to public life. He had been Secretary of Legation during James Monroe's ministry in London, and had observed the War of 1812 and the nationalistic interlude that followed it from a seat in the Pennsylvania state legislature. When the Bank was reorganized in 1819, Monroe persuaded his protégé to accept an appointment as one of its five government directors. Within the next three years Biddle achieved such a mastery of banking and finance that he was the logical choice to succeed Langdon Cheves as president of the institution. After Jackson's challenge, Biddle moved quickly to change local directors and modify policies to conform to what he understood to be the President's wishes. He accepted assurances at Cabinet level that there would be no difficulty about recharter if the issue were not raised before the election of 1832. Since the original charter would run through 1836, there was no reason for the question to be raised four years earlier.

Clay had other ideas. The Kentuckian had been nominated for President by the National Republicans in December, 1831, and the recharter of the Bank appealed to him as campaign material. Counting noses, and allowing for the crossing of party lines by members who owed the Bank money or could be persuaded to borrow some before a vote was taken, Clay satisfied himself that a recharter bill would pass both houses. It would be a bill, he reasoned, that Jackson could neither sign nor veto without losing a segment of his heterogeneous following. The Bank recharter was introduced according to Clay's plans, and with Biddle himself directing much of the strategy, it was passed. Jackson promptly applied the veto, but with none of the consequences his rival had envisaged.

In many of its operations the Bank was as much an agency of the government as was the Treasury itself, but it was much more powerful and infinitely more difficult to control. Jackson needed no prodding either from western expansionists or New York businessmen to convince him the Bank had outlived its usefulness. It was enough for him that the "people"—the small farmers, the urban workers, the adventurers in both geographical and economic senses whom he particularly represented—deemed themselves injured by it. The crushing defeat at the polls of those who had made recharter a partisan issue was in Jackson's eyes a mandate to destroy the "monster," not in four years when its charter would expire but by direct action at once. He prepared the ground in his message of December, 1832, questioning the safety of the public funds on deposit with the Bank. The follow-up came in the spring of 1833, after the nullification controversy had been settled, and the members of Congress were safely out of Washington.

The reluctant Secretary of the Treasury, Louis McLane, was "promoted" to the State Department in place of Livingston, who was being sent to Paris to deal with an impending debt crisis, and the Treasury was given to William J. Duane, whose only qualification was that his father, a Jeffersonian editor, had opposed the first Bank of the United States. The ink on his commission was hardly dry before the new Secretary was ordered to transfer the government funds from the B.U.S. to certain private banks selected for that privilege by Amos Kendall, in his dual capacity as a Treasury auditor and as Jackson's confidential advisor. Secretly backed by Vice-President Van Buren, who preferred the slower but less disrupting process of attrition, and by McLane, who would rather not destroy the Bank at all, Duane balked.

Jackson tolerated delay only long enough to oversee personally the preparation of an elaborate document justifying removal of the deposits. Francis P. Blair of the *Globe* wrote the first draft, which was revised by Attorney General Roger B. Taney, but the ideas were Jackson's own. Both Blair, who had been a banker himself back in Kentucky, and Taney, who was a very able lawyer, certainly knew that the economics of their justification were specious, but as a journalistic appeal it gave smooth and plausible grounds to all those who, for their own various reasons, wanted to rid the country of the Bank of the United States. Duane, still unconvinced and uncooperative, was removed and the utterly loyal Taney moved up to the Treasury in his stead. Taney immediately announced that beginning October 1, 1833, the revenues of the government would be deposited in certain named private banks. There were initially seven of these "pet banks" as they soon came to be called: two in Boston, three in New York, and one each in Philadelphia and Baltimore. Disbursements, on the other hand, would continue to be made from the Bank of the United States while the $7.6 million of public funds then in that institution lasted. It would not be long.

The "pet banks" knew well how Biddle operated, and, not without some reason, feared reprisals. Should the B.U.S. gather in from its own branches or purchase from other banks any substantial quantity of the notes issued by the new depositories, and present them in a lump for payment in gold and silver, one or more of the favored banks might be forced to the wall. To quiet these fears, Taney secretly gave to each bank substantial drafts against the government funds in the Bank of the United States— drafts that could be used in lieu of specie to redeem their own paper. The drafts were not to be presented for payment unless it became absolutely necessary as a matter of self-protection, but the temptation proved too great. Within six weeks' time, some $2,-000,000 were thus withdrawn from the B.U.S. yet Biddle had not even been informed of the existence of the drafts! By February, 1834, the government deposits were down to $3.1 million, giving the enraged Biddle all the excuse he needed for a sharp contraction of credit. The Bank war by then was merged with the political struggle between hard-pressed Democrats, who controlled the House of Representatives, and an opposition compounded of many elements that could at will control the Senate.

The coalition between followers of Clay and Calhoun that passed the Compromise Tariff of 1833 had been to both men a union of expediency with no long-range objectives. The removal of the deposits once more gave them common ground and after a brief flirtation with the administration, whose cause he had championed in the nullification fight, Webster also teamed with the opposition. To old Federalists like Webster and to those who, like Clay, had inherited the Federalist ideology, the destruction of the Bank was economic suicide. To those like Calhoun and Tyler who had fought a losing battle against the Force Act, it was only another example of Jackson's abuse of power. Both groups called loudly and in unison for "reform," and on that basis collectively took the name of Whigs. Their theme was executive usurpation, carried to the point of judgment in a Senate Resolution censuring Jackson for assuming powers "not conferred by the constitution and laws, but in derogation of both"; and in the rejection of Taney for the Treasury post he occupied. The National Republicans were, in effect, straightening the road that led back to Federalism, giving Jackson much the same treatment their fathers had meted out to Jefferson in the embargo days. And the Nullifiers were continuing, if in a different form, the old state rights battle against central power that had been Jefferson's own. Only in the condemnation of Jackson were the two factions in complete accord, but with Biddle's substantial help behind the scenes, the power of the opposition grew. When Congress adjourned at the end of June, 1834, the Democracy was at its lowest ebb.

To understand why this was so, we must go back a little way to examine the economic structure of the country. Since the conclusion of the War of 1812 America had been moving rapidly into a new type of economy—an economy in which "enterprise" rather than "capital" was the key. In the older order of the revolutionary days, inherited from Britain and expounded by Alexander Hamilton, the wealth of certain individuals—wealth made in trade or as a result of agricultural production—became the capital which was in turn invested in new ventures. It was in this pattern that the mercantile wealth of New England, its normal outlet blocked by the embargo and the war, came to be invested in manufactures. It was not, in this early period, a change of investors. It was only a shift of investment capital by the individual to whom it belonged from one form of productivity to another.

For the new America of the postwar years—the confident,

eager America whose princely domain demanded exploitation—
the old processes were far too slow. Men had discovered that
capital could fairly easily be gotten from banks, which, under
the loose controls and the imperfectly understood operations of
the day, could manufacture what they did not have. These new
businessmen were the "enterprisers" of the new order. It was
they who made up a powerful portion of the Jackson party and
who gave it its distinctive ideology. In this sense, Jacksonianism
was not an attack on capitalism or on wealth. It was a movement
intended by a majority of those in it to make more capitalists
and to accumulate more wealth. The Jacksonian enterprisers
simply wanted more capital for themselves rather than for such
as the Lowells, the Astors, the Girards, who had hitherto controlled and wielded the bulk of it.

Such an economy of easy money, unchecked, could—and did
—lead to runaway inflation and an eventual crash. But this the
new, enthusiastic enterpriser, bent on making a fortune for himself
and developing the country at the same time, could not see. He
was ready and eager to absorb any amount of subsidy in the form
of roads and waterways, or bolstered prices, but he wanted no
government interference with his business. If a bank would lend
him money, he would make money; if his security was not
adequate now, it would be more than adequate later, after settlement had moved farther west, new towns had grown up, and old
towns like New York had grown bigger and more prosperous
through his operations.

But the Bank of the United States provided a check against
would-be unlimited borrowers, so the growing enterpriser class
disliked the Bank and heartily wished it destroyed. One of the
Bank's major functions, as an instrumentality of the Treasury,
was to provide the uniform currency required by the Constitution, but it could only do this by forcing local banks to keep
adequate specie reserves, which meant keeping the credit extended by these local banks within hailing distance of their
resources. The process required financial skill and judgment on

the part of the Bank of the United States, but the means of exercising control were automatic. Taxes, money paid to the land offices, and other government dues were paid in the form of notes issued by state and private banks throughout the country. Without regulation, these notes, which constituted the bulk of the currency in circulation, would be worth only what people thought them worth in terms of the confidence they had in each individual bank. But any bank note accepted in payment of government dues by the B.U.S. was universally worth its face value. By presenting these notes for redemption at frequent intervals the United States Bank could force all other banks to remain solvent or to close their doors.

The New York banks, bound together and their depositors protected by the newly established Safety Fund, chafed under restrictions imposed from rival Philadelphia. The western banks, whose very existence depended on liberal credit secured more by confidence in the country's future than by tangible assets, resented the power of life and death held over them by the B.U.S., and were backed by all those who owed them money.

It was inevitable that Biddle should in turn seek backing from those who were in debt to the Bank of the United States. For the first dozen years of its existence the Bank averaged about $31,000,000 in loans and discounts. For 1829 the figure rose to $39,000,000, reached $44,000,000 for 1831, and leaped to $66,000,000 for 1832—the year in which recharter was vetoed. It was true, as the Jacksonians charged, that loans were made to Congressmen and to editors, but these were only "good-will accommodations." What Biddle was really doing was making credit easy for the whole business community the country over. He had no doubt that the businessmen, including Jacksonian enterprisers, would repay him by choosing Senators and Representatives in Congress who would back the indispensibility of the Bank by their votes. This sudden expansion of credit had a negative value also; for when recharter was vetoed, giving the Bank four years to wind up its affairs, curtailment was necessary.

When Jackson removed the government deposits late in 1833, it became imperative.

The removal of the deposits played into Biddle's hand, for it gave him the justification of necessity for speeding the contraction f credit by the B.U.S. Memorials and petitions were soon pouring in to Congress, recounting business failures and community impoverishment, and praying for restoration of the deposits or outright recharter of the Bank. Even leading Democratic congressmen were staggered by the public reaction, but Jackson himself did not waver. Neither did Benton, whose Missouri constituents hated the Bank, nor did the New Yorkers who expected their own banks to rise on Biddle's fall. The tangible and articulate evidences of hard times more than anything else made it possible for the Whig coalition to rebuke the Treasury and censure the President for removing the deposits.

The Bank might even have won the fight, had Biddle not overreached himself. In his hostility to Jackson, and his overmastering desire to avenge himself on the President who was seeking his destruction, Biddle carried the contraction farther than was necessary for the present safety or ultimate liquidation of the Bank of the United States. Many of those hurt were Biddle's own sympathizers—Whig merchants and manufacturers who reprobated Jackson as thoroughly as did Biddle. Shortly after the adjournment of Congress in the summer of 1834, they called a halt, threatening to expose the whole economic squeeze if Biddle did not relax credit. Under pressure, the B.U.S. president blandly announced that the Bank's condition had so far improved as to require no further contraction. Business immediately picked up, making inevitable the conclusion that if the Bank could thus easily produce prosperity it must also have been responsible for the previous hard times. Men otherwise undecided or even friendly toward the institution now agreed that the Bank of the United States had too much power.

The Bank thus helped to bring about its own demise, ironically because Jackson's economic policies rather than Biddle's mismanagement triggered the ultimate collapse. When the government deposits were removed from the Bank of the United States, the Bank lost its power to regulate currency, and no substitute was provided by the pet banks. On the contrary, these new depositories were prime movers in rushing the country headlong into inflation. When the public funds were deposited in the original seven, it had been the understanding that no withdrawals would be made until the money in the vaults of the B.U.S. was used up. The new depositories were encouraged to expand their operations in keeping with their enlarged deposits, and so they did—not only the original seven but all of the ninety-one pet banks that were depositories of government funds by 1836. They used it, not as deposits, but as windfall capital. They increased their business in every department, but especially in the matter of loans; and inevitably aggressive Jacksonians eager to make fortunes for themselves were the most forward in taking advantage of the new business opportunities.

Without the Bank of the United States to regulate their activities by refusing their notes, specie reserves of the pet banks failed to keep pace with their expanding operations. When the government deposits in the B.U.S. were exhausted and drafts were drawn on them for payment of goverment obligations, they were shocked. Few of them could honor the drafts without being bolstered by the Treasury, and the whole bank question was back in politics. By that time the financial center of the country had moved from Chestnut Street to Wall Street; New York had replaced Philadelphia as the commercial center of America; and the political power of the Democratic party was again on the upswing.

The resurgence of the Democracy was brought about in two ways— by effective political organization, extending down through each layer of government to the individual voter; and by a shift of principles to appeal more directly to an uncommitted but growing group of urban liberals and to new voters, represented chiefly by Irish and German immigrants. In New York City, Philadelphia, even in Boston labor had become a factor since 1828. Neither the "hardy sons of useful labor" who made up the first Workingmen's party in Philadelphia in that year, nor the New York Workingmen's party, which polled over 6,000 votes— almost a third of the New York City total—the following year, were "labor" in the sense of a proletariat; they were men who practiced "trades" as distinguished from "professions," including shopkeepers but not what we think of as "common" or "unskilled" labor. With the enormous growth of industry, stimulated by the tariffs of 1824 and 1828, machine operations were replacing many hand crafts. The single master craftsman, with his journeymen and apprentices, was being undersold by relatively large-scale producers, and the status of both artisan and apprentice was in jeopardy. Organizations quickly sprang up to exert united pressure for better wages, shorter hours, and an end to imprisonment for debt. In the larger cities, these organizations were linked by Trades' Unions. As Nicholas Biddle intensified the economic pressure during the winter of 1833–1834 the "workies," now calling themselves the Equal Rights party, gained in power, giving more than enough votes to the Democrats to make up the margin of victory in New York City in the spring elections. That fall a "labor" candidate was endorsed by Tammany and won a seat in Congress.

Tammany Hall was even then the model and the symbol of the political machine, which had been extended by Crawford and Van Buren to nation-wide proportions. Its basic technique was the appeal to the individual voter through his own self-interest— a technique more difficult to apply in the 1830's than it had been in the days of Jefferson and Burr because there were more voters. Without going too deeply into detail, the means were public office, both appointive and elective; government contracts and other forms of public spending; and promises of legislation from which the individual could see tangible benefit to himself. Those commonly used to elect local officers and congressmen in 1834 and 1835 were mail and printing contracts; construction contracts for fortifications; and the promise of easy credit and business expansion if the Whigs could be prevented from restoring the deposits and rechartering the Bank.

It was only a step from the grass roots to the Congress. Representatives were elected every two years, and Senators despite their longer terms could be replaced by the state legislature as often as its majority changed. The legislature had only to pass resolutions telling the state's two Senators how to vote on a given measure. Any Senator who could not reconcile the instructions with his conscience was expected to resign, leaving the legislature free to choose a successor who shared its own views. All this was possible because the people believed in themselves, and in their own ability to decide any question of public policy, however complex. Their representatives in Congress were their agents only—never their masters. The Democrats secured their Senate majority in March of 1836 when the Virginia legislature so "instructed" Tyler out of his seat. Roger B. Taney was then nominated and confirmed as Chief Justice of the United States, John Marshall having died the previous year. In the following session the resolution censuring Jackson for removing the deposits was formally expunged from the Journal of the Senate.

During four years of divided responsibility, the country had been courting a disaster for which Whig Senate and Democratic House blamed each other freely in advance. With Jackson himself finally alarmed, both parties agreed that the remedy lay in regulation of the deposit banks and in somehow disposing of the revenue that, since the final payment on the public debt in 1832, had been flowing into the custom houses and land offices faster than a strict construction of the Constitution permitted the government to spend it. Both purposes were accomplished in a single act which limited government funds on deposit in any single bank to three-fourths of its capital; and deposited the surplus revenue with the states. Technically the Treasury might demand that the money be returned but practically, as exponents of the measure frankly argued, political expediency would preclude any such demand. The states would therefore be free to use the funds for canals or for the railroads that were rapidly replacing them in public favor. A proposal by Benton that only gold and silver be received in payment for public lands was not acted upon by Congress, but was embodied in the Specie Circular later issued by the Treasury.

The effect of these various devices was merely to hasten the inevitable catastrophe. Public land sales had risen from 3.8 million acres in 1833 to 20 million in 1836, the overwhelming bulk of the increase being bought for speculative purposes with money supplied by the pet banks. The Specie Circular hastened the process by siphoning gold and silver from the eastern commercial cities to the West where people reasoned that, since the government no longer trusted the banks, they had best hoard their precious metals. Without specie, land could not be bought from the land offices, but millions of acres could be had from speculators for bank paper. So the lands were sold, resold, and sold once more at ever-mounting prices. The effect of the Deposit Act was equally unhappy, for scores of pet banks held more government funds than the act permitted and were forced to relinquish the excess. This they could do only by calling in their own loans on short notice, putting great pressure on the business community. In order to make the first deposit of the surplus revenue with the states on January 1, 1837, as required by the Deposit Act, still more money had to be called in, adding an other increment to the pressure.

A further element in the impending debacle was the unbalanced nature of American foreign trade. Going back to 1816, when America first broke the bonds of her colonial dependence upon Europe, the volume of foreign trade had steadily risen, but it had been primarily trade with Great Britain, and it had been onesided. In the fifteen-year period from 1816 through 1830, exports of domestic produce had averaged $56,000,000 a year, about half of it cotton. In the same period, however, imports had averaged $67,-000,000 a year—a yearly excess of imports over exports of $11,-

000,000. Both exports and imports rose sharply after 1830, but the imports rose more sharply than the exports: $168,000,000 in 1836 against $106,000,000 in exports. For the six-year period 1831–1836 the aggregate excess of imports over exports was $188,000,000. For the entire twenty-one-year period from 1816 the excess amounted to more than $350,000,000.

Throughout this period, the bulk of the government income came from customs duties on these same imports. So rapid indeed was the expansion of trade that even the progressively lowered duties fixed by the tariff compromise of 1833 brought about an appreciable lowering of the customs receipts for only two years. In a word the tariff, even at its 1832 peak had not excluded any substantial quantity of British goods. On the contrary, the enormous physical and economic growth of the United States between 1816 and 1836 had been enough to absorb both domestic and foreign production, even at tariff-inflated prices, but payment had been deferred in much the same way that local bank credit had been extended—by paying off each obligation with part of the proceeds from a new and larger loan. The aggregate excess of imports over exports thus represented a British investment in America. The trade balance that should normally have been redressed by exports or by transfer of precious metals was in fact absorbed by British purchases of shares in American enterprises, and of American state bonds. In effect, Britain was doing in the United States precisely what she had been doing in Latin America: lending the money that was to be used to buy her manufactured goods. She did this, not to bolster the alien economies concerned but to provide the expanding market that alone would keep her own expanding industry in operation.

The system functioned smoothly because the potential wealth of America in her prairies, her forests, her as yet untapped mineral reserves, and above all in the ingenuity and daring of her people, was always more than enough to secure her indebtedness to Europe, just as the potential value of the western lands was always more than sufficient to secure the loans made against them by bankers with faith in the future. The enormous growth of foreign trade and of foreign investment were only two aspects of the explosive growth of the American economy. Both were intimately related to the nation-wide movement for better and faster transportation, touched off by the success of the Erie Canal. Pennsylvania launched a canal construction program, using inclined planes and stationary steam engines to cross the Alleghenies, that would aggregate a thousand miles before railroads made the system obsolete. Ohio, with a water route between Cincinnati and Cleveland, had linked the Mississippi River system with the Great Lakes by 1834. As early as 1828 Washington, too, had sought a commercial route to the West with President Adams launching the Chesapeake and Ohio Canal, symbolically, on Independence Day; but in Baltimore, on the same day, ninety-year-old Charles Carroll of Carrollton, last surviving signer of the Declaration of Independence, laid the cornerstone of the Baltimore and Ohio Railroad. By 1836 there were more than 1,200 miles of railroad in the United States, while canal mileage, in operation or under active construction, exceeded 10,000 miles. European investment in these transportation ventures was physical as well as financial, for much of the actual labor was performed by immigrants. Ten thousand entered the country in 1825; 27,000 in 1828; 60,000 in 1832. The figure for 1836 was 76,000, including 30,000 Irishmen and 20,000 Germans.

The bulk of the foreign-born who had been in the country long enough to obtain citizenship—and some who had not—adapted easily to the pattern of Democratic politics, ultimately giving the party a radical cast in New York and Pennsylvania. For the most part hand workers, many of these foreign-born citizens were quickly identified with the labor movement, helping to give it in New York the balance of power it had achieved by 1834. When the victorious Democrats repudiated the principles for which their Equal Rights allies had stood, the labor faction resumed independent status. By the fall of 1835 the Equal Rights party had enough vocal and muscular followers to rout the Democrats from a Tammany Hall meeting. The Democrats turned off the gas by which the building was lighted but the Equal Rights men produced ample supplies of the new friction or "locofoco" matches, and proceeded with their meeting. They were soon being called in derision Locofocos themselves, and under that title, proudly worn, most of them again moved into the Democratic ranks.

The immigrants of the late 1820's and 1830's were also involved as victims in various less wholesome political movements. Many—probably most—of them were Catholic, and their presence precipitated in time both nativist and Protestant movements by those with whom they came increasingly into competition. Discrimination was often patent, and exploitation was the rule rather than the exception. The pick-and-shovel men working on the canals and railroads were paid as little as fifty cents for a fifteen-hour day, with a substantial ration of whiskey to keep them happy. It was the same technique that had been used to part the Indians from their tribal lands and from the furs they brought in for trading; but the Irish and German immigrants needed only a little time, a little familiarity with their adopted country, to realize how they were being duped, and to see a remedy in the ballot box.

All these forces bore upon the election of 1836, but the determining factor was approval or disapproval of Andrew Jackson and his policies. The Whig coalition, unable to agree on a candidate, ran Webster for the North, Senator Hugh Lawson White of Tennessee for the South, and for the West aging, all-but-forgotten General William Henry Harrison, hero of Tippecanoe and of the Battle of the Thames. The Democrats, more than a year before the election itself, put up Van Buren, and for Vice-President, Richard M. Johnson of Kentucky, whose long battle against imprisonment for debt had made him the darling of the Workingmen-turned-Locofocos. Van Buren won with ease but neither he nor his party overlooked the fact that an independent Locofoco ticket in New York City had beaten both Whigs and

Tammany Democrats. To win back this radical faction, with its evidence of long-run political strength, the northern Democracy would be forced in the direction of social reform, as that term was understood in the first half of the nineteenth century, and ultimately toward an antislavery position and disruption along sectional lines. Yet for the time being, with New England and the West both dominated by the opposition, Van Buren had no choice if he would sustain his administration but to win back the South from her unnatural alliance with the Whigs.

The gathering economic storm gave the new President little chance to show his skill at peacemaking. In London news of the Specie Circular had been received with a mixture of alarm and dismay. Britain, as we have seen, was the largest purchaser of both American cotton and American securities. America, in turn, was a heavy purchaser of British goods. Inflation in the United States had already raised the discount rate on American currency in London from 4 to 4½ to 5 percent. In a moment of panic the Bank of England now refused to accept the paper of certain British houses with large American interests. A sudden reduction in the demand for cotton followed, with the resulting lowered price. Early in March, 1837, just as Van Buren was beginning his uneasy term of office, a New Orleans cotton broker failed. Other New Orleans failures followed on the heels of the first, and in chain reaction, failure spread to New York. On May 8 and 9 frightened depositors withdrew a million dollars in gold and silver from New York banks. Not even the strongest could withstand the mounting pressure, and the following day, by mutual agreement, New York banks suspended specie payments. This panicky shutdown was, in turn followed by banks in other cities. Van Buren called Congress to meet in special session on the first Monday in September.

Before the appointed day arrived the collapse was complete. Real estate prices dropped to as little as 10 percent of the level of less than a year earlier. Cotton plunged to half its value of only a few months before. The same western lands that had so recently passed from hand to hand at steadily rising prices could not now be sold at any price. The government revenues were accumulating in the custom houses and land offices when they ought to be in circulation because the general suspension of specie payments had left no banks legally qualified to receive the public funds. Unemployment in the industrial states was general, distress in one form or another almost universal. Soup kitchens in the eastern cities fed the hungry. Business everywhere was at a complete standstill.

Van Buren was no longer forced or able to reconcile his views with Jackson's. In a hard-hitting and unequivocal message that left his detractors speechless, Van Buren laid down a program of economic recovery designed to appeal at the same time to radicals and conservatives, to the unemployed workies of the northern cities and to the land-poor planters of the South. There were interim measures to relieve debtors, adjust claims, and provide revenue, including a request that the deposit of a now nonexistent surplus with the states be suspended. But the financial engine of recovery as well as of future prosperity was to be a system under which the Treasury could collect and disburse the public funds without the aid or intervention of banks of any kind. This measure came to be known as the Independent Treasury or the Subtreasury. The idea had been under exploration, both within the government and by economists unconnected with public service, since Jackson's first attack on the Bank of the United States. It was a favorite measure of the Locofocos, who were hostile to all banks, but it was also calculated to entice the cotton planters, with their dependence on foreign exchange, by providing a uniform and stable currency.

Van Buren's program was abhorrent to the Whigs, who would accept nothing less than a complete restoration of the now defunct Bank of the United States. It was unacceptable also to many Democrats some of whom saw in it a further step toward the consolidation of power in Washington, while others feared it as an opening wedge for the radicals. But Calhoun supported the Subtreasury and brought enough of his old state rights following back to the Democratic fold to give the party a majority in Congress, and to insure the ultimate establishment of the Independent Treasury. Even before the party realignment was complete, recovery in the West and in the great commercial cities had begun. The New York banks set the pace, resuming specie payments in 1838, just a year after the suspension. They were backed by the transfer of a million pounds in specie from the Bank of England, with a promise of more should it be needed. The banks in other cities followed the lead of New York. The Specie Circular was repealed by Congress and business activity slowly gathered momentum, its sights on an even more distant star.

9

Half Slave, Half Free

DURING VAN BUREN's administration the fluid party lines of Jackson's time began to harden around an issue that had little or nothing to do with the economic crisis. The existence of slavery in half the states of the Union controlled political attitudes, influenced international relations, obstructed territorial expansion, and modified the national economy. Slavery had been the unacknowledged ghost at every political feast since the Missouri Compromise. Its abolition now became the mainspring of every movement for social reform; its defense the core of American conservatism.

It was a question that created fanatics on both sides. To the moralist the evil of slavery was so clear and obvious that he could not see how any man of good will and good sense could defend it. The slaveholders—and most of those who lived in the South, whether they personally held slaves or not—saw every criticism of the institution as a threat to their livelihood and a danger to their own freedom. The northern intellectual, stimulated by writers, lecturers, active reformers at home and abroad; inspired by revolutionary undercurrents in Europe and by the revolutionary accompaniments of Jacksonian Democracy, was prepared by the 1830's to take his stand on the egalitarian philosophy of the Declaration of Independence. In the South the acceptance of slavery as a permanent way of life had already produced an emotional blight that would persist long after its reason for existence had passed and its origin had been forgotten. After the Missouri Compromise forced the issue, every attack upon the labor system of the South met the kind of organized, obstinate resistance that inevitably called forth greater effort from the attackers. Proponents on both sides were intelligent, resourceful and dedicated to a degree unparalleled before or since.

The Missouri debates had also given impetus to a stream of abolition literature that reached flood proportions in the next decade and a half. Indeed the fateful debates were still going on in January, 1821, when Benjamin Lundy, a young Quaker who had learned to hate slavery when apprenticed to a saddler in Virginia, began publishing the *Genius of Universal Emancipation*. First established in Ohio, Lundy soon moved the paper to Tennessee, and in 1824 to Baltimore. While lecturing in the North he met William Lloyd Garrison, who became associate editor of the paper in 1829.

The sectional battle over the tariff of 1828 had meanwhile aired once more the relation of slavery to the struggle for power between state and federal governments. The labor system of the South was well on the way to political immolation when David Walker's impassioned *Appeal to the Colored Citizens of the World* struck deeper than any political argument could have done. Himself a free Negro, Walker had been born in North Carolina, had traveled widely in the South before taking up his residence in Boston, and had read extensively. He knew well the institution of American Negro slavery, and his *Appeal*, closely reasoned and argued with a stirring, primitive eloquence, was in fact addressed to the southern slaves, who were bidden to burst their bonds no matter what the cost in blood. The pamphlet went through two further editions, each enlarged and more militant than its predecessor, before Walker died, reputedly by violence, in 1830. So dangerous was the *Appeal* considered in the slave states that ships in southern harbors were searched for copies. In Georgia the legislature made it an offense punishable by death to circulate such documents among the slaves. In neighboring South Carolina, with her more intellectual orientation, Governor Stephen D. Miller answered Walker's arguments with what was probably the first reasoned attempt to defend the morality of slavery.

The publication of the Walker pamphlet coincided with the beginning of a period of religious enthusiasm, marked by widespread "conversion" phenomena, and the steady growth of a moral fervor that was soon guided like the equally amorphous reform movements into abolitionist channels. Garrison, whose association with Lundy had been of brief duration, published the first number of the *Liberator* in Boston on January 1, 1831. Unlike Lundy, who was seeking places to colonize the freed slaves in Haiti, Texas, and Canada, Garrison was concerned only with emancipation itself, and not overly squeamish about how it might be achieved. "I am in earnest," he wrote in the first number, "I will not equivocate—I will not excuse—I will not retreat a single inch—and *I will be heard*." Like Jackson's propagandist, Francis Preston Blair of the Washington *Globe,* Garrison never doubted that the ends would always justify the means.

The *Liberator* had been delighting and infuriating its readers for about eight months when a slave rebellion in Virginia, led by Nat Turner, an eloquent and often "inspired" preacher among his people, resulted in the massacre of fifty-one white men, women and children within twenty-four hours. The revolt was quickly suppressed and all those who took part in it executed or exiled, but its effects were lasting and profound. With her classical education, the South knew well the history of slave uprisings in ancient Greece and Rome, and her reaction followed the classical mold. Slave codes were tightened, punishments made more severe, and enforcement made swifter and more certain. Curfews were imposed for all Negroes and in time it became a criminal offense to teach any slave to read or write. The state of Georgia even put a $5,000 price on Garrison's head. But to the northern abolitionists, Nat Turner's rebellion merely presented another evidence of the immorality of slavery. In North and South alike a connection was seen, though never proved, between the Virginia holocaust and Garrison's *Liberator*.

The southern slaveholder had always prided himself on his tolerance, even forgiveness, toward his slaves. The occasional runaways were balanced by the thousands who, whatever their inner thoughts, made no overt attempt to escape, served loyally if not always diligently in the tasks assigned to them, and accepted as no more than their due the general tendency of their owners to overlook small transgressions. The slave-owner, even while he insisted that his Negroes were too close to their ancestral savagery to be trusted with their freedom, protested over and over again that their lot was easier and more rewarding than that of the Irish immigrant laborers or the factory hands of the northern states, and held the crusading abolitionists responsible for stirring up whatever trouble his human chattels gave him after 1830. There were, to be sure, those who belied in various ways their professed beliefs: Men who, like John Randolph, emancipated their own slaves in their wills and provided land in the North on which they might live in freedom; and women who defied the code to teach the three R's to bright youngsters who might indeed be blood relatives or stepchildren of their own. The majority of southerners, however, were probably consistent within the inconsistent limits of their own dogma.

In the South one seldom heard the term "slave." They were called "hands" or "servants" according to whether they worked outdoors or in the house. The master usually referred to the skilled workers among them by trade, as "my mason," "my blacksmith," "my carpenter"; and to the group collectively as "my people," or "the Negroes," or "the force." Except on the small farms, each slave had a patch of ground where he raised vegetables, or cotton if he preferred, the proceeds of which would be his own. Except in harvest season, week-ends were usually free. The slaves were often encouraged to attend church, usually a small, local affair with a slave or free Negro preacher.

Indeed, the conversion of these millions of souls to Christianity is even today one of the foremost arguments advanced in defense of the system.

In addition to the huge river-bottom plantations—often owned by absentees who entrusted the entire management to hired over-seers—there were smaller units of a few hundred or a thousand acres in piedmont or upcountry. On these middle-class planta-tions, the owner was at least nominally in residence, though he often as not practiced law, engaged in business activity, or sat in Congress. Like that of his tidewater compatriot, cotton was his cash crop, but he also raised small grains, cattle, hogs and poultry —enough usually to feed his household and the twenty to one hundred slaves who made up his establishment. About half of the cotton crop was still produced by small farmers with not more than five or six slaves, but the defense of the system, after Garrison and Nat Turner, became as important to these as it was to the large plantation owners.

The North for the most part had only vague and contradictory impressions of the slave in the South. The auction block, the slave mother begging for her child, the lash—all depicted in the crude woodcuts and more artistic steel engravings of the day—were often the limits of his information. But the slave market in Washington, within sight of the Capitol itself, was a festering sore that left an indelible imprint and served to keep smoldering the fires of moral indignation. The fugitive slave law of 1793 entitled a master or his agent to return a runaway by force on the basis of no better identification than his unsupported word under oath. As the demand for slaves rose with the spread of cotton culture, perjury became profitable and "slavecatching" a recognized if reprobated occupation. The northern response was a series of personal liberty laws, beginning with Pennsylvania's in 1825, to protect free Negroes from being kidnaped as fugitives. Another response was the "underground railroad" by which run-aways were smuggled from one rendezvous point to another across border states and free soil to Canada. The number of slaves who made good their freedom by flight was never large—probably no more than a fraction of a percent—but the nuisance and propaganda values of the underground railroad were out of all proportion to its actual success. In a sense, indeed, these organized northern efforts to help the runaways were of equal or greater help to the masters, for they provided a safety valve by removing the more resourceful, more rebellious of the Negroes and thus made it easier for the South to perpetuate the system. By bringing free men into direct contact with some of the more abhorrent aspects of slavery, however, the underground railroad helped immeasurably to hasten its doom.

On the other hand, the North was also familiar with the unemployed, largely illiterate ex-slaves or free-born Negroes who crowded into ghettos in the northern towns and filled the jails far out of proportion to their numbers. Their cheap labor provoked the hostility of the competing Irish immigrants, and in not a few instances their very presence aroused the animosity of those who would, in the abstract, do all in their power to abolish slavery. In addition to the Christianity of which his master was so proud, the southern slave learned to be indolent, untruthful, and dishonest because there was no positive motive or incentive for work. In the interests of his own survival, he developed the psychological protective coloring so many of his descendants exhibit still. These qualities, carried over into a free, competitive world, could lead only to personal and social disaster.

On another level the North observed as in a separate compartment of existence, and the South refused to see at all, the achievements of such as Benjamin Banneker, the Negro mathematician and astronomer who had helped L'Enfant to lay out the city of Washington; and Ira Frederick Aldridge, who had gone with Kean to England where, with "his own black hands" instead of the usual gloves, he played Othello to his benefactor's Iago, and by the 1840's was conceded to be one of the greatest Shakespearean actors of his day. The runaways Frederick Douglass and William Wells Brown were closer to the problem and devoted their own considerable talents to the antislavery cause.

More significant for the slavery controversy than even the *Liberator* or Nat Turner's rebellion was the appearance in the House of Representatives in December, 1831, of ex-President John Quincy Adams. Asked by a group of Quakers to present petitions for the abolition of slavery and the slave trade in the District of Columbia, Adams' first speech in the House was in compliance, though the petitioners were not his own constituents. He asked only that the petitions be referred to the appropriate committee. No sinister meaning was then inferred, the House so ordered, and in due time the Committee on the District of Columbia reported that it would not be expedient to do as the petitioners asked. That was the beginning, from which mighty events would presently flow. Adams had neither said nor done anything to mark him as an abolitionist. Except in the privacy of his diary, he had not even taken an unequivocal antislavery position. Yet the judgment of those who chose him as their instrument was unerring. Adams' contribution to the antislavery cause would prove incalculable.

Adams and his colleagues in both houses of Congress soon turned their attention to the tariff and the bank, but the question of slavery still engrossed the Virginia legislature, where Jefferson's old plan for gradual emancipation—the same plan that had been attached as a rider to the bill admitting Missouri a decade earlier—was being soberly debated. The measure passed the House of Burgesses, but in January, 1832, it failed in the upper chamber by a single vote. It was another point of no return in the slavery controversy. Later in the year Thomas R. Dew, professor of political economy at the College of William and Mary, published a review of the debate in the legislature on the emancipation bill. It was the first full-scale defense of slavery as a positive good, amplifying and enlarging the position taken earlier by Governor Miller of South Carolina. It was precisely the argument for which the South yearned, because it gave a moral base and justification for an institution of which she believed she could not rid herself.

This moral defense of slavery came just as the nullification crisis in South Carolina brought into sharp focus the nature of the political defense. Only in the compact theory of the Constitution could a state or region whose interests differed from those of the majority find safety. If the South could not agree on nullification of the tariff, she would resist abolition with greater unity. So it was that Jackson's proclamation against the Nullifiers shocked many who were otherwise well disposed, for in the unified nation Jackson envisaged, slavery ceased to be a local institution and became everybody's responsibility. So it was that Garrison hailed it in the *Liberator* as "an exceedingly powerful and eloquent exposition of the Constitution and Laws." The Force Act that followed showed how easily the majority could carry out its will, should abolition ever become the prevailing sentiment in the more populous northern states.

The antislavery cause received an enormous boost in the late summer of 1833 when Parliament abolished slavery in the British West Indies. It was the culmination of a long crusade in which the British Antislavery Society had been the spearhead of the final drive, and which was itself a reflection of the widespread revolutionary movement that was changing dynasties on the continent, extending the franchise in Britain and America, sending new groups of hopeful idealists to the New World. An Antislavery Society, with Garrison as its salaried agent, was already in existence in New England. A similar society was established in New York shortly after news of the British action reached America. In December, 1833, the American Antislavery Society was formed, and was pledged to immediate emancipation, by which was meant the immediate application of a gradual plan such as that so narrowly rejected in Virginia.

The dominant personality in the new organization was that of Theodore Dwight Weld, who had been "converted" by the Reverend Charles Grandison Finney, revivalist and crusader without peer. Weld, in turn, had converted the wealthy New York philanthropists, Arthur and Lewis Tappan, who promptly became large contributors to the Lane Theological Seminary in Cincinnati, with which Weld was then associated. Another Weld convert to the antislavery cause was former Alabama slaveholder James G. Birney, who brought to the movement legal acumen, organizing skill, and a dedication as great as Weld's own. Birney and the Tappans joined Weld in the American Antislavery Society; and the Tappans went along also in the simultaneous launching of Oberlin College. This small Ohio school, founded without barriers of sex or race, would become a fertile breeding ground for abolitionists. The dynamic Finney himself took the chair of theology, while Weld spread the word far and wide as lecturer and preacher. Among those inspired to join the antislavery movement by this "Holy Band" were Joshua Giddings, long-term Congressman from the Western Reserve district of Ohio; and the Reverend Lyman Beecher's children, Henry Ward who became the greatest preacher of his day, and Harriet whose contribution would be *Uncle Tom's Cabin*.

A further evidence that a solid milestone had been reached came in December, 1833, when antislavery sentiment in Congress first became strong enough to make of the hated institution a political issue. Petitions for the abolition of slavery and the slave trade in the District of Columbia multiplied in both houses, and only the political hopes of the Whig coalition prevented introduction of legislation to carry out the ends asked. For the moment northern and southern interests had drawn together to protect the Bank of the United States from Andrew Jackson, a battle they would most assuredly lose if they fell to squabbling among themselves.

There was no such restraint to a campaign of propaganda. The American Antislavery Society took the lead, with scores of local societies that mushroomed throughout the free states adding to the impact of a drive that was being worked up to crisis proportions during 1834. Pamphlets, broadsides with simple texts, and woodcuts carried their message, however crudely, even to those who could not read. Some of these documents were designed to reach the slaves themselves; others were intended to arouse the consciences of those many southerners who were not happy with the system they had inherited, but did not know what to do about it. Many and ingenious ways were devised for delivering this abolition literature. Sometimes it was consigned to agents who saw personally to its distribution. Sometimes propaganda sheets, and especially pictures designed for those who could not read, would be slipped in with various manufactured articles being delivered to the South. More boldly still, lists of names of leading citizens were compiled and the publications were sent to them by mail. One of the most damaging of the pamphlets was an *Appeal to the Christian Women of the South* by Angelina Grimké, the daughter of a Charleston slaveholder, who would marry Weld in 1838. Her sister Sarah's *Epistle to the Clergy of the Southern States* created almost as much havoc. The Grimké sisters, who started as abolitionists, soon found themselves crusading for women's rights in order to justify their participation in the antislavery battle.

To the South this propaganda campaign was incendiary, vicious, perhaps murderous; for who could say what might happen should such explosive materials fall into the hands of another Denmark Vesey or Nat Turner? On this subject even men otherwise controlled lost their heads, and the rift opened between North and South by the tariff began to widen into a gulf. The whole South was aflame by the spring of 1835, when Martin Van Buren, a northern man from a state in which the abolitionists were strong, was nominated for President by the Democrats. The explosion came in July. A steamboat from New York delivered quantities of abolition literature to the Charleston post office. Some of the documents were addressed to clergymen and other leading citizens. Some, in bulk lots, were consigned to post offices throughout the slave states. The Charleston postmaster impounded the material and wrote hastily to Amos

Kendall, now Postmaster General, for instructions. Before they arrived, however, indignant citizens broke into the post office and the offending publications were burned in the streets.

Following Kendall's advice, Jackson asked Congress to authorize the Post Office to bar incendiary publications from the mails; but to the South this remedy was as bad as the disease. If the Postmaster General could decide what was incendiary, and had power to bar it from the mails, then no southern paper, no pamphlet in defense of slavery, no speech by a southern orator could be circulated except on sufferance. The alternative proposed by the South did not become law, but it was nevertheless put into practice by the postal authorities. It was simply that each state should decide for itself what literature should be banned from the mails within its borders, and the Post Office should take measures to enforce these state regulations. This solution worked well enough to turn the energies of the abolitionists into other channels.

More effective were the petitions now flooding Congress and threatening to monopolize the time of the members in more and more acrimonious debate. Beginning in 1831 antislavery petitions had been coming in, by scores, by hundreds, by thousands, and it would soon be by hundreds of thousands. Originally from Quaker meetings, then from abolitionist societies or groups, they were coming by the end of 1835 from plain citizens in cities, towns, and hamlets throughout the northern and western states. They came from men and women alike, who had no axes to grind except a personal dislike of slavery or a religious conviction that it was wrong to own one's fellow man. Antislavery petitions came from virtually every congressional district in the free states, and as the number of signers grew they found more congressmen ready to abet them.

Up to the first session of the 24th Congress, meeting in December, 1835, such petitions had always been referred to an appropriate committee and in due time the petition had been denied, if indeed any notice at all were taken. There was now a change of attitude. The southern members, alarmed by the number and persistence of the petitioners, sought some formula for disposing of them without even the nominal recognition of their existence implied by rejection. It was then that the House passed what came to be known as the gag rule, to the effect that "all petitions, memorials, resolutions, propositions, or papers, relating in any way, or to any extent whatever, to the subject of slavery, shall, without either being printed or referred, be laid upon the table, and that no further action whatever shall be had thereon." When the roll was called, John Quincy Adams then and at every session thereafter until the gag rule was rescinded, vigorously denounced the rule as a violation of the rights of his constituents, of the rules of the House, and of the Constitution of the United States.

In the battle over reception of the abolition petitions, the lines were sectional rather than partisan. On that issue the South could accept Harrison or Webster no more than she could accept Van Buren. The gag rule was re-enacted after the election, but not before Adams had again been heard, and had made it clear that the right of petition itself was in jeopardy. The panic of 1837 and the special session of Congress, with its first tentative reconciliation of Van Buren Democrats and Calhoun Nullifiers, only spurred the abolitionists to mightier efforts.

Into this charged atmosphere of doubt and distrust, with all the complications introduced by economic catastrophe where violence lay just below the surface, the lone star of Texas suddenly blazed forth to beckon or repel. As President, Adams had twice sought unsuccessfully to buy Texas; and Jackson too had tried and failed. Yet the largely American population of the area was growing fast, and growing restive. Sam Houston, protégé of Jackson, ex-governor of Tennessee, by adoption a Cherokee Indian and by inclination an adventurer, brought matters to a head. Moving to Texas in 1832, Houston began recruiting followers who came largely from the South; men who brought a predilection toward cotton culture, and who generally brought slaves as well. Many of them—perhaps most—believed that Texas ought to be, if it was not already, a part of the United States. This belief was shrewdly encouraged by southerners who realized that only the equal balance in the Senate so far maintained by the Missouri Compromise could protect them from the growing power and militancy of the abolitionists. Without Texas there was no other area from which new slave states could be carved to balance the burgeoning territories in the northwest. Without Texas slavery was therefore doomed, and possibly the Union as well.

Of almost equal significance was the subversion of the Mexican Republic by General Antonio López de Santa Anna, who as dictator had little choice but to suppress if he could the incipient revolt in Texas. Texas and Mexico had actually been at war with each other for some six months, a Texan Constitution on the United States pattern had been drafted and ratified, and Sam Houston had been given command of the Texan army when the massacre at the Alamo in March, 1836, struck fire all over America. On April 21 Houston caught Santa Anna by surprise, defeated decisively a much larger Mexican army, and took the dictator himself a prisoner. Texan independence was assured. In October Houston was inaugurated first President of the Republic of Texas. The following year the Texan Congress voted all but unanimously to ask for annexation to the United States, and the Texan Minister in Washington so informed President Van Buren on August 4, 1837.

Northern opinion was alert for just this eventuality. Even while the Texas Revolution was going on, Benjamin Lundy condemned it in a series of articles in the *National Gazette*. Lundy had himself received a substantial grant of land in Mexico for the avowed purpose of showing that slave labor was not necessary, even in the tropics. To him, the Texan Revolution appeared no more than a gigantic plot by the "Slave Power" to extend the peculiar institution. The Quaker abolitionist convinced Adams, who spoke powerfully and at length against annexation only a month after the battle of San Jacinto. The American Antislavery Society prepared to join the fight against Texas, and petitions opposing annexation were added to the familiar ones asking for abolition in the District of Columbia. By the time the Texan request for annexation was actually made, the issue had become too sensitive for any politician dependent as Van Buren was upon both northern and southern support. The President kept his own counsel for three weeks. Then a few days before the special session was to meet, he rejected the request without giving Congress an excuse to debate the issue.

Every ounce of Van Buren's skill was needed to hold northern and southern Democrats together long enough to pass urgent financial legislation. When Congress met in December, 1837, for the regular session, its members knew that the antislavery forces had been given a martyr with the death of abolitionist editor Elijah P. Lovejoy at the hands of a mob in Alton, Illinois. Stimulated by the Lovejoy murder as well as by the Texas question, antislavery petitions in this session swelled to more than 200,000, signed by literally millions of citizens in the free states. With a northern population of only some 10,000,000, this evidence of antislavery strength was something to set politicians on both sides of the Mason-Dixon line to calculating.

Even though they were not received by Congress, or printed, or read, the influence of these abolition petitions was incalculable. The mere canvass of citizens for signatures brought the question of slavery to the fore for many who had not thought much about it, one way or the other. The whole congressional fight to evade any action was also a factor, when reported by the press, by private letter, and by word of mouth, in crystallizing sentiment in the North and hardening resistance in the South. In this slavery controversy the West had lost its identity. There was only slave or free soil, and those who differed on this question were ready, before the end of the fourth decade of the 1800's, to believe only evil of each other. In happier times it would not have been possible for two members of Congress to duel with rifles at close range over a matter of punctilio, but in February, 1838, Jonathan Cilley, a state rights Democrat from Maine, was killed in just such an encounter by William Graves, a slaveholding Kentucky Whig.

The antislavery crusade now took a new and more ominous turn, posing new issues and shaking party ties. In the House, young William Slade of Vermont had got the floor before the gag rule was imposed for the 1837–38 session and had succeeded in delivering a biting philippic against slavery before a hasty adjournment was taken. At the same time, one of the Vermont Senators, Benjamin Swift, offered a new kind of petition in the upper chamber—resolutions from his state legislature protesting the annexation of Texas or the admission of any more slave states to the Union, and affirming the power of Congress to abolish slavery and the slave trade in the District of Columbia. The Vermont Senators were instructed to work toward these ends, and the state's lone Representative was requested to do likewise.

Southern Representatives and Senators—all of them then in Washington except Benton and Clay—met together that evening to plan their own strategy, but they could not agree. There were younger men in the House who wanted to leave the Union then and there; and there were conservatives like Calhoun who were content to reassert the compact theory of the Constitution, which they believed would now be backed up by the united strength of the slave states. In the end, the House re-enacted the gag rule, while the Senate, with Locofoco Democrats supporting southern Nullifiers, passed resolutions affirming the compact theory and its state rights corollaries, and specifically placing slavery in the category of matters not delegated to the general government by the sovereign states.

Only five years earlier a President of the United States had proclaimed in ringing and memorable words the indivisible sovereignty of the nation, and a Congress of the same mind had passed the Force Act. The times and the men were now different, the issue no longer a question of the equitable assessment of taxes but the way of life of seven million persons, more than a third of them Negro slaves. The spokesmen for the South would use every weapon short of war, and ultimately even war itself, to preserve a status quo as obsolete as the arguments that sustained it; but the case for nationalism had been made and would prevail. In the House an attempt by the Democratic coalition to legislate Texas into the Union was talked to death by Adams, who managed to hold the floor for the last three weeks of the session. Texas herself took the next decisive step, withdrawing her annexation request on October 12, 1838.

The reunion of northern and southern Democrats in a renewal of the old Jeffersonian alliance was a tenuous thing at best, for the growth of antislavery sentiment in the free states might well force northern Democrats to choose between that cause and involuntary retirement from politics. For the time being, however, the alliance meant that the abolitionists would be checked so far as it lay in the power of a congressional majority to do so. In the off-year elections of 1838 enough state rights southerners returned to the Democratic fold to keep the party in power, but the Whigs, with antislavery support, showed gains throughout the northern states. In New York William H. Seward, ex-Antimason who leaned strongly toward the antislavery cause, won the Whig nomination for governor and, aided by the internal squabbles of the Democrats, was elected. Thurlow Weed, another Antimason-turned-Whig, began a flirtation with the abolitionists that would lead to marriage. The antislavery forces could use their strength negatively also, as they demonstrated by defeating a Whig governor of Ohio because he had returned a fugitive slave in strict compliance with the law.

Whig gains were not enough to offset the return of the South to the Democratic column. When the 26th Congress met in December, 1839, the gag was made the twenty-first standing rule of the House, rendering any discussion of the slave question thereafter a matter of sufferance by the majority. But James G. Birney had already been proposed as an independent candidate for President of the United States, and would receive the formal nomination of the Liberty Party in the spring. Before Congress met again the Democratic coalition of North and South would fall apart, General Harrison would be washed into office on a tidal wave of hard cider, and the antislavery movement would enter its political phase.

10

Sectionalism and Democracy

THE CAMPAIGN of 1840 brought 2.5 million voters to the polls—more than half again as many as in 1836 and double the total of 1832, though the population increase in the same eight-year span was only about 30 percent. Many of these good citizens had suffered as well as profited by Jacksonian policies, but it was easier to blame the suffering on Van Buren, who had been unfortunate enough to be in the White House when economic retribution came. Depression still lingered as Whigs and Democrats squared off, but few were the wiser for it, or less confident in their country's future. This was still an exciting, adolescent America in which it was fashionable one month to journey for miles to hear Emerson, Weld, or the Grimké sisters, and the next to see the latest marvel discovered by young P. T. Barnum, who had recently been exhibiting an aged Negro woman billed as the nurse of George Washington and alleged to be 161 years old. Equally popular were stump speakers, itinerant evangelists, and traveling medicine men with their herb cures and their local versions of Europe's phrenology and mesmerism. This was an America—for all its campaigning for free public schools, for shorter working hours, and for individual salvation—that worked from sunup to sundown and enjoyed few diversions. In such an atmosphere, political showmanship was as natural as the invention and propagation of tall tales. Both were part of the American way of life.

This showmanship was never better exemplified than in the campaign of 1840. Because they had no other choice, the Democrats renominated Van Buren, who had accepted for the North the economic policies of the Locofocos and for the South the constitutional principles of the Nullifiers. In this unnatural union the Whigs, bound neither by men nor doctrine, saw their own opportunity. With scant regard for party services, Clay was pointedly shelved and Webster was passed over in favor of the innocuous Harrison; and to give the ticket southern appeal John Tyler of Virginia, ex-Jacksonian Democrat and a Calhoun Nullifier still, was nominated for Vice-President. A belittling remark by a disappointed Clay supporter to the effect that Harrison's ambitions reached no higher than a barrel of hard cider and a log cabin gave the campaign its symbols. Soon log cabins and barrels of cider were everywhere while people who turned out to watch the fun sang lustily that "Tippecanoe and Tyler, too" would send down to everlasting defeat little Van who was a "used up man."

And so it happened. Harrison's popular majority was 140,000, his electoral preponderance almost four to one. The Whig hero carried both Jackson's Tennessee and Van Buren's New York, as well as traditionally Democratic Pennsylvania. Yet more significant than the magnitude of Harrison's victory, or even the fact that a majority of the American people were willing to trade principles for entertainment, were the seven thousand antislavery votes polled by James G. Birney. With these votes opposition to slavery became the cause of a national political party which under different names would continue to gain followers until its object was achieved.

Harrison's victory ended with the counting of the ballots. With no common policy or program to which all Whigs could adhere, the party quickly split into Clay and Webster factions. Clay, dominating the Senate, bullied the President into calling a special session of Congress to meet in June, 1841, but the State Department and with it the first round of infighting went to

Webster. It would not in fact be either of the Whig leaders who would gain the upper hand. Harrison, sixty-eight when he entered the White House and unaccustomed to the kind of life he was suddenly called upon to live, caught cold while personally shopping at the public market. The cold, neglected, turned to pneumonia and the old soldier died on April 4, 1841, just one month after his inauguration. Two days later Tyler took the presidential oath, and began the slow, tortuous journey that would take him back to the Democracy by way of Texas. It was a journey that would align him with the South and slavery against the North and abolition. Party lines would tend to merge with sectional as the single issue of slavery came steadily to dominate American life.

No administration—not even Van Buren's—had faced a more unhappy beginning. Again thwarted in his own ambition by the failure of his party to nominate him, Clay intended to control Tyler as he had meant to manipulate the more pliable Harrison. He intended it still, even after Tyler announced the retention of Harrison's Cabinet, for aside from Webster the members were or would be his partisans. Thomas Ewing, former Ohio Senator, at the head of the Treasury would be the key figure in Clay's scheme of things, but able, intelligent and dedicated John J. Crittenden of Kentucky, in the relatively untaxing post of Attorney General, would be still as he had been for more than a decade Clay's good right arm.

Between the imperious Kentuckian and the persuasive Webster, now recognized rivals for the Whig succession, stood the lean, hawk-nosed figure of John Tyler, who was not a Whig at all. An obstinate man, proud as Virginians were taught to be proud, and not a little vain, Tyler had entered politics under the aegis of the Jeffersonian state rights school, had gone all the way with the Nullifiers, and in spite of the place the Whigs had given him on their ticket, was at heart a Democrat still: a Democrat, moreover, who would rather be consistent than right.

When the members of the new Whig Congress gathered in

Washington toward the end of May, 1841, for the special session, Clay appeared to be in full control. He had a legislative program ready, designed in part to cope with the still lingering hard times and thus justify this early meeting of Congress, and in part to consolidate the Whig triumph. Although majorities were sometimes slim when sectional interests were touched upon, the components of Clay's program, one by one, were driven through. The Independent Treasury, in operation scarcely a year, was wiped from the statute books. The tariff, which under the Compromise of 1833 had only one year to go before the uniform 20 percent level was reached, was modified without upsetting the Compromise by imposing duties on articles previously free. Clay's favorite scheme to ensnare the West by distributing among the states the proceeds from the sale of the public lands was also enacted, but only with a qualification that distribution should cease if import duties rose above 20 percent, and a rider making permanent the pre-emption policy that had been periodically reaffirmed since 1830. The rider gave the squatter first option to buy at the established price of $1.25 an acre the land he may have occupied for years. In effect it established the principle of deferred payments, opening the public domain to those who had no money to buy until the land itself had earned it for them. The importance of this principle in the settlement of the West cannot be overestimated.

But the key measure of Clay's ambitious program was the re-establishment of a national bank. Called a "Fiscal Bank of the United States" because Tyler had used that curiously cryptic term, Clay's scheme sidestepped the constitutional objection that had been hurled at both its predecessor institutions by a location in the District of Columbia where the jurisdiction of Congress in such matters was not challenged. Otherwise it followed and improved upon the charter of the Second Bank of the United States. It was a statesmanlike measure and one that might have served the country well, had it been allowed to function. It was not. John Tyler, torn between his obligations to the party that elected him and his past opposition to a national bank, delayed decision as long as the Constitution allowed. Then on August 16, 1841, he vetoed the bill. The members of his Cabinet were disgusted and Clay was furious.

A new bank bill, designed to overcome what were believed to be the President's objections, was quickly drafted and shown to him by Webster. Although changes suggested by Tyler had been made, he again returned a veto when the new bill came to him for signature. Two days later the entire Cabinet, excepting only Daniel Webster, resigned, and the Whig majority in Congress read the President out of the party. Although the time before adjournment was short, a new Cabinet was nominated and confirmed by Democratic votes. It was a cabinet of Lilliputians with Webster a Gulliver at their head. He alone remained, not because he saw eye to eye with Tyler on domestic policies but because he believed that negotiations with Great Britain in which he was then engaged were too important for the nation's future to be trusted to other hands.

Relations between the two countries had in fact been worsening for a decade until they were now dangerously close to war; just how close Webster himself would not know for another week, for Palmerston's blunt assertion of the right to board American vessels in search of slavers, dated August 27, 1841, would not reach the State Department until after the adjournment. Fortunately the Melbourne government was supplanted in a matter of days by the Tory ministry of Sir Robert Peel, and the conciliatory Lord Aberdeen replaced the sword-rattling Palmerston in the Foreign Office.

Matters in dispute went back to the abolition of slavery in the British West Indies in 1833, and subsequent British pressure for emancipation in the United States; and to the case of the *Enterprise,* an American vessel storm-driven to Bermuda, where the slaves she carried were set free by British authorities because slavery was illegal on British soil. This British interest in American shipping by way of stamping out the slave trade was matched by American intervention in Canada to speed along in the name of liberty a rebellion against the Crown; and by the ease with which the states fell back upon their "sovereignty" when British investors sought to salvage something from the $150,000,000 they held in American state bonds. There were border disputes at both ends of the long frontier: in the east, where the contested boundary between Maine and New Brunswick had brought rival lumbering interests into armed conflict in the "Aroostook War" of 1839; and in Oregon, where the joint occupation that had served both countries well for more than twenty years was beginning to chafe the land-hungry Americans.

It was the aftermath of the Canadian rebellion that had brought about the immediate crisis. The uprising had occurred late in 1837 in the lower peninsula of Ontario. The rebel leader, William L. Mackenzie, set up his headquarters in Buffalo, and proceeded to swell the ranks of his "army" with unemployed Americans. Rebel forces bivouacked on Navy Island across the Niagara River were supplied from the New York side by the American-owned steamer *Caroline*. Canadian authorities ordered the vessel destroyed, and destroyed she was, but unfortunately the deed took place in New York waters and a New York citizen was killed in the process. The rebellion collapsed soon afterward. The whole affair was only a distant memory in November, 1840, when a former Canadian deputy, Alexander McLeod, was heard to boast in a Lockport, New York, bar that he had helped to burn the *Caroline*. He was promptly arrested, and in due time indicted for murder.

At this point the two governments stepped in, the British to take official responsibility for the destruction of the *Caroline* and to demand McLeod's release; the American to protest its own lack of jurisdiction over a crime committed against a state. By the time Webster succeeded Forsyth as Secretary of State, the British government was threatening war if anything happened to McLeod and British public opinion was ready to back the government. Webster conceded that the official character of the act gave to all connected with it immunity from prosecution, but Governor Seward made no such concession and the trial went on as scheduled. The most Webster could do was to provide McLeod with counsel, in the person of Attorney General Crittenden.

Tension was eased early in October when McLeod was acquitted on the strength of a belated alibi for the night in question. But another Bahama slave case soon had the two countries at loggerheads once more, and northern and southern Congressmen at one another's throats. In the midst of the most acrimonious debate yet heard on slavery, Lord Aberdeen made known his intention to send to America a special envoy with full powers to treat on all outstanding issues. The envoy was to be Alexander Baring, Lord Ashburton, whose banking connections had brought him into long and friendly association with America and whose American wife was a further hostage to the success of his mission. Still another, and perhaps the greatest, of his assets was Daniel Webster, who was personally and politically indebted to the house of Baring.

The slavery debate was still in progress when Ashburton reached Washington in April, 1842, with British conduct in the case of the brig *Creole* furnishing the immediate text. The *Creole* had been carrying a cargo of surplus slaves from Virginia to Louisiana when the Negroes had seized the ship and brought her to the sanctuary of the British flag in the Bahamas. A few of the mutineers had been arrested for murder, but most had been allowed to vanish into freedom and none at all had been surrendered to American authorities. In Congress Joshua Giddings, speaking for his own abolitionist constituents in Ohio and for the antislavery forces the country over, excused the British action and condemned slavery. For this he drew upon himself the censure of the House—a censure the more gratifying because it was really meant for the otherwise invulnerable Adams. The ex-President had earlier offered a petition of certain citizens of Haverhill, Massachusetts, asking the dissolution of a Union that condoned human bondage. For the next ten days, Adams was unmuzzled because a motion for censure had been made and he spoke therefore in his own defense. He could not be called to order, and he took full advantage of this unfamiliar freedom to so overwhelm, annihilate, and destroy his foes that the southerners were glad to drop the charges in order to quiet the old man's acid tongue. Giddings was less formidable, but the censure strengthened both the man and his cause. Giddings had promptly resigned his seat and was now back in Ohio's Western Reserve facing a special election that would return him to Congress with the all but unanimous approval of his constituents.

The settlements reached under the Webster-Ashburton Treaty were principally remarkable for the good temper in which they were negotiated, and for the clearly implicit desire of both governments to stop squabbling and be friends. The Maine boundary was settled by a compromise line; both the United States and Canada were guaranteed free navigation of all border waters; and each party agreed to police its own ships in an effort to stamp out the slave trade. But nothing was done about debts; the old and bitterly contested question of impressment was not mentioned because Ashburton's instructions forbade it; the right of search and seizure claimed by Britain was passed over; the *Caroline* case was allowed to slip into limbo without further action; Oregon was set aside for a future negotiation; and the *Creole* controversy was acknowledged only in the insertion of a mutual extradition clause. Aside from the Maine boundary (and many thought Webster gave up too much there), the treaty actually changed things very little if at all. What it did do was to bring Britain and the United States closer together, and make easier friendly settlement of all outstanding matters at some future time.

The truth was that Britain and America were coming to need each other as they never had before. Thanks to increased acreage consequent upon depression-stimulated migration, the West now had grain in greater quantity than she could sell and was suffering the inevitable price decline. Britain, on the other hand, had been shaken by a succession of bad harvests, and was almost at the point of modifying her corn laws to permit the importation of the American surplus. The West would then need better transportation to the Atlantic ports. Railroads were beginning to prove their worth in competition with the canals still feverishly being built, and cheap British rails might solve the problem. Cyrus McCormick's reaper, years in the perfecting, was being manufactured on a commercial scale to swell still more the harvest of western wheat. In helping to provide a market for this surplus, the antislavery leaders saw an opportunity to strengthen the area in which lay their own long-term hopes and they prepared for a brief interval to make common cause with southern slaveholders; for the same free trade that would benefit the cotton planters would also mightily promote western growth, and with it the political power that would ultimately destroy the hated institution. Men like Garrison, who had called upon the North to secede from a compact that protected slavery, and would soon inspire the American Antislavery Society to pronounce the Constitution of the United States, in the words of Isaiah, "a covenant with death and an agreement with Hell," belonged to an adolescent past. The antislavery movement had ceased to be a crusade; it had become a party, seeking its ends through the familiar channels of politics.

The tariff of 1842—the "Black Tariff" southern cotton planters called it—was not a fair test of sentiment on the issue. It was a political knife thrust into John Tyler's back by Henry Clay, and twisted by Tyler himself, possible only because of the still persisting hard times and the desperate condition of the Treasury. Clay used his control of the Whig majorities in both houses of Congress to hold up all revenue bills until the President in desperation asked an increase in duties to meet the necessary expenses of government. A bill prepared by Buffalo's Millard Fillmore was then passed, to which Clay's distribution scheme was again attached. Tyler unwarily based his veto on that point, and so had no excuse for another veto when the same bill came back to him without the rider. Western Whigs were reluctant; some southern Whigs did not go along at all. But Democratic Senators James Buchanan of Pennsylvania and Silas Wright of New York voted for the tariff, thereby committing the northern wing of the party to protection and publicly ratifying the dissolution of the North-South alliance. As the price of cotton, slowly climbing since 1837, tumbled to an average of 6.2 cents for 1843—the lowest it had ever been up to that time—Calhoun resigned his Senate seat to campaign for the Democratic nomination against Van Buren, whose hat had been in the ring since his defeat in 1840.

Tyler was now torn between the Democratic factions as he had once been torn between Democrats and Whigs. For the North he had signed the tariff of 1842; for the South, where his heart still lay, he would now annex Texas. It was in part a matter of political expediency, but in a deeper sense it was an economic and social necessity if the institution of slavery, in which Tyler believed as firmly as did Calhoun, was to be preserved and with it the economy of cotton and the southern way of life. Texas, if it was not absorbed by the United States and that without delay, would almost inevitably fall into the orbit of Great Britain, whose interests were very different from those of the South. As the first and still the greatest industrial nation in the world, a steady supply of customers was more important to Britain than cheap labor, and customers meant free men with money in their pockets. It was in part to make up for the rising cost of agricultural production in her own West Indian colonies since the Emancipation Act of 1833 and in part to enlarge the American market for her manufactures that British policy avowedly looked toward ultimate emancipation in the United States. Should she acquire hegemony over Texas, or even a strong treaty interest there, she could secure the abolition of slavery in that country. Peel had explained as much to Parliament soon after he became Prime Minister in 1842, and Aberdeen had repeated the explanation to delegates—including Americans—attending a world convention of abolitionists in London the following summer. For the time being Tyler did nothing to counteract the British position, but late in 1843, after Webster had been succeeded in the State Department by Judge Abel P. Upshur of Virginia, the President stated the case for annexation of Texas. Van Buren Democrats had meanwhile supplanted Clay Whigs in control of Congress and a sectional battle loomed in which not Texas but slavery would be the issue.

Unmoved by the clamor of extremists on either side, Upshur drafted a treaty of annexation, persuaded Sam Houston, serving his second term as President of Texas, that the treaty would be ratified by the necessary two-thirds of the Senate, and was awaiting the arrival of a Texan envoy with authority to sign the document when fate intervened. On February 28, 1844, a gun aboard the new steam battleship *Princeton* exploded while the ship was being displayed to a group of distinguished visitors on a Potomac cruise. Among the dead were Upshur and Secretary of the Navy Thomas W. Gilmer; those narrowly escaping death included Senator Benton and the President himself. All work on the Texas treaty halted until the Cabinet could be reconstituted. Calhoun, already withdrawn from the presidential contest, went into the State Department for the dual purpose of completing the annexation of Texas and reopening the Oregon negotiations. The South Carolinian took over the office on April 1, 1844. The Texas treaty was signed on the twelfth but was held up for ten days while an attempt was made to appease Mexico.

The new Secretary, catching up on official correspondence, found on his desk a letter from the newly arrived British Minister, Richard Pakenham, transmitting Aberdeen's assurances that Britain had no intention of interfering in Texas provided no one else did. Obsessed as he was with the problem of the South, Calhoun made of his answer a detailed defense of slavery. The Pakenham letter went to the Senate along with the treaty and other documents relating to Texas. Though it was confidential, the letter was promptly leaked to the press by Senator Benjamin Tappan of Ohio, elder brother of the two New York abolitionists,

Arthur and Lewis Tappan, who were also the financial angels of the Liberty Party. It appeared in William Cullen Bryant's New York *Evening Post,* house organ of the Locofoco Democrats, on April 27. That same day saw the publication in the Washington *Globe* of a letter from Van Buren opposing both annexation and the extension of slavery. The *National Intelligencer,* on the Whig side, simultaneously published a similar letter from Clay equivocating but opposing immediate annexation. With the public thus fully aroused, the Texas treaty could only be debated in terms of the extension of slavery, and in those terms it would most assuredly be defeated. It was, by a vote of more than two to one, with even Benton, who had been for a dozen years the spokesman for western Democracy, now in opposition.

Not Van Buren and Benton alone, but the party itself was changing. In its amplified concern for the welfare of the common man, the Democracy was coming closer to its twentieth-century equivalent, even though by so doing it took for the moment a sectional rather than a national stand. The Locofoco wing of the Democracy, born of labor unrest in the 1830's, was now the authentic voice of the party in the North, and through Van Buren, with his uncanny sensitivity to every popular breeze, it dominated the party councils. The Locofoco doctrines had also been read into the law. Chief Justice Taney in the Charles River Bridge case (1837) had subordinated the rights of contract to the needs of the people; and Chief Justice Lemuel Shaw of Massachusetts, Whig though he was, had upheld the right of labor to organize and to strike (Commonwealth *v.* Hunt, 1842). In the northern industrial states labor had become a political force not to be ignored with impunity. Yet it was precisely this class of factory workers, artisans, and unskilled laborers whose condition the South was fond of comparing unfavorably with the lot of her slaves, and so could never admit to places of responsibility and power.

On the intellectual side socialistic doctrines that had arisen in

Europe out of the world-wide depression of the 1830's had been propagated in America chiefly by men associated with the left-wing Democracy: William Leggett and Parke Godwin of the New York *Evening Post,* and Albert Brisbane, propagator in America of the Fourierist doctrine of association. In Europe the reform movement would achieve the abolition of serfdom, and through Marx and Engels would give birth to doctrines that would long outlive the age that spawned them. In America, as we have seen, much of the reforming zeal was channeled into the antislavery cause by the 1840's, and any politician who accepted the support of the political radicals had necessarily to come to terms with the abolitionists.

He had also to countenance, if not actively support, such belated drives for legal equality as that represented by the People's Party of Rhode Island. Of all the states in the Union, only Rhode Island had not changed her constitution since colonial days. Though she had been the first industrial state, her political institutions had lagged far behind her economic development with a franchise still restricted to a small body of freeholders. Years of agitation resulted in a convention, held without sanction of law or the blessing of the constituted authorities in the fall of 1841; and a constitution submitted to and ratified by the people—those who could as well as those who could not vote. Under this unauthorized constitution, Thomas Wilson Dorr was elected governor in the spring of 1842. Dorr himself was in discreet, self-imposed exile, but with the vocal and financial backing of the New York Democracy and the more direct support of a band of volunteers, he prepared to assume the power voted to him by the disfranchised majority of his native state. At the demand of the legitimate government of Rhode Island, Tyler intervened with federal troops, the rebellion collapsed, and Dorr was sentenced to prison for life—a sentence of which he served only twelve months before being released under a general amnesty act passed by the legislature. But Dorr's cause was firmly identified with the Locofoco Democracy, with Van Buren, with all those Democrats who believed as Jefferson had believed in the worth and dignity of man.

With each new move of the northern Democracy toward the egalitarian side of the Jeffersonian tradition, the southern Democrats intrenched themselves more deeply behind the barrier of state sovereignty. The rift between North and South had become a chasm by the time the Democratic Convention met in Baltimore toward the end of May, 1844. Though Van Buren had the largest single block of votes, he had not enough to prevent re-enactment of the two-thirds rule, or enough to secure a nomination under it. Neither had Lewis Cass, who was the favorite of the West; nor Calhoun, who was still backed by southern conservatives despite his own withdrawal. In this situation James K. Polk, who had carefully groomed himself and his supporters for just this role, emerged as a "dark horse" candidate. Jackson's endorsement had been secured in advance. As a slaveholder himself he was acceptable to the Calhoun faction; and his party services to Van Buren as Speaker of the House could not be denied. Moreover, he was prepared to run on the same platform Van Buren had endorsed in 1840, which gave the New York delegation no excuse to reject him. As the Polk movement gained strength, Van Buren's floor manager read a letter from the ex-President withdrawing his name, and Polk was quickly made the unanimous choice of the convention. Silas Wright was then nominated for the Vice-Presidency, an honor he learned of minutes later in the Capitol, where Samuel F. B. Morse received the message over his magnetic telegraph, operated in Baltimore by his partner, Alfred Vail. Wright declined the honor, and the word was sent back the way it had come. The delegates in Baltimore would not believe it, however, until they had sent a deputation to Washington to learn it from Wright's own lips. They then nominated Senator George M. Dallas of Pennsylvania, whose father had been Secretary of the Treasury under Madison.

After Tyler, the Whigs were only too glad to come back to Clay, though his stand against annexation would inevitably make

Texas a dominant issue in the campaign. Polk's slogan—the re-annexation of Texas and the re-occupation of Oregon—was specious on both counts, for neither had ever really been American soil, but it served to enlist antislavery as well as proslavery expansionists behind the Democrats. Polk won, but New York, which he carried by a bare 5,000 votes, was the measure of his victory. Birney, still the Liberty Party candidate, had taken 16,000 votes in New York, more than enough of them from nominal Whigs to have elected Clay. So Polk, the slaveholding expansionist who was pledged to annex Texas, was in fact elected by the votes of New York abolitionists who were almost willing to agree with Garrison that annexation would of itself dissolve the Union.

The sectional differences were indeed so pronounced by this date that even the churches, after long and turbulent travail, had begun the historic division into northern and southern congregations—into those that held slavery to be a sin and those who believed the institution to be ordained by God. Men were searching their own souls and taking sides in a way they had not done before. In December of 1844, when Congress met for the short session, the same men who had accepted the gag rule twelve months earlier now rescinded it by a strictly sectional vote that had nothing to do with party.

Tyler meanwhile had accepted Polk's election as a mandate to annex Texas, but he did not propose to let his Democratic successor have the credit for this favorite measure of his own. Time was pressing, with Britain and France both active in the Texan capital and Houston by no means cold to their blandishments. A joint resolution providing that the rejected treaty should be the law of union between Texas and the United States was drafted, rammed through a divided Congress, and signed by the President shortly before the expiration of his term. It was dispatched to Texas with suitable assurances as to the disposition of army and navy units in case Mexico should offer more than vocal objections, and a convention in Texas ratified on July 4, 1845.

The South used the brief preponderance Texas gave her in the Senate to make one final, unsuccessful bid for a political alliance with the West, but reduction of the tariff was no longer a primary goal. She required now above all else the armor of intervention by the Federal Government to protect her domestic institution from the onslaught of the antislavery forces. For this protection she was prepared to return benefits in kind, but her position in the new administration was weak. Wisely, Polk had steered clear of both Democratic factions, giving the State Department to the pedestrian Buchanan instead of retaining Calhoun or offering it to Wright. The War Department went to William L. Marcy, once of the Albany Regency but now spokesman for the anti-Van Buren Democrats in New York. The Treasury was given to Robert J. Walker, Pennsylvania-born Mississippian who had been the outstanding champion of Texas in the Senate and was now the foremost advocate in public life (Calhoun alone excepted) of the free-trade policy. Van Buren went into opposition with all the following he could still command. Calhoun returned to the Senate where he stood alone, neither for nor against the administration, but hopeful to the last that the archaic southern way of life might somehow be preserved by legislative fiat in a world of change.

The perennial offer of southern politicians to the West now included, in addition to a further liberalization of public-land policy, the prospect of a European market for western grain, and improved transportation to Atlantic ports and eastern centers of trade. The tariff of 1846, drafted by Walker and steered through Congress behind the scenes by the Secretary of the Treasury himself, was the nearest approach to free trade the country had known since Jefferson's time. At many points, on its hazardous legislative journey, it was challenged, modified, bitterly attacked; but in the end it passed. In the eyes of Americans and Englishmen alike, the Walker Tariff was bound up with repeal of the corn laws, and its passage was deliberately delayed until word came by courier from Halifax, where the enterprising James

Gordon Bennett of the New York *Herald* had arranged to intercept the mail steamers, that the British part of the tacit bargain had indeed been made good. The tariff was then passed by a combination of southern and western votes, easily in the House but in the Senate only after cracking the party whip. Even then it required the casting vote of the Vice-President to break a final tie and destroy the protective policy so dear to his own state of Pennsylvania.

To complete the bargain, the Senate passed a bill to graduate the price of the public lands, and to improve at the expense of the Federal Government the navigation of the Mississippi, Missouri, Arkansas, and Ohio rivers. The river-improvement scheme came out of an internal improvements convention held in Memphis, Tennessee, and presided over by Calhoun. Navigable waterways, argued that prince of rationalizers, should now be treated as in the category of lakes and inland seas, affecting the commerce of too many states to be considered as anything less than a national concern. It was a far-reaching concession, but a necessary one, for despite the momentary predominance of the South in the Senate, and of the North in the House, the West would in time have the political strength to impose her will on both. It was a bid to wean the West from her abolitionist leanings by tying her in interest to the South, through whose waters her commerce would pass to New Orleans or to future railheads at strategic points along the river system.

In the House of Representatives, where each member thought in terms of the reception he would get when he returned home to his district, the inland waterways bill was dissected and reassembled with many changes. It was no longer confined to the four rivers originally mentioned, all parts of a single system. Indeed, if the members had had their way, it would have included every creek and bayou and dry canyon in the land. It went back to the Senate a typical Rivers and Harbors bill of the pork-barrel type that would become far more familiar to a later generation. The Senate accepted the changes, but the President did not. The bill was vetoed, and in reprisal the House tabled the graduation bill.

The truth was that the South was already too much in the minority to deliver the necessary votes, even on a matter her own chosen leaders felt to be of vital concern to her. The West had helped to pass the Walker Tariff as much for herself as for the South. With the Great Lakes already at her command, and the prospect of easy access to cheap British rails, there was no reason why she should tie herself to any southern scheme of river transportation. Her future lay in commercial alliance with the North and East, where the centers of domestic population lay and whence she could tap the shorter great circle routes to Europe, now that steam was replacing sail to overcome the natural advantages offered by the Gulf Stream and the trade winds of the South.

It was Oregon that finally tipped the scales in favor of the North and abolition, overbalancing in influence both Texas and the southwestern lands that would come as a consequence of the war with Mexico. For a generation Oregon had been little more than a fur-trading post, since 1821 dominated by the Hudson's Bay Company and virtually governed by the company's factor, Dr. John McLoughlin. The trappers and Yankee skippers were followed in the early 1830's by missionaries like Jason Lee and Marcus Whitman, and around the missions in the fertile valleys of the Columbia and the Willamette, cultivated lands began to spread in widening circles. In 1836, Washington Irving's story of the first American settlement on the Columbia, *Astoria,* touched off new interest in the far northwest. Then in 1842 Whitman and a lone companion journeyed on horseback from Oregon to plead for American intervention, and the "Oregon fever" set in.

Oregon became the new frontier for the northern states just as Texas had been for a decade the goal of southern expansionism. Independence, Missouri, already the starting point of the Santa Fe Trail, was soon crowded with chastened easterners, ready to trade the furniture and other useless items they had carried thus far for the provisions and equipment they would need to complete their trek. Long wagon trains guided by hunters and trappers threaded their way through the lands of the Sioux and the Blackfeet. Benton abandoned Texas to plead for Oregon and California. Young Parkman braved the wilderness to observe the Oregon Trail at first hand. In the years 1843–1845 some five thousand Americans moved to Oregon, enough of them from New England to give a Yankee twang to the speech and a Yankee twist to the thought of their new home. Despite Polk's sword-rattling "fifty-four-forty or fight" neither the American nor the British people had any stomach for a war that even more than in 1775 or 1812 would have seemed fratricidal to both sides. The 49th parallel, extended from the Lake of the Woods to the Rockies by the Treaty of 1818, was continued west to the sea. Brigham Young had brought the Latter-day Saints to the shores of Great Salt Lake, where the new Canaan was rising; and California, beautiful, deceptive magnet then as she is today, would soon revolt from Mexico and offer herself, as Texas had before her, to the United States. Polk's war with Mexico would fill the gap between old and new frontiers.

Although its ordeal by fire still lay ahead, the United States by 1846 had indeed become a nation. The number of her states had increased from sixteen in 1800, totaling less than half a million square miles, to twenty-six with an aggregate area three times as great, and territories not yet ready for statehood swelling the total still more. The five and a quarter million Americans of 1800 had grown to twenty million, with growing diversity of racial stock, of cultural background, of religious faith. In terms of national wealth, of industry, of agriculture, of science, even of art and literature, 1800 was a remote and primitive age. In the crucible of time the external conflicts had been or were soon to be resolved. The colonial dependence on Europe was gone, and the United States of America was on the way to becoming a world power with all the responsibility, all the potency for evil or for good, that term implies.

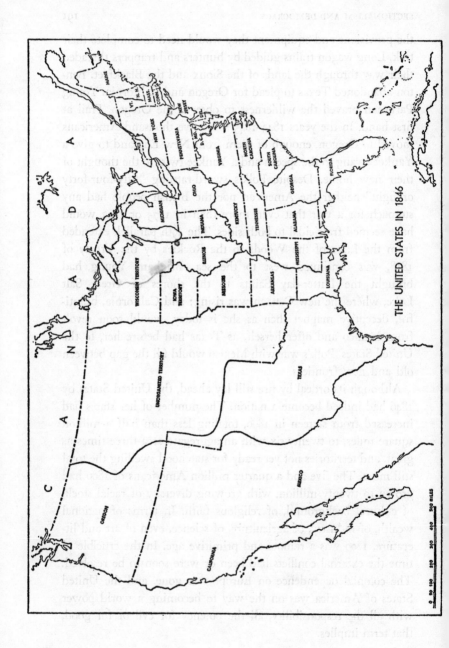

THE UNITED STATES IN 1846

Politically the period of almost half a century between the Kentucky Resolutions and the Oregon settlement was character-ized by sectional strife and sectional compromise. First one re-gion, then another, would uphold the powers of the general government or fall back upon the sovereignty of the states, ac-cording to whether a contemplated course of action was felt to be in her interest or to her disadvantage. The truth was that the United States of the nineteenth century was in many respects a forerunner of the great powers of the modern era—a nation occu-pying a vast territory, with a heterogeneous economy in which measures helpful to one interest might well be hurtful to another. France and Britain still relied on the exploitation of alien peoples in colonial empires; Spain and Russia were still sunk in feudal-ism; Germany and Italy had not yet been born. Only in America was the typical economy of the twentieth century being worked out, with all the false starts, mistakes, and growing pains that are the normal lot of the pioneer. Had it not been for the moral issue raised by the existence of slavery, American sectionalism would undoubtedly have worked itself out earlier than it did. As it was, the crisis for the South came when she began to regard the slave system as permanent. No society can endure, to paraphrase Lin-coln, half static and half dynamic, and so the conflict that might otherwise have been avoided became irrepressible.

In the context of 1846 the internal struggle was capable of only one ultimate solution. Slavery in the nineteenth century was an anachronism, its defenders destined to be overwhelmed and dis-credited by the forces—economic as well as moral—that were molding the modern world. With the Walker Tariff and Polk's veto of the internal improvement bill that might still have joined something of interest between West and South, the doom of the "cotton kingdom" was sealed even before it reached its apogee. The unity for which the South had been striving since the Mis-souri Compromise was near at hand, but it was a unity that could now achieve no more than military defeat.

The dogma of state sovereignty had been kept alive, in spite of the nationalistic forces released by the second war with Britain, by the urgent need of a substantial agricultural interest to protect itself against a more profitable and more aggressive industrialism. The slave-based nature of the agricultural interest gave a moral character to the industrial challenge, but the contest did not differ in essence from the upheavals then beginning in Europe out of which would come the end of serfdom, and ultimately the concept of a balanced economy in which subsidies—to agriculture as well as to industry—would be freely used as instruments of policy. In the Kentucky Resolutions, Jefferson had been responding not to his own times alone but to 2,000 years of history which had shown men forever grasping for power and power as universally corrupting men. The kind of particularism represented by state rights became obsolete when the advance of the industrial revolution concentrated physical power at the only governmental level with resources adequate to support the new technology, and enough disinterestedness to seek reconciliation of conflicting interests.

That point had been reached in the United States by the middle 1840's. Neither tyranny nor love of liberty was dead, but both took new forms in keeping with the changing times. The preponderance of physical and moral strength now lay with those who believed, with Jackson, Webster, and Abraham Lincoln—then about to enter Congress from Illinois—that the United States was indeed one nation, indivisible, committed by all her heritage from the past and all her faith in the future to seek liberty and justice for all in a society without barriers of race or creed.

Bibliographical Essay

IN THE ABSENCE of footnote citations, the scholarly reader of such a volume as this has a right to know something of the sources on which it is based. At the same time the more casual reader, if he has been inspired by what he has read to pursue the subject more deeply, is entitled to some guidance in the selection of further reading. For both purposes the literature of American history—specifically that portion of it lying between 1800 and 1846—may be most profitably discussed in categories. Many of the works mentioned, and often whole groups of sources, will not be available to the average reader. They belong rather to the dedicated scholar who is willing to travel from collection to collection, to use photostats and microfilms, to forget union hours and to ignore fatigue. But in this world of easy communciation, interlibrary loans, and inexpensive reprints, anyone who has the will may delve deeply and profitably into the story of the American past, with emphasis wherever he himself may choose to place it.

I. PUBLIC DOCUMENTS. The various branches of government, federal, state and local, generate and publish every year enormous quantities of material, much of it worthless from the historical point of view, but some of it of the greatest value. The debates in Congress, more illuminating and wide-ranging than they have since become for an age that delegates too much to committees, may be followed in the *Annals of Congress* (March 3, 1789-May 27, 1824), the *Register of Debates* (December 6, 1824-October 16, 1837), and the *Congressional Globe,* which begins with the session of Congress opening December 2, 1833. The official *Journals* of House and Senate are primarily valuable for the record of voting and for the text of resolutions and amendments. The multivolume *American State Papers,* in nine subject-matter series including Foreign Relations, Military Affairs, Indian Affairs, Public Lands, and Manufactures, carry into the 1830's, containing the type of material that later came to be issued as House and Senate Documents—predominantly committee reports, reports from the executive departments, and hearings. Many of these same documents also appear as appendices in the *Annals* and the *Register.* Similar documents exist at the state level, but are not uniform in coverage, or readily accessible. There is a convenient collection of *State Documents on Federal Relations* edited by Herman V. Ames (1906).

The *Diplomatic Correspondence of the United States,* and *Treaties and Other International Acts of the United States,* both issued by the State Department in continuing series, are indispensable for the study of foreign relations. The State Department also publishes the *Territorial Papers of the United States,* containing both official documents and correspondence dealing with the affairs of each territory before its admission to statehood. For Texas, which never was a territory, the same purpose is served in part by the *Diplomatic Correspondence of the Republic of Texas,* edited by George P. Garrison and published by the American Historical Association as supplements to its annual reports of 1907 and 1908. Court records, beginning with those of the Supreme Court, often have social, political, and economic value as well as legal significance. *Messages and Papers of the Presidents,* compiled by J. D. Richardson, is a standard source that has gone through various editions, but covers strictly public communications.

II. Diaries, Correspondence, and Personal Papers. Letters, diaries, business and plantation records, and similar papers constitute one of the most extensive and most valuable of historical sources, much of it still to be mined for its cultural, psychological, economic and political wealth as well as for its historical significance. Too much of this material remains in manuscript and so is of limited accessibility, but there are major collections in print or in process of publication. Inevitably the most available papers are those of men identified with politics. *The Papers of Thomas Jefferson,* superbly edited by Julian P. Boyd and beautifully printed by the Princeton University Press, have not yet reached the period of Jefferson's Presidency, but older editions though incomplete are readily available, notably those of P. L. Ford, 10 vols., 1892-99 (reissued in 12 vols., 1904-05); and A. A. Lipscomb and A. E. Bergh, 20 vols., 1903-04. In *The Complete Jefferson* (1943) Saul Padover brings all of Jefferson's systematic writings together. Another convenient selection of Jefferson material is the *Adams-Jefferson Letters,* a wide-ranging fifty-year correspondence edited by Lester J. Cappon (2 vols., 1959). The *Writings of James Madison,* edited by Gaillard Hunt (9 vols., 1900) includes the bulk of the Madison papers. In contrast, the *Writings of James Monroe,* edited by S. Hamilton (7 vols., 1901), is of little value, a circumstance for which Monroe himself rather than his editor must be held responsible. Following Monroe in the presidential succession comes John Quincy Adams whose famous diary, published by his son as the *Memoirs of John Quincy Adams* (12 vols., 1874-77), is a running commentary on American history in the making from John Adams to Polk. Though its judgments are frequently caustic, it is an invaluable source for the entire Jefferson-Jackson period. A single-volume condensation by Allan Nevins is excellent for all but the most exacting needs. The *Writings of J. Q. Adams,* edited by W. C. Ford, was never completed, stopping short with the seventh volume, which comes up to 1823. It is valuable, however, for the period it covers. *The Corre-*

spondence of Andrew Jackson, edited by J. S. Bassett (7 vols., 1926-35), is not complete but is still of major importance. Van Buren is less well documented, with only an occasional letter in the published papers of those to whom he wrote, or printed in one of the historical journals. The same is true for Harrison, Tyler, and Polk, though the *Diary of James K. Polk during his presidency, 1845-1849,* M. M. Quaife, ed. (4 vols., 1910), is of first importance. Again Professor Nevins has supplied a useful single-volume edition.

Of those who did not make the White House but sometimes overshadowed those who did, the *Writings of Albert Gallatin,* Henry Adams, ed. (3 vols., 1879), is tantalizingly incomplete. A new edition of the *Papers of Henry Clay,* edited by James F. Hopkins and Mary W. M. Hargreaves, is in process of publication by the University of Kentucky Press; but only the first volume, covering the years 1797 through 1814, has so far been issued. For the later years, the student must still consult the older *Works of Henry Clay,* Calvin Colton, ed. (10 vols., 1904). A new edition of the *Papers of John C. Calhoun* is also in process; of this the first volume, 1801-17, skillfully edited by the late Robert L. Meriwether, appeared in 1959. Older editions of Calhoun papers include the *Works of John C. Calhoun,* Richard K. Crallé, ed. (6 vols., 1854-57); *Correspondence of John C. Calhoun,* edited by J. Franklin Jameson and published as Vol. II of the Annual Report of the American Historical Association for 1899; and a volume of *Correspondence Addressed to John C. Calhoun, 1837-1849,* Chauncey S. Boucher and Robert P. Brooks, eds., Annual Report of the American Historical Association, 1929. The National Edition of the *Writings and Speeches of Daniel Webster* (18 vols., 1903) approaches completeness for the systematic pieces, while much of the more revealing private correspondence will be found in C. H. Van Tyne's edition of the *Letters of Daniel Webster* (1902) and scattered through various journals and in volumes primarily devoted to the papers of others. The first five volumes of the *Writings of Sam Houston,* edited by Amelia W.

Williams and Eugene C. Barker, cover the period from 1813 through the annexation of Texas.

In more specialized areas, *Jacobin and Junto* (1931), edited by Charles Warren, gives a colorful Republican commentary on New England Federalism by way of selections from the diary of Dr. Nathaniel Ames, whose brother, Fisher Ames, was the darling of the Essex Junto. Another New England Republican comments on his times from his post as United States Consul at Bordeaux during the Napoleonic period in *A Yankee Jeffersonian: Selections from the Diary and Letters of William Lee of Massachusetts written from 1796 to 1840,* Mary Lee Mann, ed. (1958). Other documents dealing with the separatist movements of Jefferson's time were collected by ex-President J. Q. Adams in the course of a bitter newspaper controversy with surviving adherents of the Junto, and were published as *Documents Relating to New England Federalism,* Henry Adams, ed. (1877). The story of the Burr-Hamilton duel is told through the original documents in *Interview in Weehawken,* edited by Harold C. Syrett and Jean G. Cooke (1960), a form of publication that could well be extended in many directions with profit to the scholar and pleasure to the general reader. Professor Syrett is also responsible for a small but very useful volume of Jackson documents, *Andrew Jackson: His Contribution to the American Tradition* (1953). *The Correspondence of Nicholas Biddle dealing with National Affairs, 1807-1844,* edited by R. C. McGrane (1919), is far from complete but is nevertheless essential to an understanding of the Bank fight of the 1830's. The compound of emotionalism and moral dedication that swayed northern antislavery leaders colors almost every page of the *Letters of Theodore Dwight Weld, Angelina Grimké Weld, and Sarah Grimké, 1822-1844,* Gilbert H. Barnes and Dwight L. Dumond, eds. (2 vols., 1934) and Dumond's *Letters of James Gillespie Birney, 1831-1857* (2 vols., 1938). There is a delightful mingling of cultural, social, political, and economic history in the *Diary of Philip Hone, 1828-1851,*

Allan Nevins, ed. (1936), which enlarges upon the two-volume edition by the same editor in 1927.

There is much of cultural history in the *Life, Letters and Journals of George Ticknor,* edited by Anna Ticknor and G. S. Hilliard (2 vols., 1876); and still more in Ralph Waldo Emerson's *Journals* (10 vols., 1909-1914). Emerson's *Letters,* edited by Ralph L. Rusk (6 vols., 1939), provide many insights into both literary and intellectual history for the 1830's and 1840's. A great deal of material originating with lesser figures has also been published in book form, while the historical journals, especially those sponsored by state historical societies, are filled with invaluable documents of this kind. Despite this extensive publication of sources in the last few years, however, the scholar working in the 1800-46 period will still find it necessary to go to numerous manuscript collections, of which those of the Library of Congress are outstanding. Among the more familiar Library of Congress collections used in the preparation of this volume were the Jefferson papers, Madison papers, Van Buren papers, Jackson papers, and Polk papers.

III. CONTEMPORARY NARRATIVES OF TRAVEL AND SOCIAL COMMENTARY. The America of the early nineteenth century attracted observers of every kind, from the merely curious to the professional writer who expected his reflections to pay off; from the trained subject-matter specialist to the businessman or diplomat who could not resist the temptation to add his rivulet of comments to the growing flood. There was in all this a sense of participating in something of historical importance, not always consciously recognized but implicit in most of the writings that fall into this category. Psychologically as well as politically the United States was a new nation, dominating a new world whose resources had only begun to be suspected, and upholding social doctrines at variance with those accepted by most of the civilized countries of the day. Too many books fall into this category for individual mention of more than a representative handful. Among useful guides are Jane L. Mesick, *The English Traveller in America, 1785-1835* (1922); and Frank Monaghan, *French Travellers in the United States, 1765-1932* (1933). Convenient anthologies include *America through British Eyes*, edited by Allan Nevins (1948); and *A Mirror for Americans: Life and Manners in the United States, 1790-1870, as Recorded by American Travellers*, Warren S. Tyson, ed. (3 vols., 1952).

For wilderness exploration the journals of Lewis and Clark remain fresh and fascinating. There have been many editions, beginning with that edited by Nicholas Biddle, with Jefferson's own introduction, in 1814 down to the excellent abridgment by Bernard De Voto in 1953. Another perennial mine of information and opinion is Alexis de Tocqueville's *Democracy in America*, the best edition in English translation being that of Phillips Bradley (1945). The notebooks kept by de Tocqueville on his American tour in 1831-32 have been edited by J. P. Mayer and published under the title *Journey to America* (1959). Margaret Bayard Smith, *The First Forty Years of Washington Society*, Gaillard Hunt, ed. (1906), is a well-chosen selection from a large collection of chatty and informative letters from one who knew well the people and events of which she wrote. Harriet Martineau's *Society in America* (2 vols., 1837) is both more objective and more critical than Mrs. Smith but lacks the leaven of intimacy that gives to the latter's work its quality of credibility. More critical still are Charles Dickens' *American Notes* (1842), which sometimes descend to the level of caricature. More conventional travel narratives are those of Thomas Hamilton, *Men and Manners in America* (2 vols., 1833); Joseph J. Gurney, *A Journey in North America* (1841); and Charles Lyell, *Travels in North America* (2 vols., 1845).

IV. AUTOBIOGRAPHIES AND MEMOIRS. Unlike diaries, correspondence and contemporary narratives, the autobiography or personal memoir is generally written long after the events described in it, after memory has dulled and hindsight has added a prescience that transcends actuality. Such documents are not to be discounted as source materials, but they must be used with caution and critical judgment.

Jefferson left a short autobiographical sketch of dubious value, but Bernard Mayo, in *Jefferson Himself* (1942), has selected from Jefferson's voluminous writings and arranged in chronological sequence everything of autobiographical value to give us a synthetic but nonetheless authentic self-portrait that is as readable as it is fascinating. The intricacies of New York State politics, and national politics as they were molded by those who learned the art in the New York school, have been explained from all sides by major participants. The *Autobiography of Martin Van Buren,* edited by John C. Fitzpatrick and published as Vol. II of the Annual Report of the American Historical Association for 1918, is as notable for its omissions as for the events it includes. Written in Van Buren's verbose and circumlocutory style, the book is not easy reading, but is rewarding for those who can bring to it enough background to fill in between the lines. More entertaining but no more candid is the *Autobiography of Thurlow Weed,* Harriet A. Weed, ed. (1883), which is principally valuable in the Jefferson-Jackson period for the election of John Quincy Adams and for the transition from National Republicans to Whigs. The *Reminiscences of James A. Hamilton* (1869), one of Alexander Hamilton's sons, has valuable material on Van Buren's side of Jacksonianism and on the absorption of Jackson by the Crawford Radicals, but is biased by Hamilton's later conversion to Whiggery. Jabez D. Hammond's *History of Political Parties in the State of New York* (2 vols., 1842) and Fitzwilliam Byrdsall's *History of the Loco-Foco or Equal Rights Party* (1842) are contemporary accounts by men deeply involved in the movements of which they write. Both books are basic sources for all who have written on New York politics since that time.

Other significant personal narratives of the period include the *Autobiography of Amos Kendall,* William Stickney, ed. (1872), which throws much light on the Jackson period if one can discount the nationalistic partisanship of Kendall's old age, which spanned the Civil War; and the *Autobiography of William H. Seward,* F. W. Seward, ed. (1877), which is useful for the sectional conflict of the 1830's and 1840's. Winfield Scott's *Memoirs of Lieut.-General Scott, LL.D.* (1864) is concerned largely with his own honor and glory, but manages in spite of his vanity to contribute to an understanding of both military history and politics. Charles J. Ingersoll's *Historical Sketch of the Second War Between the United States of America and Great Britain* (2 vols., 1845-1849) is an indispensable primary source. Himself one of the War Hawks of 1812, Ingersoll writes from extensive contemporary documents as well as from personal acquaintance with the chief actors in the war. Of more specialized value are the *Memoirs of the Reverend Charles G. Finney* (1876), whose evangelistic fervor shines through the otherwise rather dull record of countless souls saved at numerous revivals, and makes understandable the impetus he gave to the antislavery movement.

Ashbel Smith's *Reminiscences of the Texas Republic* (1876) is valuable for Texan history. Peter Harvey's *Reminiscences and Anecdotes of Daniel Webster* (1882) has been at the right hand of everyone who has written of Webster since that date. The *Autobiography of Peggy Eaton* (1932) was dictated in 1873, too long after Peggy's heyday to be anything but confused, though it is still vigorous and colorful. Horace Greeley's *Recollections of a Busy Life* (1868) has pertinent material for the late 1830's and 1840's, while Boston editor Joseph T. Buckingham's *Personal Memoirs and Recollections of Editorial Life* (1852) spans the entire Jefferson-Jackson period. Nathan Sargent's *Public Men and Events from the Commencement of Mr. Monroe's Administration, in 1817, to the Close of Mr. Fillmore's Administration in 1853* (2 vols., 1875) contains valuable first-hand matter by one who was first a Philadelphia editor, then a Washington correspondent, but is far less comprehensive than Thomas Hart Benton's *Thirty Years' View* (2 vols., 1854-56). Benton made extensive—but selective—use of documents to produce a work that cannot be ignored, though it is biased by time and by Benton's own changing views and associations.

V. CONTEMPORARY PERIODICALS. Perhaps better than any other class of materials, newspapers convey the emotional shades and nuances of a period. In the first half of the nineteenth century every shade of opinion, each school of doctrine, had its journalistic champion. The Washington papers, then as now, were pre-occupied with politics. The *National Intelligencer,* originally spokesman for the Jeffersonians, followed Adams and Clay into the Whig ranks. The *Globe* throughout its life was solidly Democratic, using every art and trick of journalism to advance the Jackson cause. Other papers came into being solely to serve the purposes of individual candidates, only to perish quietly when the cause was lost. Papers came and went with astonishing frequency, but a few of the longer-lived and more useful for this study were the Boston *Sentinel,* Philadelphia *Franklin Gazette,* Albany *Argus,* Baltimore *American,* Richmond *Enquirer,* Charleston *Courier* (notable for its Washington correspondence of the 1830's and 1840's), and the Charleston *Mercury.* The New York papers set the tone and pioneered the techniques. The *Evening Post,* under Bryant, was a solid Democratic sheet, in the main conservative but with a radical interlude in the 1830's when the influence of its assistant editor, William Leggett, was strongest. The *Tribune* was a paper of causes, including that of antislavery. But James Gordon Bennett's *Herald* was the prototype of the modern daily, to be read by the historian both for what it says and for how and where it says it.

Before the days of far-flung telegraphic networks, newspapers copied liberally from one another. Political news from Washington, commercial stories from New York or Boston, crop reports from South and West, the latest in exploration and discovery, all were eventually repeated over the country, with or without local commentary, so that access to one paper over a fair stretch of time will supply a wide range of information and opinion. If that one paper happens to be *Niles' Weekly Register,* a magazine-size sheet that began publication in Baltimore in 1811, the reader is blessed indeed, for there is no better repository for the source documents of the times.

Magazines also came and went, and were as highly individualistic as their editors. The *North American Review,* emanating from Boston, and the *Southern Review* from Charleston were patterned on English models, featuring unsigned essays in political, social, economic, and literary criticism. The *Democratic Review* was more wide-ranging in its interests than its name implies, but it was basically a political organ. Of purely literary journals there were many, but few of long duration. Outstanding were the *New England Galaxy,* the *Southern Literary Messenger* of which Poe was for a time the editor, and Margaret Fuller's *Dial,* mouthpiece of the New England transcendentalists.

VI. CONTEMPORARY BOOKS. To understand any period of history one must read the books written in it. For the Jefferson-Jackson period there is no substitute for reading Irving and Cooper, Poe and Hawthorne, Emerson and Thoreau, and Melville. Editions are numerous, and available wherever there is a public library or a bookstore.

VII. GENERAL HISTORIES. There are numerous histories covering all or part of the period of this volume. All use essentially the same sources, with due allowance for additional materials available to more recent scholars, but there is wide variance in point of view. Each age has its own special requirements of the past, and the historian who is true to his own times will seek out these special requirements for emphasis. Thus the history of history becomes a revealing phase of the national story. Among the older, comprehensive works that should still be read, although both have been superseded in many particulars of detail and of interpretation, are John Bach McMaster's *History of the People of the United States from the Revolution to the Civil War* (8 vols., 1883-1913); and Edward Channing's *History of the United States* (6 vols., 1905-25). Henry Adams' *History of the United States during the Administrations of Thomas Jefferson and James Madison* (9 vols., 1889-91) is a classic that approaches the validity of a primary source because of its extensive use of the Adams family archives. Though by no means laudatory, the account is surprisingly sympathetic to have been written by a great-grandson of John Adams. George Dangerfield's *Era of Good Feelings* (1953) covers the period from the War of 1812 to the election of Jackson in readable and well-organized form, with more than the usual space devoted to related events abroad. Glyndon G. Van Deusen, *The Jacksonian Era, 1828-1848* (1959), a volume in the New American Nation series, takes up where Dangerfield leaves off with a thorough and scholarly account of the Jackson-Polk period. *The Age of Jackson* (1945) by Arthur M. Schlesinger, Jr., covers the ground of both Dangerfield and Van Deusen in more free-wheeling style. It is a challenging study that must be taken into account by all who would write of the Jackson period. The familiar sectional interpretation is represented in Frederick Jackson Turner, *The United States, 1830-1850* (1935), the final statement of Turner's historical emphasis on the frontier. The most articulate of the sections is explored at greater length in C. S. Sydnor, *Development of Southern Sectionalism, 1819-1848* (1948). Ulrich B. Phillips' *The Course of the South to Secession,* E. Merton Coulter, ed. (1939), is a provocative study of southern ideological development, while Avery Craven's *The Coming of the Civil War* (1942) traces the long, slow build-up over half a century of the causes of sectional conflict.

One- and two-volume histories of the textbook type are numerous, and the more recent ones are well enough written to be read with pleasure. It would be unfair to single out any particular one for special mention. All are accurate, the differences being primarily of organization and of emphasis.

VIII. SPECIALIZED HISTORIES. As with the general histories, the number of specialized volumes is impressive and the quality high, with ample room for reader preferences. For social history the History of American Life series remains standard. The relevant volumes are John A. Krout and Dixon Ryan Fox, *The Completion of Independence, 1790-1830* (1944); and Carl Russell Fish, *The Rise of the Common Man, 1830-1850* (1927). Both are readable and informative, but leave the reader with the feeling that he has barely entered the portals of a new and fascinating world. Alice Felt Tyler's *Freedom's Ferment* (1944) deals more specifically with social and religious movements prior to the Civil War.

Economic history is no longer a single subject but has been broken down into numerous subtopics. For economic thought the second volume of Joseph Dorfman's *Economic Mind in American Civilization* (1946) is a thorough and surprisingly readable account. The two-volume work of John R. Commons and his associates on the *History of Labour in the United States,* though it appeared in 1918, is still of great value. Pursuing a special phase of the subject, Philip S. Foner's *History of the Labor Movement in the United States* (1947) gives a sympathetic account of the beginnings of organized labor in the Jackson period. The *History of Manufactures in the United States* by Victor S. Clark (3 vols., 1929) is an unsurpassed mine of information. The agricultural story is fully told in Percy W. Bidwell and John I. Falconer, *History of Agriculture in the Northern United States, 1620-1860* (1925), and its companion work, Lewis C. Gray, *History of Agriculture in the Southern United States to 1860* (2 vols., 1933). Benjamin Hibbard's *History of the Public Land Policies* (1924, 1939) rounds out the agricultural story. Special phases of economic history are usefully treated in Edward Stanwood, *American Tariff Controversies of the Nineteenth Century* (2 vols., 1903); and in John W. Oliver, *History of American Technology* (1956). Bray Hammond's *Banks and Politics in*

America, from the Revolution to the Civil War (1957) gives the best and most readable account of both first and second Banks of the United States. It is also an excellent analysis of the inevitable interrelations of business and government.

In diplomatic history it is impossible to choose between Samuel Flagg Bemis, *A Diplomatic History of the United States* (4th ed. 1955), and Thomas A. Bailey, *A Diplomatic History of the American People* (6th ed. 1958), each of which includes ample guides to the more abundant literature of the subject. For constitutional history a similar choice rests between the similarly titled works of Andrew C. McLaughlin (1936) and Homer C. Hockett (1939). Leonard D. White's pioneer studies in administrative history, *The Federalists* (1948), *The Jeffersonians* (1951), and *The Jacksonians* (1954) are essential to a full understanding of the history of American government in the early nineteenth century. The Presidency as distinct from the executive departments, complete with campaign issues and platforms, is succinctly treated in Edward Stanwood, *A History of the Presidency,* revised edition by Charles K. Bolton (2 vols., 1928); and more recently in Eugene H. Roseboom, *A History of Presidential Elections* (1957).

The literary currents of the Jefferson-Jackson period are nowhere better treated than by Van Wyck Brooks in *The World of Washington Irving* (1944), *The Flowering of New England* (1936), and *The Times of Melville and Whitman* (1947). Oliver W. Larkin's *Art and Life in America* (1949) is a superb blending of general history with the specialized history of American art. Intellectual history is told imaginatively by Vernon L. Parrington in *Main Currents of American Thought* (3 vols., 1927-30), and unimaginatively but with meticulous detail by Merle Curti in *The Growth of American Thought* (1943, 1951). Ralph H. Gabriel, *The Course of American Democratic Thought* (1940, 1956), is a well-proportioned account of the influence of the democratic idea. Louis Hartz, on the other hand, in *The Liberal*

Tradition in America (1955), re-creates the American past as a sort of prologue to the age of Franklin D. Roosevelt.

IX. BIOGRAPHY. Biography remains the best introduction to history for the lay reader. It gives him a character with whom he may identify, and a single unified point of view from which he may observe the events of a period. For the historian, on the other hand, these very virtues constitute the chief dangers inherent in the biographical approach. The historian's point of view must be that of his own times, and he cannot allow himself to be restricted or conditioned by the attitudes and perceptions of one of his actors. For the most part the biographical works mentioned here are those of characters whose names have appeared in the text of this volume. The most recent scholarship is generally—but by no means universally—the best.

Indispensable alike to the historian and to the lay reader of serious purpose is the *Dictionary of American Biography* (20 vols., 1932). The DAB is both a mine of information in itself and a selective guide to the sources up to the date of its appearance. A subject-matter index and alphabetical lists of entries by occupation and birthplace will be found most useful.

Among individual life stories, let us begin with those of Jefferson and his contemporaries. The best Hamilton biography now available is John C. Miller's *Alexander Hamilton* (1959), but the reader whose primary interest lies in the direction of economics will find challenge in Broaddus Mitchell, *Heritage from Hamilton* (1957). John Adams has still to receive his due from biographers. The only relatively modern study that purports to be complete is that of Gilbert Chinard, *Honest John Adams* (1933), but it is distressingly brief for so important a subject. Professor Chinard has also given us a good single-volume Jefferson, stressing the intellectual side of that many-sided man: *Thomas Jefferson, the Apostle of Americanism* (1929). Claude G. Bowers' *Jefferson and Hamilton* (1925) and *Jefferson in Power* (1936) are vivid and dramatic, giving a colorful and generally accurate though frankly partisan picture of the times. Albert Jay Nock's *Jefferson* (1926, 1960) is perceptive, readable, and penetrating in its judgments. Nathan Schachner, *Thomas Jefferson* (2 vols., 1951) is well written and factual, though lacking in depth. The definitive life will, of course, be that of Dumas Malone, *Jefferson and His Time,* of which, however, only two volumes have so far appeared: *Jefferson the Virginian* (1948), and *Jefferson and the Rights of Man* (1951).

Apart from Jefferson himself, there are many contemporaries whose lives throw light on the period of Jeffersonian dominance. Most important of these, and most fortunate in his biographer, is James Madison. Irving Brant's fine full-scale work includes *The Virginia Revolutionist* (1941), *The Nationalist* (1948), *Father of the Constitution* (1950), *Secretary of State* (1953), and *The President, 1809-1812* (1956). The sixth and final volume, *Commander in Chief,* is scheduled for publication in the fall of 1961. James Monroe, perhaps because there is less substance there, has been less happily enshrined on the library shelves. The best of a handful of single-volume Monroe biographies is that of W. P. Cresson, *James Monroe* (1946). Aaron Burr has received perhaps more than justice from Samuel H. Wandell and Meade Minnegerode, *Aaron Burr* (2 vols., 1925). Raymond Walters, Jr.'s *Albert Gallatin: Jeffersonian Financier and Diplomat* (1957) is a well-rounded and readable life of one of the most influential of all the Jeffersonians. The orthodox view represented by Walters is challenged by Alexander Balinky, *Albert Gallatin: Fiscal Theories and Policies* (1958), which argues that Gallatin subordinated fiscal to political considerations—a charge that could probably be made without prejudice of every Secretary of the Treasury. In *John Randolph of Roanoke* (2 vols., 1922) William Cabell Bruce has given us the only full-length biography. It is factual, though badly organized, and remains useful though it fails to grasp the essence of its brilliantly erratic subject.

In addition to these predominantly political figures, representative biographies of men with other preoccupations include

Henry H. Simms, *Life of John Taylor* (1932) for the development of democratic thought; Kenneth W. Porter, *John Jacob Astor, Business Man* (2 vols. 1931); Constance McL. Green, *Eli Whitney and the Birth of American Technology* (1956); and James R. Jacobs, *Tarnished Warrior: Major General James Wilkinson* (1938). This last-named work illustrates what appears to be an American tendency to overdo the rascality of our few accepted rascals, perhaps so that we shall not have to endow any of our heroes with feet of clay.

Members of the Federalist opposition, though in themselves worthy and often important figures, have not attracted biographers for many years. It is in itself a commentary on the changing interpretation of history that biographers are most reluctant to devote their talents to re-creating men who are currently for any reason unpopular. Thus Federalists have been roundly snubbed by an age that admires Jefferson. William W. Story's *Life and Letters of Joseph Story* (2 vols., 1851) is one-sided but still valuable as a source for the constitutional controversy of the Jefferson-Jackson period. The *Life and Correspondence of Rufus King,* Charles R. King, ed. (6 vols., 1894-1900), approximates a compendium of source documents. More objective, and excellent for the period of the embargo and the Hartford Convention is Samuel Eliot Morison, *The Life and Letters of Harrison Gray Otis, Federalist, 1765-1848* (2 vols., 1913). Albert J. Beveridge's *Life of John Marshall* (4 vols., 1916-1919) was a pioneer in modern biographical writing, still indispensable despite its obvious bias. Of the same genre as the lives of Story and Marshall, and in its judicious detachment better than either, is John T. Horton's *James Kent: A Study in Conservatism, 1763-1847* (1939).

Most of the dominant personalities among the War Hawks of 1812 who went on to become the empire builders of the Era of Good Feelings have been given appropriate biographical treatment. The notable exception is William H. Crawford, treated only in a laudatory, inadequate and obsolete little volume by

John E. D. Shipp pretentiously called *Giant Days: or, The Life and Times of William H. Crawford* (1909). Even without an adequate collection of papers—his were destroyed by Crawford himself—there is material for a more extended and better-balanced study than this. Bernard Mayo's projected multivolume life of Clay has regrettably been sidetracked since the publication in 1937 of the first, excellent volume, *Henry Clay: Spokesman of the New West,* which carries the story only to the declaration of war in 1812. Glyndon G. Van Deusen's *The Life of Henry Clay* (1937) is a competent, though unexciting, single-volume treatment, which is much too condensed for the magnitude of its subject. The best Webster available is that of Claude M. Fuess, *Daniel Webster* (2 vols., 1930), though it does not entirely supersede the older, authorized *Life of Daniel Webster* (2 vols., 1870) by George Ticknor Curtis. A more specialized study but one that perhaps comes closer to capturing the real Webster is Richard N. Current's *Daniel Webster and the Rise of National Conservatism* (1955). Margaret L. Coit's *John C. Calhoun, American Portrait* (1950) is dramatic, colorful, and generally factual though short on interpretation. *John C. Calhoun* (3 vols., 1944-51) by Charles M. Wiltse is more detailed and better rounded for the politics and economics of the period. Indispensable to an understanding of the times are *John Quincy Adams and the Foundations of American Foreign Policy* (1949) and *John Quincy Adams and the Union* (1956) by Samuel Flagg Bemis, which together constitute a biography that is the envy of scholars and a delight to the general reader.

Competent and useful biographies of lesser figures first nationally prominent in the interregnum between Jefferson and Jackson are: Freeman Cleaves, *Old Tippecanoe: William Henry Harrison and his Times* (1939); Harriet Horry Ravenel, *Life and Times of William Lowndes of South Carolina, 1782-1822* (1901); Joseph Howard Parks, *Felix Grundy, Champion of Democracy* (1940); Leland Winfield Meyer, *Life and Times of Colonel Richard M. Johnson of Kentucky* (1932); Francis P. Weisenberger, *Life of John McLean* (1937); J. Fred Rippy, *Joel Roberts Poinsett, Versatile American* (1935); Charles Winslow Elliott, *Winfield Scott: The Soldier and the Man* (1937); and Charles H. Ambler, *Thomas Ritchie, a Study in Virginia Politics* (1913).

Andrew Jackson and his friends have attracted less biographical attention than might have been expected, considering the high esteem in which they have been held since the early 1930's, but the tide is probably still rising. The most readable work and to date the best life of Jackson himself is that of Marquis James, *Andrew Jackson, the Border Captain* (1933), and *Andrew Jackson, Portrait of a President* (1937). Scholarly and still useful for its interpretations is John Spencer Basset, *Life of Andrew Jackson* (2 vols., 1911), but James has used extensive manuscript sources not available to Bassett. For the scholar, reading James Parton's three-volume *Life of Andrew Jackson* (1860) is still a rewarding experience. It is doubtful if any more recent biographer has been Parton's equal as master of his craft. A full-scale modern treatment of Martin Van Buren is long overdue, but it is understood to be in the making by Robert V. Remini, whose *Martin Van Buren and the Making of the Democratic Party* (1959) is a scholarly but in the main unexciting forerunner. Van Buren has received less than adequate treatment from Denis Tilden Lynch, *An Epoch and a Man: Martin Van Buren and His Times* (1929), and more popular but even less adequate handling by Holmes Moss Alexander, *The American Talleyrand: The Career and Contemporaries of Martin Van Buren, Eighth President* (1935). William B. Hatcher's *Edward Livingston: Jeffersonian Republican and Jacksonian Democrat* (1940) is the only study available, though it does scant justice to one of the major characters of the time. John A. Garraty's *Silas Wright* (1949) is the well-documented and readable story of a man who just missed greatness. Wright was one of those who made Van Buren possible. In his *Roger B. Taney* (1935), Carl Brent Swisher analyzes Taney's political as well as his judicial role in a sympathetic account from a strictly Jacksonian point of view. William Nisbet

Chambers, in *Old Bullion Benton, Senator from the New West* (1956) has given us a fascinating and perceptive study of a controversial figure whose solid bulk sooner or later looms across the path of every student of the age of Jackson. Frank B. Woodford's *Lewis Cass, the last Jeffersonian* (1950) is more accurate in detail than it is in its choice of subtitle.

In *Emily Donelson of Tennessee* (2 vols., 1941) Pauline W. Burke shows us the Jackson era through the eyes of the President's niece and White House hostess, a welcome departure from the heavily political emphasis of other books. Thomas P. Govan's *Nicholas Biddle, Nationalist and Public Banker, 1788-1844* (1959) is a fully documented account of Biddle's side of the Bank war, and a challenging defense of the conservative position in the 1830's. Theodore D. Jervey's *Robert Y. Hayne and his Times* (1909), though outmoded, throws much light on national events through the eyes of a man who claimed both Jackson and Calhoun as friends. The only life of Buchanan is George Ticknor Curtis, *Life of James Buchanan* (2 vols., 1883), prepared at the instigation of the family. It is valuable for the documents it reprints, but is far too dull to be read as anything but a duty— a dullness that is probably inherent in the subject, since Curtis did much better with Webster. Marquis James, *The Raven* (1929), is a colorful and readable life of Sam Houston. George Bancroft, who has a place both as man of letters and as Jacksonian politician, is well portrayed in Russell B. Nye, *George Bancroft, Brahmin Rebel* (1945).

Following the swiftly moving administrations of Jackson and Van Buren, the dominant political figures are Tyler and Polk. Lyon G. Tyler, last of John Tyler's fourteen children, has left a thoroughly partisan but valuable legacy in his *Letters and Times of the Tylers* (3 vols., 1884-1896). The emphasis should be on "Letters" rather than "Times." Oliver P. Chitwood's *John Tyler, Champion of the Old South* (1939) is in proper proportion and factually correct but pedestrian and devoid of insight. E. I. McCormac's *James K. Polk* (1922), as the only complete biography of Polk, must still be used, but it has already been superseded in part by Charles Grier Sellers, Jr., *James K. Polk, Jacksonian* (1957). This excellent first volume of what will be a two-volume life carries its subject to the eve of his nomination for the Presidency. Samuel Flagg Bemis, ed., *American Secretaries of State and their Diplomacy* (10 vols., 1927-29) contains individual sketches of all who served in the State Department throughout the 1800-1846 period. In Richard Hofstadter's challenging volume on the *American Political Tradition and the Men Who Made It* (1948), the essays on Jefferson, Calhoun, and Jackson are provocative for the same period.

Getting away from political figures, Carlton F. Maybee, Jr.'s *American Leonardo: Life of Samuel F. B. Morse* (1943) is valuable both for art and science. Richard W. Leopold's *Robert Dale Owen* (1940) has material on the New Harmony community, in which the younger Owen was associated with his father, and on later reform ventures. John Gill's *Tide without Turning: Elijah P. Lovejoy and Freedom of the Press* (1958), though more "literary" than scholarly, catches well the deeply dedicated nature of the reformers.

X. MONOGRAPHS AND SPECIAL STUDIES. Books and journal articles falling into this category constitute both the largest and in many ways the most useful body of materials with which the historian must deal. Each represents an exploration of some special theme, or aspect of a period, in far greater detail than anyone attempting to write about the period as a whole could possibly include, while the sum of hundreds of such monographs represents an evaluation of a far greater body of source materials than any single individual could hope to review in a lifetime. The writers of monographs and scholarly articles are in effect screening and interpreting a huge body of documents, thereby giving necessary guides as well as suggested conclusions to those whose task it is to cover larger periods in more sweeping fashion. It would not be feasible to list here even a relatively small percentage of the special studies that have entered in some degree into the preparation of this volume. The dedicated scholar will search the indexes of such invaluable journals as the *American Historical Review* (AHR), the *Mississippi Valley Historical Review* (MVHR), the *Journal of Southern History* (JSH), and the proceedings and periodical publications of the historical societies that flourish in every state of the Union. The more general reader, in terms of his own special interests, may find further inspiration or enlightenment among the titles noted here.

For the background of Jefferson and the Jeffersonian movement there is no better place to start than with Carl Becker's masterly analysis of the eighteenth-century mind in *The Declaration of Independence* (1922), and *The Heavenly City of the Eighteenth Century Philosophers* (1932). Charles A. Beard's *Economic Origins of Jeffersonian Democracy* (1915) is as challenging today as when it first appeared, a work that has in one aspect or another influenced all who have written on the period since. For the ideas of Jefferson and his contemporaries, the reader should consult Charles M. Wiltse, *The Jeffersonian Tradition in American Democracy* (1935, 1960); Adrienne Koch, *The Philosophy of Thomas Jefferson* (1943); Edward McNall Burns, *James Madison, Philosopher of the Constitution* (1938); and Eugene T. Mudge, *The Social Philosophy of John Taylor of Caroline* (1939). Merrill D. Peterson's *The Jefferson Image in the American Mind* (1960) is a meticulous and meaty study of the changing emphasis in the Jeffersonian heritage. The Alien and Sedition Acts have been fully explored by John C. Miller, *Crisis in Freedom* (1951); and James M. Smith, *Freedom's Fetters* (1956). The politics of the Jeffersonian movement are explored from opposing points of view in Manning J. Dauer, *The Adams Federalists* (1953); and Noble E. Cunningham, Jr., *The Jeffersonian Republicans: The Formation of Party Organization, 1789-1801* (1957). The circumstances that led up to the Louisiana Purchase are well treated in Arthur P. Whitaker, *The Mississippi Question, 1795-1803* (1934). Outdated but still useful is Charles Raymond

Brown, *The Northern Confederacy According to the Plans of the Essex Junto, 1796-1814* (1915). Most recent of many studies of an ever-intriguing subject is Thomas P. Abernethy, *The Burr Conspiracy* (1954).

For an understanding of the events leading up to the War of 1812, James F. Zimmerman's *Impressment of American Seamen* (1925); and Louis Martin Sears' *Jefferson and the Embargo* (1927), are of solid value. Julius W. Pratt, *Expansionists of 1812* (1925), traces the causes of the war to matters unrelated to commerce. For the military story the reader should consult Francis F. Beirne, *The War of 1812* (1940); and Alfred T. Mahan's classic *Sea Power in its Relation to the War of 1812* (2 vols., 1915). *The West Point Atlas of American Wars* (1959), edited by Col. Vincent J. Esposito, contains textual analyses almost as useful as its illuminating maps. A guide to the older literature will be found in Warren H. Goodman, "The Origins of the War of 1812: a Survey of Changing Interpretations," *MVHR,* Vol. XXVIII (Sept. 1941), pp. 171-86.

Specialized materials that clarify aspects of the period of expansion following the War of 1812 include Ray Allen Billington, *Westward Expansion* (2nd ed., 1960), which follows the Turner thesis of the frontier as a determining factor in American history; and Richard C. Wade, *The Urban Frontier: The Rise of Western Cities, 1790-1830* (1959), which relates urban growth to such factors as the appearance of the steamboat on western rivers. The role of the steamboat is definitively explored in Louis C. Hunter, *Steamboats on the Western Rivers* (1949). A sidelight on the economy of the South is in Alfred Holt Stone, "Cotton Factorage System of the Southern States," *AHR,* Vol. XX (Apr. 1915), pp. 557-65. Samuel Rezneck's "Depression of 1819-1822, a Social History," in the same journal for October 1933, Vol. XXXIX, pp. 28-47, is the best analysis of the first American postwar slump.

There is a voluminous literature on slavery and the Missouri Compromise. Political aspects of the compromise are illuminated by contemporary documents printed in *The Missouri Compro-*

mises and Presidential Politics, 1820-1825, Everett S. Brown, ed. (1926). Early L. Fox's *The American Colonization Society, 1817-1840* (1919) is exhaustive on that peripheral subject. Thomas P. Martin, "Some International Aspects of the Anti-Slavery Movement, 1818-1823," *Journal of Economic and Business History,* Vol. I (Nov. 1928), pp. 137-48, suggests an element of British as well as northern pressure. Slavery in operation is discussed by Robert R. Russel, "The General Effects of Slavery upon Southern Economic Progress," *JSH,* Vol. IV (Feb. 1938), pp. 34-54; and more recently by Kenneth M. Stampp, *The Peculiar Institution: Slavery in the Ante-Bellum South* (1956), both of whom conclude that the institution was economically profitable. While this was doubtless true for individual large-scale plantations, I cannot agree that it was generally true for the section as a whole. I regard it rather as one of the major causes of southern poverty (relative to the North) from about 1820 on.

For the imperialistic implications of American expansion on the Continent, Edgar B. Wesley's *Guarding the Frontier; a study of Frontier Defense from 1815 to 1825* (1935) is suggestive. Albert K. Weinberg's *Manifest Destiny* (1935) is one of those focal studies that give historians a new point of departure. Arthur P. Whitaker's *The United States and the Independence of Latin America* (1941) is an excellent summary. The British role in Latin America is treated from different aspects in Edward Tatum, *The United States and Europe, 1815-1823* (1936); and J. Fred Rippy, *British Investments in Latin America, 1822-1949* (1959). A fascinating comparison is suggested between the lines in Ralph W. Hidy, *The House of Baring in Anglo-American Trade and Finance* (1949). The definitive study of the Monroe Doctrine is that of Dexter Perkins, *The Monroe Doctrine* (3 vols., 1927-37). The general reader will find the *History of the Monroe Doctrine* (1955) by the same writer perhaps more profitable reading.

The classic treatment of parties is that of Wilfred E. Binkley, *American Political Parties*(3rd ed., revised and enlarged, 1958), which traces the origin and role of political parties and analyzes party leadership. William O. Lynch, *Fifty Years of Party War-fare, 1789-1837* (1931), stresses tactics rather than intellectual explanations. There are many detailed studies of local party politics that add up to the larger picture, including such as Gustavus Myers, *History of Tammany Hall* (1901), upon which all subsequent writers in the field have drawn; Arthur B. Darling, *Political Changes in Massachusetts, 1824-1848* (1925); and Philip S. Klein, *Pennsylvania Politics, 1817-1832: A Game without Rules* (1940). The particular election that brought Jackson to power is analyzed in detail in Florence Weston, *The Presidential Election of 1828* (1938).

On the doctrinal side, Marvin Meyers, *The Jacksonian Persuasion: Politics and Belief* (1957) is a provocative interpretation in terms of psychological and sociological factors. Charles G. Sellers, Jr.'s pamphlet, *Jacksonian Democracy* (1958) is a good summary with an extensive bibliography. Louis W. Koenig's essay on Van Buren in his *Invisible Presidency* (1960) tends to enlarge Van Buren's role in developing the policies of the Jackson era. From a more critical point of view, Richard P. McCormick, "New Perspectives on Jacksonian Politics," *AHR,* Vol. LXV (Jan. 1960), pp. 288-301, suggests that the Jackson movement, on the basis of the votes it actually commanded, was something less than "popular." Thomas P. Abernethy, *From Frontier to Plantation in Tennessee* (1932), scoffs at Jackson's pretensions to democracy; while Richard R. Stenberg, "Jackson, Buchanan, and the 'Corrupt Bargain' Calumny," *Pennsylvania Magazine of History and Biography,* Vol. LVIII (Jan. 1934), pp. 61-85, finds evidence of the use of calculated misrepresentation as a tool of party.

The Great Debate, although the final test of nullification was precipitated largely by economic causes, was basically a legal conflict, which the jurists resolved in favor of national power. The standard historical account of the nullification episode is that of Chauncey S. Boucher, *The Nullification Controversy in South Carolina* (1916). In terms of ideological content the classic treatment is that of David F. Houston. *A Critical Study of Nullifica-*

tion in South Carolina (1896). Results of later scholarship are presented in Frederic Bancroft, *Calhoun and the South Carolina Nullification Movement* (1928); and John G. Van Deusen, *Economic Bases of Disunion in South Carolina* (1928). Calhoun's position as political theorist is well handled in a brilliant essay by Richard Nelson Current, "John C. Calhoun, Philosopher of Reaction," *Antioch Review,* Vol. III (Summer 1943), pp. 223-34. The legal answer to the compact theory of the Constitution and the state rights dogma derived from it was stated by two contemporaries in works that are as important for American law as Coke and Blackstone for the law of England. New York Chancellor James Kent's *Commentaries on American Law,* in four volumes, was published between 1826 and 1830. Supreme Court Justice Joseph Story published his three-volume *Commentaries on the Constitution of the United States* in 1833, with the Force Act still on the statute books. Both of these jurists took cognizance of debates in Congress and of the whole body of controversial literature as well as of the familiar chain of court decisions. By way of footnote to the constitutional controversy, Lord Acton, writing of the "Political Causes of the American Revolution" in 1861 took for granted that the Union was permanently dissolved, and traced the causes of its fall in the ancient struggle of liberty against power in terms that would have seemed to Calhoun and Webster but echoes of their own debates. The essay is reprinted in *Essays on Freedom and Power* (1948).

Shifting from law to morals, Oliver W. Elsbree's *Rise of the Missionary Spirit in America, 1790-1815* (1928) shows how the conviction of responsibility for the salvation of one's fellows led into the whole reform movement. Invaluable background materials for the moral crusades of the 1830's and 1840's are also supplied in Charles I. Foster, *An Errand of Mercy: The Evangelical United Front, 1790-1837* (1960). Whitney R. Cross, *The Burned-over District: The Social and Intellectual History of Enthusiastic Religion in Western New York, 1800-1850* (1950) is a necessary point of departure for further study of the urge toward perfection that gripped so many Americans of that time. The first two chapters of William G. McLoughlin, Jr., *Modern Revivalism: Charles Grandison Finney to Billy Graham* (1959) are excellent for the role of religious awakening in the reform movement. The more specific impact of religion upon philosophical and literary currents is well treated in William R. Hutchison, *The Transcendentalist Ministers: Church Reform and the New England Renaissance* (1959). The whole gamut of reform, from religion to the abolition of slavery, is explored in Clifford S. Griffin, *Their Brothers' Keepers: Moral Stewardship in the United States, 1800-1865* (1960).

Education is as well documented as religion, and a sampling is quite as difficult to make. Paul Monroe's *The Founding of the American Public School System* (1940) is a useful summary. Sidney Jackson's *America's Struggle for Free Schools* (1941) deals with the crucial period 1837-1842 in the key areas of New York and New England, with attention to economic, religious, and political forces. Neil G. McClusky's *Public Schools and Moral Education: The Influence of Horace Mann, William Torrey Harris and John Dewey* (1958) is excellent for the work of Horace Mann. Valuable for intellectual and moral history in general is Arthur A. Ekirch, Jr., *The Idea of Progress in America, 1815-1860* (1944). In *The American as Reformer* (1948), Arthur M. Schlesinger, Sr., has written a wise and suggestive little book that opens many doors and peeks through some keyholes.

The economic and social forces that steered the 1830's toward collapse have been explored too often for repetition, but new books continue to cast light into familiar corners. Ralph C. H. Catterall, *The Second Bank of the United States* (1903), is still useful to the scholar but for all practical purposes has been superseded by Bray Hammond's *Banking and Politics* mentioned in a earlier connection. Against the economic background of the times, the rise of the Whigs is treated in George Rawlings Poage, *Henry Clay and the Whig Party* (1936). Whig conservatism was balanced by the beginnings of a radical labor movement, fully developed in Walter Hugins, *Jacksonian Democracy and the Working Class* (1960), which tended to push northern Democrats farther to the left. The impact of immigration is classically treated in Carl Wittke, *We Who Made America* (1939); and Marcus L. Hansen, *The Atlantic Migration, 1607-1860* (1940). For various aspects of the depression of the late 1830's and early 1840's, Reginald C. McGrane's *The Panic of 1837: Some Financial Problems of the Jacksonian Era* (1924), and the same writer's *Foreign Bondholders and American State Debts* (1935) are still valuable, as is Samuel Rezneck's "The Social History of an American Depression, 1837-43," *AHR,* Vol. XL (July 1935), pp. 662-87.

The slavery controversy, in all its many facets and ramifications, continues to provoke a spirited and often penetrating series of polemics. For background two old volumes are without peer: William E. Dodd, *The Cotton Kingdom* (1919); and Ulrich B. Phillips, *Life and Labor in the Old South* (1929). Both are by southern historians, both tend to be sympathetic to the southern cause, but neither has been superseded. Basic to an understanding of the controversy as a whole are Gilbert H. Barnes, *The Anti-Slavery Impulse, 1830-1844* (1933); and Dwight L. Dumond, *The Antislavery Origins of the Civil War in the United States* (1939). Special aspects of the larger theme are dealt with by W. S. Savage, *The Controversy over the Distribution of Abolition Literature, 1830-1860* (1938); and R. B. Nye, *Fettered Freedom: Civil Liberties and the Slavery Controversy, 1830-1860* (1949). Arthur Young Lloyd, *The Slavery Controversy, 1831-1860* (1939) is a convenient summary but is somewhat biased toward the southern position. Wilbur H. Seibert, *The Underground Railroad from Slavery to Freedom* (1898) remains the basic work on the subject, but the interested reader will probably prefer Henrietta Buckmaster's compelling and dramatic account in her *Let My People Go* (1943). Robert R. Russel plows what has become familiar ground in *Economic Aspects of Southern Sectionalism* (1924). Eric Williams, *Capitalism and Slavery* (1944), analyzes the relation between the British economy and the British anti-slavery movement, and the impact of both upon the United States. William S. Jenkins, *Proslavery Thought in the Old South* (1935), summarizes the varieties of intellectual legerdemain by which the ante-bellum southerner rationalized his refusal to give up his slaves. W. J. Cash's brilliant study, the *Mind of the South* (1941) is required reading, as is Jesse T. Carpenter's psychoanalytic study of *The South as a Conscious Minority* (1930). Stanley M. Elkins' *Slavery: A Problem in American Institutional and Intellectual Life* (1959) does not quite succeed in explaining the psychology of the slave himself.

The period from the accession of Tyler to the Oregon Treaty is a period of many emphases, each well exploited in monographic literature. Jesse Slidell Reeves, *American Diplomacy under Tyler and Polk* (1907), is still a useful guide. Hugh S. Soulsby, *The Right of Search and the Slave Trade in Anglo-American Relations, 1814-1862* (1933); and Albert B. Corey, *The Crisis of 1830-1842 in Canadian-American Relations* (1941), both deal conveniently with specific issues between Great Britain and the United States. On another outstanding point of friction between the two English-speaking countries, Ephraim D. Adams, *British Interests and Activities in Texas, 1838-1846* (1910), contains much valuable material. Justin H. Smith's *The Annexation of Texas* (corrected edition, 1941) is the standard authority on that subject.

The political forces of the early 1840's received detailed treatment in Herbert D. A. Donovan, *The Barnburners* (1925); and in Oscar Doane Lambert, *Presidential Politics in the United States, 1841-1844* (1936). Arthur May Mowry's *The Dorr War* (1901) is the definitive study of a related episode. Less closely but more ominously connected is the subject of John Nelson Norwood's study, *The Schism in the Methodist Episcopal Church, 1844* (1923). The interrelations of Oregon, slavery, and the tariff are suggestively discussed in Thomas P. Martin, "The Upper Mississippi Valley in Anglo-American Anti-Slavery and Free

Trade Relations, 1837-1842," *MVHR*, Vol. XV (Sept. 1928), pp. 204-20; the same writer's "Free Trade and the Oregon Question, 1842-1846," *Facts and Factors in Economic History* (1932), pp. 470-91; and Frederick Merk, "The British Corn Crisis of 1845-46 and the Oregon Treaty," *Agricultural History,* Vol. VIII (July 1934), pp. 95-123.

Index

CHARLES M. WILTSE brings to the understanding of American history twenty-five years of experience in government. He came to Washington in the idealistic early years of the New Deal; remained to cope with the harsher problems of industrial mobilization in the War Production Board and its Korean-War counterpart, the National Production Authority; and is currently Chief Historian of the Army Medical Service, for which he is writing the administrative history of the Medical Department in World War II. In addition to the varied demands of a civil-service career, Dr. Wiltse has found time to follow up an early interest in Jeffersonian Democracy with a definitive three-volume life of John C. Calhoun, completed with the aid of two Guggenheim Fellowships. He earned his Ph.D. at Cornell University, where he was Sage Fellow in Philosophy, and was awarded an honorary Litt.D. from Marshall College, at which he had been president of his freshman class. During intervals of insolvency in his academic career he was a book salesman in San Francisco and a sports writer in West Virginia.

AMERICAN CENTURY SERIES

WHEN ORDERING, please use the Standard Book Number consisting of the publisher's prefix, 8090-, plus the five digits following each title. (Note that the numbers given in this list are for paperback editions only. Many of the books are also available in cloth.)

I Wonder As I Wander by Langston Hughes (0068–7)
Science in Nineteenth-Century America ed. by Nathan Reingold (0069–5)
The Course of the South to Secession by Ulrich Bonnell Phillips (0070–9)
American Negro Poetry ed. by Arna Bontemps (0071–7)
Horace Greeley by Glyndon G. Van Deusen (0072–5)
David Walker's Appeal ed. by Charles M. Wiltse (0073–3)
The Sentimental Years by E. Douglas Branch (0074–1)
Henry James and the Jacobites by Maxwell Geismar (0075–X)
The Reins of Power by Bernard Schwartz (0076–8)
American Writers in Rebellion by H. Wayne Morgan (0077–6)
Policy and Power by Ruhl Bartlett (0078–4)
Wendell Phillips on Civil Rights and Freedom ed. by Louis Filler (0079–2)
American Negro Short Stories ed. by John Henrik Clarke (0080–6)
The Radical Novel in the United States: 1900–1954 by Walter B. Rideout (0081–4)
A History of Agriculture in the State of New York by Ulysses Prentiss Hedrick (0082–2)
Criticism and Fiction by William Dean Howells and *The Responsibilities of the Novelist* by Frank Norris (0083–0)
John F. Kennedy and the New Frontier ed. by Aïda DiPace Donald (0084–9)
Anyplace But Here by Arna Bontemps and Jack Conroy (0085–7)
Mark Van Doren: 100 Poems (0086–5)
Simple's Uncle Sam by Langston Hughes (0087–3)
Stranger at the Gates by Tracy Sugarman (0088–1)
Waiting for Nothing by Tom Kromer (0089–X)
31 New American Poets ed. by Ron Schreiber (0090–3)
Documents of Upheaval ed. by Truman Nelson (0092–X)
Black Pow-Wow by Ted Joans (0093–8)
Half a Man by M. W. Ovington (0094–6)
Collected and New Poems: 1924–1963 by Mark Van Doren (0095–4)
From Plantation to Ghetto (Revised) by August Meier and Elliott Rudwick (0096–2)
Tambourines to Glory by Langston Hughes (0097–0)
Afrodisia by Ted Joans (0098–9)
Natural Process ed. by Ted Wilentz and Tom Weatherly (0097–7)
The Free World Colossus (Revised) by David Horowitz (0107–1)

THE MAKING OF AMERICA

Fabric of Freedom: 1763–1800 by Esmond Wright (0101–2)
The New Nation: 1800–1845 by Charles M. Wiltse (0102–0)
The Stakes of Power: 1845–1877 by Roy F. Nichols (0103–9)
The Search for Order: 1877–1920 by Robert H. Wiebe (0104–7)
The Urban Nation: 1920–1960 by George E. Mowry (0105–5)

AMERICAN PROFILES

Thomas Jefferson: A Profile ed. by Merrill D. Peterson (0200–0)
Franklin D. Roosevelt: A Profile ed. by William E. Leuchtenburg (0201–9)
Alexander Hamilton: A Profile ed. by Jacob E. Cooke (0202–7)
Mark Twain: A Profile ed. by Justin Kaplan (0203–5)
Theodore Roosevelt: A Profile ed. by Morton Keller (0204–3)
Woodrow Wilson: A Profile ed. by Arthur S. Link (0205–1)
John C. Calhoun: A Profile ed. by John L. Thomas (0206–X)
Ralph Waldo Emerson: A Profile ed. by Carl Bode (0207–8)
William Jennings Bryan: A Profile ed. by Paul W. Glad (0208–6)
Martin Luther King, Jr.: A Profile ed. by C. Eric Lincoln (0209–4)
George Washington: A Profile ed. by James Morton Smith (0210–8)
Jonathan Edwards: A Profile ed. by David Levin (0212–4)
Benjamin Franklin: A Profile ed. by Esmond Wright (0214–0)